QUEER FREEDOM : BLACK SOVEREIGNTY

SUNY SERIES, AFRO-LATINX FUTURES
Vanessa K. Valdés, editor

QUEER FREEDOM : BLACK SOVEREIGNTY

ANA-MAURINE LARA

Cover image: *How Some Folks Get to Space without a Rocket (Planetary Travel)*—a collage by Mirlande Jean-Gilles. © Mirlande Jean-Gilles.

Published by State University of New York Press, Albany

For information, contact State University of New York Press, Albany, NY
www.sunypress.edu

Library of Congress Cataloging-in-Publication Data
Names: Lara, Ana-Maurine, author.
Title: Queer freedom : Black sovereignty / Ana-Maurine Lara.
Description: Albany : State University of New York Press, [2020] | Series: SUNY series, Afro-Latinx futures | Includes bibliographical references and index.
Identifiers: LCCN 2020006762 | ISBN 9781438481104 (paperback) | ISBN 9781438481098 (hardcover) | ISBN 9781438481111 (ebook)
Subjects: LCSH: Sexual minorities–Dominican Republic–Social conditions. | Blacks–Dominican Republic–Social conditions. | Blacks–Race identity–Dominican Republic. | Sexual minorities–Identity—Dominican Republic.
Classification: LCC HQ73.3.D65 L37 2020 | DDC 306.76097293–dc23
LC record available at https://lccn.loc.gov/2020006762

10 9 8 7 6 5 4 3 2 1

For my young relatives:
may our worlds be a better place
because we are in it.

For my queer : Black ancestors and
ancestors yet to come—the brujas and
the storytellers, the artists and the
teachers, the ones who run and the
ones who stay behind, the ones who
speak and the ones who stay silent,
the brave ones and the cowards,
the ones we have yet to imagine.
All we have for you is love.

For you, we call in the Four
Directions, the forces of the Sky
and Earth, and all of the Elementos.

We begin here, with story, roadmaps,
a question: are we free : sovereign?

El día más soleado cae llovizna sobre mi pecho
la india dice que casándose está una bruja con su pareja
y niños y niñas admirados van
corriendo, saltando de aquí para allá
como celebrando una boda real.
La reina de las brujas te llevará
allá por la enrama' a bailar gagá.

—XIOMARA FORTUNA, *Bruja*

CONTENTS

Tisa Bryant once shared two key questions with me: Who do I love? And to whom am I accountable? These questions are everything. Here, I want to start off by saying that very often, the answers to these questions overlap, but not exclusively so. Similarly, to whom I am accountable also often includes people for whom I am grateful. And here, I would like to mention those for whom I am grateful—specifically and especially in the process of bringing this book into being. Now, the introduction to this book includes a moyugba and a naming of those who I am calling into the room from among the living. So this is not that. This is a thank-you, a gracias, mezi, a seneka kakom, a tlazokamati of a different ilk. I did not intend to write this book, but it is the book I have intended. I am filled with such deep gratitude that it is hard to express in words.

I want to say thank you to all of the healers, servidores, tradition keepers, dancers, drummers, and community leaders who have received me in their homes for so many years, and who continue to do so, offering me fresh-brewed coffee, a glass of cold water, and simply time together. I am so joyful that you are here in this ceremony with me, celebrating together as we have done for so many years now. Thanks to all of the abuelas, brujas, medicine women and men, paleros, vuduistas, santeros, obas, babalawos, iyalorishas, guardians, and liboristas who continue to share their knowledge with me, often with so much love, joy, and kindness. Thank you to all of the seres that protect you, so that you can continue transferring your knowledge to all of the generations yet to come. Thank you, also, for having my best interests in mind and taking care of me so well. Thank you, especially, to the community in San Cristobal, which, through laughter, el compartir, and work has taught me so much; Wanga, Naina, Francisca, and Canuma, who are all amazing; Guadalupe Tonalmitl Retíz Yanez, Rosa Tupina Yaotonalcuauhtli, Beatrice Ilhuicatlahuilli Villegas, Yvette Mendéz, Xiuh Lalis, Abebbe Oshun, Adela, Amantina, Doña Carmen, La China—amazing leaders and elders who serve their communities and, in so doing, teach me and all of us. In our visits together, we have learned so much—tlazokamati for your entrega and love for all of our peoples; Vanessa K. Valdés, who invited me to the Let the Spirit Speak! Conference at City College so many years ago, and who then opened up the door so that this ceremony could take place. Your rootedness in your vision and connection to spirit enabled this ceremony to be midwifed as a book through the SUNY Afro-Latinx Series. I am honored to be part of that vision, and to be wrapped in this river; Rebecca Colesworthy, thank you for your excitement, gentle guidance, and editorial acuity. Thank you for understanding this poet; all of the senior scholars who have walked with me and then, having shown me snippets of possibility, have gently drawn me forward, in particular Joni L. Jones/Omi Osun Olomo, Jafari S. Allen, Inderpal Grewal, Kamari Clarke, Lynn Stephen, Michelle McKinley, Michael Hames-Garcia, Ginetta Candelario, April Mayes, Carlos U. Decena, Fatima L. Portorreal, Matt Richardson, Omi'seke Natasha Tinsley, J. Kehaulani Kauanui, Gina Ulysse, Erica L. Williams, Rosamond King, Angelique Nixon, Solimar Otero, Elizabeth Alexander, and many, many others. I hope that I continue to be worthy of the honor you bestowed upon me by taking my work, my inquiries, and my methods seriously; my colleagues, in particular the bad-ass women of the Yale Black Feminist Reading Group (Dana Asbury, Kristin Baxivanos, Sofia Betancourt, Diana Burnett, Jalylah Burrell, Adom Getachew, Sarah Haley, Jennifer Leath, Key Jo Lee, Christine Slaughter, Heather Vermeulen), who taught me how to put our work in conversation, and to Kemi Balogun and Margaret Rhee, who offered insight into what was going on here when I wasn't sure; all of my friends who held space for me while I worked through some of the harder aspects of this ceremony—thank you, Courtney Morris, Lauren F. Guerra, drea brown, Sheree Ross, Jai Dulani, D'Lo, Anjali Alimchandani, Maram Epstein, Justine Lovinger, Alejandro Quiahuitl Martínez, Angela Mictlanxotchil Anderson, Cristina Hernández; my kinfolk, especially Lennox, Niko, Leo, Luciana, Victor José, Ernesto, Enrique, Mom, Papí, Tía Magalí, Tía Lupina, Alice, Carol, and Lauren;

my ancestors, those named and unnamed, who walk with me sharing in the love I hold for them and reflecting it back to me; Alaí Reyes-Santos, who has been a partner, a friend, a cheerleader, and an interlocutor at all stages of the development of my research and writing, including making me hot chocolate when I thought I could go no further. Seneka kakom for being my partner in so many adventures and in this work we are doing of building treaties toward a world where our ancestors are collectively and indefinitely free : sovereign forever. Mafarefun Yemanya. D'annishibuii.

opening
ceremony

Las afrodescendientes no somos feministas de habitación propia,
sino de barracón.

—AÍDA BUENO SARDUY[2]

---

1   This drawing is a vêvê, a landing point for the misterios, the energies present
within these pages who will traverse this ofrenda along with us (the author, readers,
those encountering). *Ofrenda* means offering. Ofrendas reflect the person's heart
and, often, their capacity to demonstrate love, generosity, respect, and reciprocity.
Each part of this ofrenda contains vêvê. As roadways, vêvê remind us to take note
of our physical and emotional presence within ceremonial time and space. In their
becoming, they guide us into an alternate temporal corporeality. In their scatter-
ing, they bring us back to the material world. Footnotes in this text are also part of a
vêvê. Here, they are symbolic doorways, placeholders and landing points signaling
where the reader might need to go to know more, to contemplate, to connect—not
just with what lies behind the note but with our own physical and emotional experiences of the text. Sometimes, they will lead you to translations or to sources.
Sometimes, just to an ancestor, an embodied presence, a question. As vêvê, footnotes in this ofrenda do multiple kinds of work at once, across and through queer :
Black time-space.
2   I encountered Aída Bueno Sarduy's quote through Yuderkys Espinosa Miñoso,
a longtime Afro-Dominican lesbian feminist theorist. She posted this article on her
social media. The quote roughly translates to "Afro-descendent women, we are not
feminists [created] in our own rooms, but rather of shared work quarters." I needed
to know more about this person who made something so intuitive to me suddenly

I desire decolonization as in I desire the full realization of our lives, as queer peoples, as Black peoples, as Indigenous peoples.[3] These decolonial desires are not metaphors; they are re-oriented desires for the recuperation of body-lands, water-memories, and altars-puntos through the continuous mobilization of the spiritual force of the people.[4] By spiritual force, I am referencing a queer : Black genealogy born out of a genealogy that begins with the unnamed women who birthed my father's lineage in hiding from the violent beings descending on her lands to enslave and murder her people; it begins with the unnamed women who also birthed my father's lineage on a ship, or when she arrived in the Caribbean—these lands new and foreign to her; it begins with an enslaved negra who ran the first hospital (place of care, place of refuge) for her comadres and compadres and maybe even her lovers—Celsa Albert Batista calls her Micaela;[5] it begins with the generosity, astuteness, and diplomacy of Anacaona in the face of invasion; it begins with the sovereign government established by the rebel leader named Ana Maria following a successful uprising in Nigua in 1791; it begins with the unnamed women who laid prayers down in the forest so that Dutty Boukman could realize the war against the blancs and mula-tres, plantation owners all of them; it begins before we were named women and indias and negras and mulatas and pardas and trigueñas and dominica-nas; it begins by speaking the names of Mamá Tingó. Olivorio. Ana Maria.

---

come into sharp focus. See Sara Beltrame, "Aída Bueno Sarduy: 'Las afrodescen-dientes no somos feministas de habitación propia, sino de barracón,'" *El Salto*, December 12, 2018, https://www.elsaltodiario.com/feminismos/aida-bueno-sar-duy-antropologa-no-somos-feministas-de-habitacion-propia-sino-de-barracon. Please note that all images throughout are provided by the author, unless otherwise specified.

3   Years ago, I was introduced to Frantz Fanon's *Wretched of the Earth*, which pro-vided me with the language to begin to comprehend my experiences of colonization and decolonization. In this book, he writes, "Decolonization is quite simply the sub-stitution of one 'species' of mankind by another. The substitution is unconditional, absolute, total, and seamless." Frantz Fanon, *Wretched of the Earth* (New York: Pen-guin, 1995), 1. This quote lives within me, as do the works of Carrie Mae Weems, Wangechi Mutu, Cauleen Smith, and so many other Black women artists. The co-existence is uncomfortable, as is the transformation. I propose, in this ceremony, substitution, expansion, reconfiguration.

4   Eve Tuck and K. Wayne Yang, "Decolonization Is Not a Metaphor," *Decolon-ization: Indigeneity, Education & Society* 1, no. 1 (2012): 1–40.

5   Celsa Albert Batista, *Mujer y esclavitud en Santo Domingo* (Santo Domingo, DR: Ediciones CEDEE, 1993).

Lemba. Anacaona. Caonabo. Candelo. Metresili. Coatlicue. Ayida Wedo. Ogún Balendyo. Anaisa Pye. Micaela. Yemanya. Zumaco. Chalchihuitlicue. I include the ancestors Zora Neale Hurston. Audre Lorde. Gloria Anzaldúa.[6] James Baldwin. Toni Cade Bambara. Prince. Ida B. Wells. Essex Hemphill. June Jordan. Gloria Naylor. Paula Gunn Allen. Marsha Gomez.[7] Harriet Tubman. Sojourner Truth. Berta Caceres. Emilsen Manyoma.[8] Marielle Franco. Aida Cartagena Portalatin. José Esteban Muñoz. Michel Foucault. Aimé Césaire. Frantz Fanon.

In this ceremony, I call in, with love, those who—through their work—continue to create the enramada that enable this ceremony to take place, especially M. Jacqui Alexander, Jafari Sinclaire Allen, Carlos Andújar Persinal, Cheryl Boyce Taylor, Dionne Brand, Sharon Bridgforth, Ginetta Candelario,

---

6   Gloria Anzaldúa did not identify as queer : Black; however, she was friends with and informed by queer : Black activists, artists, and scholars. I include her here to demonstrate how my own understanding of queerness : blackness is deeply informed by reading her work. I could not come to an understanding of my particular experiences of queerness : blackness and queer : latinidad—either in the context of the United States or transnationally—without engaging Anzaldúa's thinking about nepantla, borderlands, and conciencia. The fact that I even have to articulate why she is included here speaks to ways in which we delimit queer : Black boundaries as always already exclusionary of borders/nepantlas—as though there are no queer : Black people in Laredo or Tijuana, as though there is not a deep history of queer : Black movement across these spaces—as though borders and nepantlas don't also emerge from the sea. There is work for us to do.

7   Paula Gunn Allen (Laguna Pueblo) and Marsha Gomez (Mississippi Choctaw, Mexica) also did not identify as queer : Black. But Allen gave me language to think about the movement of my [queer : Black] body-land on this mainland, what my relationship is to place and to family and to memory. Marsha Gomez was an artist and activist who was fiercely devoted to Native women's struggles, while at the same time always making community with queer : Black people. Our paths crossed because of Latina lesbian organizing; in our encuentros, she taught me about the power of and need for joy and bringing people close as preparation for war. Although Allen and Gomez did not identify as queer : Black women, their lives and work have been critical to my understandings of queerness : blackness—a queerness : blackness that is informed by the questions and embodied work of North American Native and Xicana women.

8   See Alexis Pauline Gumbs, "Don't Touch My Crown: The Failure of Decapitation and the Power of Black Women's Resistance," Bitch Media, April 27, 2017, https://www.bitchmedia.org/article/dont-touch-my-crown/failure-decapitation-and-power-black-womens-resistance.

Kamari Clarke, Kimberlé Crenshaw, Angie Cruz, Ochy Curiel, Angela Davis, Carlos U. Decena, Qwo-Li Driskill, Yuderkys Espinosa Miñoso, Chris Finley, Stephen G. Fullwood, Lorgia García-Peña, Lyndon Gill, Thomas Glave, Avery Gordon, Alexis Pauline Gumbs, Joy Harjo, Saidiya Hartman, Daniel Health Justice, E. Patrick Johnson, Joni L. Jones/Omi Osun Olomo, John Keene, Kamala Kempadoo, Rosamond King, Lawrence La-Fountain Stokes, Irene Lara Silva, Quisqueya Lora, Lisa Lowe, María Lugones, Nelson Maldonado-Torres, Yolanda Martínez San Miguel, April Mayes, Katherine McKittrick, Xhercis Méndez, Shani Mootoo, Angelique Nixon, Achy Obejas, Solimar Otero, Mark Padilla, Loida Maritza Perez, Fátima Portorreal Liriano, Anibal Quijano, Alaí Reyes-Santos, Tracy Robinson, Ileana Rodríguez, Juana María Rodríguez, Nelly Rosario, Rubén Silié Valdéz, Andrea Smith, Barbara Smith, C. Riley Snorton, Hortense Spillers, Omise'eke Natasha Tinsley, Silvio Torres-Saillant, Frank Wilderson.[9] As I begin this ceremony, I call in all those I have not yet named here, those spiritual forces that incorporated into realized personhood and took actions to deepen our understandings of freedom : sovereignty. After the dust of ceremony has settled, this ofrenda is what can be found.[10]

I desire queer : Black decolonization, that is, queer freedom : Black sovereignty. I know this desire is not just my desire. I know this because of how this same desire is articulated with and through relationship with others. I know this because M. Jacqui Alexander has generated the grounds for thinking about the "truth of spirit." She writes, "Since colonization has produced fragmentation and dismemberment at both the material and psychic levels, the work of decolonization has to make room for the deep yearning for wholeness, often expressed as a yearning to belong that is both material and existential, both psychic and physical, and which, when satisfied, can subvert and ultimately displace the pain of dismemberment."[11] In this sense, Alexander's theorizations of spirit and the spiritual build on Audre Lorde's ideas of the erotic as the intangible creative force that draws us into an insistence on living and

---

9 There are so many more scholars and artists I could name whose work has been key to my own work and thinking. Those named here are the ones whose work and/or conversations I revisit repeatedly. I hear their voices or see their faces when I write their names or when I think about the libations they have poured down and the forces they have called up so that the rest of us can be and do.

10 Sylvia Wynter, "The Ceremony Must Be Found: After Humanism," *Boundary 2* (1984): 19–70.

11 M. Jacqui Alexander, *Pedagogies of Crossing: Meditations on Feminism, Sexual Politics, Memory, and the Sacred* (Durham, NC: Duke University Press, 2005), 281.

freedom, as the "knowledge [that] empowers us, becomes a lens through which we scrutinize all aspects of our existence."[12] As reframed by Alexander, "We have a sacred connection to one another, and this is why enforced separations [colonization, fragmentation, dis-rememberment] wreak havoc on our souls." Because of this, Alexander proposes that decolonization "make room for the deep yearning for wholeness," and that it begin with recognition of interdependence and our deep yearning to belong.[13] That "deep yearning to belong" is grounded in erotic autonomy, what Alexander theorizes as a sexual agency and creative spiritual power that is the "sacred connection to one another."[14] By decolonization, I am referring to a subject that is constituted by sacred connection not just to another human being, but to all that is life on this planet. I am also speaking about Qwo-Li Driskill's call for a sovereign erotics, a reconfiguration of how bodies are connected to and inscribed by "nations, traditions, and histories."[15] These relations require us to interrogate how our diverse genealogies are bound to "land, memory, and history, but also specifically to the body."[16] Examining our relationships to island bodies[17] (our own and others'), to land, to water, to memory, to war is central to a process of decolonization. This ofrenda serves as a method that enables the process of imagining land restoration, the interruption of trauma, the possibilities of new histories, and the erotic autonomy[18] of queer : Indigenous and queer : Black beings. Taking up the spirit of the people, this book is an ofrenda that presents theoretical possibilities emerging from the options and tactics

12   Audre Lorde, *Sister Outsider* (Freedom, CA: Crossing Press, 1984), 57.

13   Alexander, *Pedagogies of Crossing*, 282.

14   Alexander, *Pedagogies of Crossing*, 282.

15   Qwo-Li Driskill, "Stolen from Our Bodies: First Nations Two-Spirits/Queers and the Journey to a Sovereign Erotic," *Studies in American Indian Literatures* 16, no. 2 (2004): 52.

16   Lisa Tatonetti, "Indigenous Fantasies and Sovereign Erotics: Outland Cherokees Write Two-Spirit Nations," in *Queer Indigenous Studies: Critical Interventions in Theory, Politics, and Literature*, ed. Qwo-Li Driskill et al. (Tucson: University of Arizona Press, 2011), 162.

17   Rosamond S. King, *Island Bodies: Transgressive Sexualities in the Caribbean Imagination* (Gainesville: University Press of Florida, 2014). Also see https://rosamondking.com/home.html.

18   M. Jacqui Alexander, "Erotic Autonomy as a Politics of Decolonization: An Anatomy of Feminist and State Practice in the Bahamas Tourist Industry," in *Feminist Genealogies, Colonial Legacies, Democratic Futures*, ed. M. Jacqui Alexander and Chandra Talpade Mohanty (New York: Routledge, 1997), 63–100.

mobilized by ancestors, loved ones, friends, and interlocutors and how these possibilities might enable the realization of queer freedom : Black sovereignty—queer : Black decolonization.[19]

My desires are in conflict with the ontological possibilities delimited by Christian coloniality[20] and its attendant capitalism—that is, the imposition of the logics of conversion, accumulation, and ownership that has dispossessed and continues to dispossess millions of people(s) of body-lands, water-memories, and altars-puntos.[21] Christian coloniality points to the violent and continual management of the most intimate levels of being: not just bodies, knowledge, and affect, but also that named as alma (soul, spirit, intangible essence of personhood). Christian coloniality produces and is rooted in ideas of free movement as dispossession, settlement, and salvation—teleological ends to violent means. Christian coloniality and its attendant capitalism require the valuation of some lives over others, some knowledges over others,

---

19 Here I am thinking of Chela Sandoval's articulation of tactics in *Methodology of the Oppressed* (Minneapolis: University of Minnesota Press, 2000), when she says, "The differential mode of social movement and consciousness depends on the practitioner's ability to read the current situation of power and self-consciously choosing and adopting the ideological stand best suited to push against its configurations. . . . Within the realm of differential social movement, ideological differences and their oppositional forms of consciousness . . . are understood as tactics" (59). Situating queer freedom : Black sovereignty within the realm of the spiritual allows us to consider the deep, expansive ideological differences and oppositional consciousness through which freedom : sovereignty can become possible.

20 In previously published work, I have used the term *Catholic coloniality*. As a result of many, many conversations with Christians and non-Christians, I have changed this term to *Christian coloniality*, as an effort to stave off the replication of the Black Legend within my own work, but also to draw attention to how negotiations and processes over the exercise of what constitutes Christian theology and how it is implemented was and continues to be negotiated by Christian communities around the world. I want to explicitly thank Jaqueline Jiménez Polanco, who in 2004 first spoke to me about the relationship between the Catholic church and the Dominican Republic's nation-state in the perpetuation of homophobic and anti-Black violence. My doctoral research aimed to further develop her idea through the study of ethnographic evidence.

21 Do not lose patience. In each of the subsequent chapters, I will discuss—thoroughly—what I mean by the concepts of altars-puntos, body-lands, and water-memories. Because this is a ceremony, time-space necessarily contracts and expands, and you are not expected to understand everything you encounter all at once.

some ways of being over others. The hierarchies of humanness that resulted through Christian colonization have never functioned for the well-being of all, but rather existed for the accumulation of body-land wealth and spiritual-intellectual authority for a few. An entire system of thought manifest as institutions (schools, borders, governments, etc.) has naturalized and continues to naturalize this order of things.[22] Today, the most visible manifestation of this system is the state.

The state produces unique dilemmas in the realization of queer : Black decolonization.[23] For one, the state produces and reproduces the temporal quandaries that emerge from Christian colonization: Whose time is more legitimate? Valid? Central to life and personhood? It produces the spatialization of specific temporalities and the negation and/or marginalization of those that don't reproduce the state into itself and into a Christian colonial future. The state—and the civic sphere that establishes, produces, and reproduces the State's ideologies—also legitimizes specific corporealities, over and above those it deems illegitimate. If we think of the state, and the spatio-temporalities it produces and reproduces, as the structure of time itself and as the "coordinates one uses for conceptualizing relevance,"[24] we can come to understand how the state is a problem to the realization of decolonization—that is, queer freedom : Black sovereignty, because the state requires a "singular timeline"[25] wherein the plurality of being and becoming is already configured as extraneous and, in some cases, impossible.

The state in the Caribbean (where this ofrenda gathers its materials), however, brings up additional problems. Is the state in the Caribbean a neocolonial

---

22 See Sylvia Wynter, "Unsettling the Coloniality of Being/Power/Truth/Freedom: Towards the Human, After Man, Its Overrepresentation—An Argument," *CR: The New Centennial Review* 3, no. 3 (2003): 257–337; Anibal Quijano, "Coloniality of Power and Eurocentrism in Latin America," *International Sociology* 15, no. 2 (2000): 215–32. Listen to Bob Marley's "Redemption Song"; Calle 13's "Latinoamérica"; Susana Baca's "Maria Lando"; Mercedes Sosa's "La Maza"; Manu Chao's "Clandestino"; Silvio Rodriguez's "Sueño con Serpientes"; and Xiomara Fortuna's "Rosa y Azul."
23 See Alexander, "Erotic Autonomy as a Politics of Decolonization."
24 Mark Rifkin, *Beyond Settler Time: Temporal Sovereignty and Indigenous Self-Determination* (Durham, NC: Duke University Press, 2017), 12.
25 Rifkin, *Beyond Settler Time*, 16.

state?[26] Is it a postcolonial state?[27] Is it a colonial settler state?[28] Is it an imperial colonial state? The presence of a large number of Afro-descendant peoples in the Caribbean, positioned as always already on the brink of being failed states,[29] further problematizes the question of the state and its definition.[30] How do we reconcile the presence, power, and futurity of those who were brought against their own will, through processes of colonization, and whose descendants now constitute the majority of the region's population? Here, the concept of arrivant may prove useful. Arrivant is a concept originally used by Barbadian Kamau Brathwaite[31] and that Chickasaw scholar Jodi Byrd develops to speak to the unique dilemmas of non-Indigenous peoples on Indigenous lands who themselves are subject to racial, colonial subjugation. Byrd uses this term to "signify those people forced into the Americas through the violence of European and Anglo-American colonialism and imperialism around the globe."[32] The term "provides another way to conceptualize the landscape of colonialism and Indigenous presence, overlaid in complicated ways with the practice of diaspora. The category is rooted in a Black-Caribbean poetics of being in place, gesturing to the multiple, fundamentally unsettled and unsettling relations to place that manifest, specifically, in Black geographies."[33]

---

26 See Angelique V. Nixon, *Resisting Paradise: Tourism, Diaspora, and Sexuality in Caribbean Culture* (Jackson: University Press of Mississippi, 2015).

27 See Shalini Puri, *The Caribbean Postcolonial: Social Equality, Post/Nationalism, and Cultural Hybridity* (New York: Springer, 2004).

28 See Andrea Smith, "Heteropatriarchy and the Three Pillars of White Supremacy: Rethinking Women of Color Organizing," in *Color of Violence: The INCITE! Anthology*, ed. INCITE! Women of Color Against Violence (Durham, NC: Duke University Press, 2016), 66–73; Patrick Wolfe, "Settler Colonialism and the Elimination of the Native," *Journal of Genocide Research* 8, no. 4 (2006): 387–409.

29 See Charles T. Call, "The Fallacy of the 'Failed State,'" *Third World Quarterly* 29, no. 8 (2008): 1491–507.

30 See Jodi A. Byrd, *The Transit of Empire: Indigenous Critiques of Colonialism* (Minneapolis: University of Minnesota Press, 2011).

31 See Edward Kamau Brathwaite, *Arrivants: A New World Trilogy* (1973). Though difficult to summarize so briefly, this epic trilogy attempts to grapple with the fragmentations of blackness produced by the many trajectories, misplacements, movements, and roots of people between continents, specifically between the African continent, Europe, and the Caribbean.

32 Byrd, *Transit of Empire*, xix.

33 See Manu Vimalassery, Juliana Hu Pegues, and Alyosha Goldstein, "Introduction: On Colonial Unknowing," *Theory & Event* 19, no. 4 (2016), https://muse.jhu.edu.

Arrivants are the majority in the Caribbean,[34] and arrivant states throughout the Caribbean are predicated on the perpetual negotiation of competing discourses and temporal-spatial relationships to colonialism and to sovereignty.[35] In these states the exercise of sovereignty shifts between registers, encompassing the "production of general norms by a body (the demos) made up of free and equal men and women"[36] and the ability to "exercise control over mortality and to define life as the deployment and manifestation of power."[37] As Yarimar Bonilla points out, "States continue to act as agents: they legislate, they deport, they invade, they build, and they borrow. Even as governments are toppled, states themselves persist."[38] Conceptualizing arrivant states allows us to think about the ways in which the state in the Caribbean is a project that emerged from colonialism and is a framework that contemporary polities continue to mobilize as a tool for enacting Christian colonial visions of territorialized futures. Arrivant states perpetually negotiate the racial, gender, and sexual hierarchies that were produced through Christian coloniality, most often becoming the upkeepers and protectors of Christian colonial morality at the expense of queer : Black people.[39] Lastly, arrivant states are predicated on the

---

34 Including those brought from the African continent over a 400-year period and those brought from the Asian subcontinent and China during the colonial and post-emancipation periods.

35 Take, for example, the complexities presented in any attempt to compare histories, experiences, and relationships to colonialism in Haiti, Cuba, Puerto Rico, Martinique, and Jamaica. Haiti is the result of a successful revolutionary war against France and French colonialists that took place between 1791 and 1804; Cuba was a Spanish colony until the Spanish-American War in 1898, when the US occupied it (subsequently, it became an independent state in 1902 but then became the ground for a successful left-wing revolution in 1959); Puerto Rico became a US territory in 1898 and is still in this precarious position; Martinique continues to be a département (colony) of France and, in the 2010 referendum, chose to remain so. Jamaica was granted independence from the UK in 1962.

36 J. Achille Mbembé, "Necropolitics," *Public Culture* 15, no. 1 (2003): 13.

37 Mbembé, "Necropolitics," 12.

38 Yarimar Bonilla, "Unsettling Sovereignty," *Cultural Anthropology* 32, no. 3 (2017): 331.

39 As of August 1, 2019, homosexuality (buggery, sodomy) is illegal in nine Caribbean nation-states. Across the region, notions of public morality undergird all kinds of anti-Black, anti-queer, and sexist violence. See Tara L. Atluri, *When the Closet Is a Region: Homophobia, Heterosexism and Nationalism in the Commonwealth Caribbean* (Cave Hill, Barbados: Centre for Gender and Development Studies, University of the West Indies, 2001); Joseph Gaskins, " 'Buggery' and the Commonwealth

perpetuation of discourses and policies that undergird myths of Indigenous extinction. All of these features, taken together, produce what could be construed as an arrivant state, which, rather than functioning as a space of queer freedom : Black sovereignty, in its stead perpetuates unfathomable violence and death. Linked to these arrivant states are the various intellectual apparatuses that sustain the states' spatio-temporality and logics in place through discourse, policies, and historiography.

Myths of Indigenous extinction are perpetuated throughout the continent/hemisphere.[40] In the Caribbean, these myths continue to fundamentally sustain the postcolonial state. These myths also illuminate how that same postcolonial state is a colonial settler structure that mobilizes arrivant futurities to consolidate power through continued Indigenous/Native dispossession. It is not a structure like that seen in the North American mainland, where Indigenous nations struggle to maintain sovereign political structures in the face of continued colonial settler violence perpetuated by the imperial state, civil society, and non-state entities like narcos and global businesses.[41] On

---

Caribbean: A Comparative Examination of the Bahamas, Jamaica, and Trinidad and Tobago," in *Human Rights, Sexual Orientation and Gender Identity in the Commonwealth: Struggles for Decriminalisation and Change*, ed. Corinne Lennox and Matthew Waites (London: Institute of Commonwealth Studies, 2013), 429–54. For the last point, see M. Jacqui Alexander's essay, "Not Just (Any) Body Can Be a Citizen: The Politics of Law, Sexuality and Postcoloniality in Trinidad and Tobago and the Bahamas," *Feminist Review* 48, no. 1 (1994): 5–23.

40 The central myth of Indigenous extinction is that all Indigenous peoples in the Caribbean were extinguished within the first thirty years of colonization; it is closely accompanied by myths of the dead Indian in North America. In both iterations, Native peoples of Abya Yala/Turtle Island are relegated to a romantic, idealized, but hermetically sealed, pure past. The myth undergirds many structurally violent practices, including policies of termination in the US, violence against and disappearance of Native women in Canada, and Native appropriation by the state all while killing and removing Native peoples from land by the thousands in Mexico, Colombia, Nicaragua, Honduras, and so on. In the Caribbean, it enables the perpetuation of the Indigenous ethno-state so clearly critiqued by many Caribbean scholars, at the expense of Afro-descendant peoples. Here, I argue that it also damages Caribbean Indigenous peoples, too, in that it relegates Indigenous Caribbean peoples to the realm of the ludicrous, specifically, to the realm of the impossible. In the interstices between Black and Indigenous (Native) studies, I am particularly inspired by Tiffany Lethabo King's book, *The Black Shoals: Offshore Formations of Black and Native Studies* (Durham, NC: Duke University Press, 2019).

41 See Bonilla, "Unsettling Sovereignty"; Megan Ybarra, *Green Wars: Conservation*

the mainland, Indigenous and arrivant peoples are often pitted against each other in obscuring the colonial settler state through discourses and policies based on blood logics (for example), like mestizaje[42] or multiculturalism.[43] In the Caribbean, arrivants are the majority and among them exist elites that have appropriated the colonial settler state through postcolonial mechanisms, thus producing the arrivant state.[44] The results of these appropriations are the continued disenfranchisement of the majority of people and the continued perpetuation of Christian coloniality to the detriment of queer freedom : Black sovereignty.[45]

The Dominican Republic (DR) is one such arrivant state, in which the state discourses, policies, and practices perpetuate Catholic Hispanic temporalities, corporealities, and geographies, to the detriment and continued decimation of queer : Black peoples. In this way, both the histories and futures of Indigenous and arrivant descendants become intertwined,[46] inseparable, and also central to the realization of queer freedom : Black sovereignty. Until Caribbeanist scholars—specifically those engaged with the difficult work of Afro-recuperation and reconfiguring racial histories, memories, and futures— can end myths of Indigenous extinction and the perpetuation of these myths as a product and tool of colonial settler violence, we may not be able to recover the full narrative of queer : Black resistance, survivance, and struggle across the Caribbean. The Dominican Republic is no exception. The mobilization

---

and Decolonization in the Maya Forest (Oakland: University of California Press, 2018).

42 For an example, read Taunya Lovell Banks, "Mestizaje and the Mexican Mestizo Self: No Hay Sangre Negra, so There Is No Blackness," *Southern California Interdisciplinary Law Journal* 15 (2005): 199.

43 For an example, read Juliet Hooker, "Indigenous Inclusion/Black Exclusion: Race, Ethnicity and Multicultural Citizenship in Latin America," *Journal of Latin American Studies* 37, no. 2 (2005): 285–310.

44 In *Streetwalking: LGBTQ Lives and Protest in the Dominican Republic* (New Brunswick, NJ: Rutgers University Press, forthcoming 2020), I describe the Dominican Republic as a Catholic Hispanic state, signaling how the arrivant state operationalizes specific forms of Christian coloniality, to the detriment of queer : Black peoples.

45 See Deborah A. Thomas, *Modern Blackness: Nationalism, Globalization, and the Politics of Culture in Jamaica* (Durham, NC: Duke University Press, 2004).

46 See Milagros Ricourt, *The Dominican Racial Imaginary: Surveying the Landscape of Race and Nation in Hispaniola* (New Brunswick, NJ: Rutgers University Press, 2016).

of both the myths of Indigenous extinction and the production of indias as imagined national, racialized subjects has produced a field of work in which this task is extremely difficult.[47] This ofrenda begins by articulating our collective responsibility to the first peoples of this continent to reconcile with our shared roles in Indigenous genocide and in the continued perpetuation of the colonial settler futurities through the Christian colonial arrivant state, in all of its forms. Equally, we have a responsibility to unearth complicated histories and the continued possibilities of solidarity and shared struggle in the face of Christian colonial violences within the spaces of colonial settler/arrivant states. Imagining different geographies of personhood, of being, of consciousness, and of solidarity supersedes the limits and the problems produced by the arrivant state in questions of queer freedom : Black sovereignty. In other words, the state is anathema to queer : Black present-future-past life.

This ofrenda begins with various premises. The first premise is that the structures of power, of knowledge and being, that were established through processes of colonization continue through the ongoing temporal-spatial structures that shaped colonial socio-economic-political relationships.[48] For this reason, among others, queer freedom : Black sovereignty requires us to discard the state as a site of freedom : sovereignty. The solution to this premise is not to prescribe other alternatives, but rather to open up the ceremonial reader's imagination to the possibility of other possibilities. A second premise is that the frameworks of sex, race, and gender that we currently operate with are a product of the processes of colonization and are central to interpreting the negotiations of power over and across the body-lands of "America"/Abya Yala.[49] As a result, this ofrenda is messy because it slips in between our contemporary, legible renderings of sex, race and gender while also opening up the space

---

47 See Ginetta EB Candelario, "La ciguapa y el ciguapeo: Dominican Myth, Metaphor, and Method," *Small Axe: A Caribbean Journal of Criticism* 20, no. 3 (51) (2016): 100–112. While I disagree with one of the fundamental methodological premises of this article (that mythology resides outside the realm of cultural and scholarly validity), the basic critique of the ways in which the state elides and re-inscribes itself through the figure of the ciguapa is extremely powerful.

48 See Nelson Maldonado-Torres, "The Topology of Being and the Geopolitics of Knowledge: Modernity, Empire, Coloniality," *City* 8, no. 1 (2004): 29–56; Quijano, "Coloniality of Power and Eurocentrism."

49 See Yuderkys Espinosa Miñoso, Diana Gómez Correal, and Karina Ochoa Muñoz, eds., *Tejiendo de otro modo: Feminismo, epistemología y apuestas descoloniales en Abya Yala* (Popayán, Colombia: Universidad del Cauca, 2014).

for other concepts to emerge. The third premise is that Christian theo-philo-sophical conflicts about the processes of colonization operate through these structuring processes and frameworks,[50] and as a result, I argue that the pro-cess of decolonization must take place on spiritual-religious grounds that take seriously the theo-philosophical transformations produced through these conflicts. These conflicts produced various iterations of Christianity, includ-ing the forms that developed *because of* the contexts and sites of colonization.

Christians are the world's largest religious group (31 percent of the world's population). The estimated number of Christian births outnumbering deaths in the Americas between 2010 and 2015 was approximately 38 million.[51] In Latin America and the Caribbean, there are over 400 million Catholics, and nearly 40 percent of the world's Catholic population is there. The percentage of Catholics within the region has declined in the last fifty years, from 90 per-cent of the population in the 1960s to 69 percent of the population in 2014. The decline is related to an increase in the percentage of Christian Evangelicals across the region, who constitute about 19 percent of the region's Christians. Including both Catholics and Evangelicals, Christians in Latin America make up 88 percent of those born in, raised in, and/or practicing their faith. In our contemporary world we are experiencing rapid rates of change that have provoked new formulations of ancient Christian theo-philosophical conflicts about the relationship between human beings and nature; sexuality and gender—including how these define moral authority and justice; the re-lationship between church(es) and political institutions and the implications of this relationship for governmentality. These conflicts have implications for the present-future-past of queer freedom : Black sovereignty. Though faith, belief, and practice may not always align, the presence of socially conserva-tive Christians in key positions in governments, or in political relationships with government officials, has had an impact on social policies affecting queer freedom : Black sovereignty. The Dominican Republic is one such site—it is a Christian colonial arrivant State that has produced many contradictory, simul-taneous realities. As a nepantla between Africa and the Americas, between the Atlantic and the Caribbean Sea, within the present-future-past of colonization,

---

50 See Nelson Maldonado-Torres, "Race, Religion, and Ethics in the Modern/Colo-nial World," *Journal of Religious Ethics* 42, no. 4 (2014): 691–711.

51 See Conrad Hackett and David McClendon, "Christians Remain World's Largest Religious Group, but They Are Declining in Europe," Pew Research Center, April 5, 2017, http://www.pewresearch.org/fact-tank/2017/04/05/christians-remain-worlds -largest-religious-group-but-they-are-declining-in-europe.

between Christian colonial time-space and queer : Black tempo-corporealities, the Dominican Republic is an "in-between space, an unstable, unpredictable, precarious, always-in-transition space lacking clear boundaries."[52] It is the political territory from which I will draw the majority of my evidence, despite my personal intellectual and spiritual repudiation of its validity and capacity to sustain queer freedom : Black sovereignty.

Relatedly, this ofrenda presents arguments and examples that are potentially applicable to the collective realization of decolonization among queer : Black people throughout Abya Yala, recognizing that "the queerness of Black life . . . is nothing other than the blackness of queer life."[53] For this reason, throughout this ofrenda, queer : Black will always be signaled in analogy—so as to demonstrate both the space of their incommensurability and the ways in which " 'queer' challenges notions of heteronormativity and heterosexism, [and] 'black' resists notions of assimilation and absorption."[54] Throughout the text, my use of the shorthand *queer : Black* (queer is to Black) also stands in for various configurations of this ceremony's key terms: queer, freedom, Black, sovereignty. It is an incomplete analogy, pushing the reader to reflect on their own desire for a clear and articulated resolution to the fundamental questions about what these terms imply. The unresolved analogy points to the possibilities of what awaits us on the other side of ceremony. In a very real sense, I am asking readers, those of us together in this ceremony, to be spiritually, emotionally, and physically present—to approach the production of knowledge as a collective responsibility that is both embodied and relational. Because this ofrenda is a ceremony, the meanings of these terms must be found in processes requiring embodiment and relationship: conversation, discussion, compartir, ceremony. As with jazz, bomba, atabales, and krik? krak!, this is a call and response. "Queer freedom : Black sovereignty" is the call. The responses are revealed through the reader's own experiences of the concepts presented here. I am asking all of us to enact what has been articulated by Leanne Simpson when she stated that "individuals carry the responsibility for

---

52 Gloria Anzaldúa, *The Gloria Anzaldúa Reader* (Durham, NC: Duke University Press, 2009), 243.

53 Tavia Nyong'o, *Afro-Fabulations: The Queer Drama of Black Life* (New York: NYU Press, 2019), 2.

54 E. Patrick Johnson and Mae G. Henderson, "Queering Black Studies/'Quaring' Queer Studies," in *Black Queer Studies: A Critical Anthology*, ed. E. Patrick Johnson and Mae G. Henderson (Durham, NC: Duke University Press, 2005), 7.

generating meaning within their own lives—they carry the responsibility for engaging their minds, bodies and spirits in a practice of generating meaning."[55]

Other incommensurabilities are not signaled as succinctly. For example, this ofrenda excavates queerness : blackness within an arrivant state (the Dominican Republic) already preconfigured as exclusive of both. As a result, the work of this ofrenda is also in part a challenge to the presumptions of a US readership about what queerness : blackness contains/can be/can offer. US readers—including the queer : Black folk among us—will be unable to enter, penetrate, or be a part of some of the worlds presented here. There is a space of unknowability that is delineated by language, by cultural references, by geographic references, by relationship, by narration, by the spirits, and by power itself. In this sense, "opacity is an ethical proposition, [but] it can also be understood as an ontological condition and a form of political legitimacy"[56] that offers an alternative to the violence of Christian coloniality that seeks to always know and possess that knowledge. This, like other works of queer : Black thought,[57] is a work that presupposes that opacity "is not enclosure within an impenetrable autarchy but subsistence within an irreducible singularity."[58] In this case, subsistence refers to the perpetuation of queer : Black life through various iterations of Christian coloniality, most recently rendered in the context of an arrivant state. As articulated by C. Riley Snorton, "tarrying with the unfixed, submerged, and frequently disavowed connections within blackness and transness requires that both author and reader suspend a demand for transparency, which is also, as Glissant suggests, to forgo a methodological operation that seeks to bring the submerged to the surface."[59] Extending the specificities articulated by Snorton to queerness : blackness more broadly, the reader will often find that they are being called into relationship to the ceremony and all those present within it.

---

55 Leanne Betasamosake Simpson, "Land as Pedagogy: Nishnaabeg Intelligence and Rebellious Transformation," *Decolonization: Indigeneity, Education & Society* 3, no. 3 (2014): 11.

56 Zach Blas, "Opacities: An Introduction," *Camera Obscura: Feminism, Culture, and Media Studies* 31, no. 2 (92) (2016): 149.

57 See the works of Fred Moten, Alexis Pauline Gumbs, Tavia Nyong'o, C. Riley Snorton, and Omi'seke Natasha Tinsley.

58 Édouard Glissant, *Poetics of Relation* (Ann Arbor: University of Michigan Press, 1997), 190.

59 C. Riley Snorton, *Black on Both Sides: A Racial History of Trans Identity* (Minneapolis: University of Minnesota Press, 2017), 10.

The call and response of this ceremony, the insistence on being in relation, draws on the provocations of Afrofuturism, or an "oppositionality and an historical critique that seeks to undermine the logic of linear progress that buttresses Western universalism, rationalism, empiricism, logocentrism, and their standard-bearer: white supremacy."[60] Afrofuturism "appropriates the narrative techniques of science fiction to put a Black face on the future. In doing so, it combats those whitewashed visions of tomorrow generated by a global 'futures industry' that equates blackness with the failure of progress and technological catastrophe."[61] Today, in the present-future-past, realized personhood and transformations in consciousness are close to acts of science fiction, because the context in which queer : Black life currently operates is predicated on the severe, perpetual marginalization, dislocation, and onticide of queer : Black people.[62] Queer freedom : Black sovereignty requires a reorientation so radical as to be unknowable; we can only approximate this present-future-past through imagination, dreams, memory, and the "tactical recovery of Black soul."[63] This ofrenda proposes queer : Black present-future-pasts, but it also proposes reorienting our fundamental relationship to temporal corporeality. This creates a rupture to our discursive inheritances about queer liberation[64] and Black freedom and emancipation.[65]

---

60 J. Griffith Rollefson, "The 'Robot Voodoo Power' Thesis: Afrofuturism and Anti-Anti-Essentialism from Sun Ra to Kool Keith," *Black Music Research Journal* 28, no. 1 (2008): 84.

61 Lisa Yaszek, "An Afrofuturist Reading of Ralph Ellison's *Invisible Man*," *Rethinking History* 9, nos. 2–3 (2005): 297.

62 See Calvin L. Warren, *Ontological Terror: Blackness, Nihilism, and Emancipation* (Durham, NC: Duke University Press, 2018).

63 Rollefson, "The 'Robot Voodoo Power' Thesis," 85.

64 Discourses of queer liberation often focus on seminal events like Stonewall, the devastation produced by the HIV pandemic, and the articulation of civil and human rights and protections. Queer studies has held an uneasy relationship with gay and lesbian studies from its inception—see Lisa Duggan's article "The Discipline Problem: Queer Theory Meets Lesbian and Gay History," *GLQ* 2 (1995): 179–91—and these tensions are not only methodological but also ideological. For the purposes of this ceremony, I draw on Cathy J. Cohen's seminal text "Punks, Bulldaggers, and Welfare Queens: The Radical Potential of Queer Politics?" to instead ask us to reconsider the fundamental framing of queerness itself; *GLQ: A Journal of Lesbian and Gay Studies* 3, no. 4 (1997): 437–65.

65 There is an extensive field of study and series of social movements focused on questions of Black freedom and emancipation. Key figures in this field include W. E. B. DuBois, *The Souls of Black Folk*; Saidiya Hartman, *Scenes of Subjection*;

In criollo (read: Black realized through land, read: Black realized through local histories, read: Black through solidarity with Indigenous peoples, read: Black through solidarity with other peasants, read: Black through an island framework beyond the nation-state) traditional ceremonies, the misterios (elemental forces) enter the enramada (ceremonial grounds) to heal people: to cleanse them, bless them, and assist them in navigating the world and its problems. This text is my ceremony, my ofrenda, my prayer for queer freedom : Black sovereignty—two intertwined states of being and forms of relation in which no single piece can exist without the other. Queer freedom : Black sovereignty is corporeal-temporal-spiritual. Consider this: Can we imagine a Black sovereignty in which queerness is no longer an apt metaphor for corporeal-temporal difference and people are ontologically free?[66] Can we imagine a queer freedom not predicated on Black subjugation and unidimensional, homonormative configurations of bodies, spaces, and times? History has shown that Black sovereignty has yet to translate into queer freedom. The Haitian Revolution and Black nationalism did not produce societies in which masisis and madivinesse (the holy, the divine), gays, lesbians, same-gender-loving peoples, and quares could articulate a sovereign erotic autonomy.[67] The advent of queer liberation as configured by the global, neoliberal lesbian, gay, bisexual, and transgender (LGBT) movement is currently predicated on the continued and increasing oppression of Black peoples. This is made visible in consolidation of LGBT power through imperial projects—like marriage, the military, and occupation. It, too, has not produced the queer freedom : Black sovereignty I speak of here. In all of these instances, freedom, emancipation, liberation, and sovereignty have relied on the continued dispossession of Indigenous American lands, bodies, histories, and memories.

Angela Davis, *Women, Race & Class*; Ida B. Wells; Frederick Douglass; Gregorio Luperón; Antenor Firmin; Leopold Senghor; Ramon Emeterio Betances; and José Martí. Some of the key moments in struggles for Black freedom and emancipation include the Wolof uprising of 1521, the Haitian Revolution, the American Civil War, the abolition of the slave trade and slavery, the struggle for civil rights in the US, the struggle for land and human rights in Black communities across Latin America, and decolonization from European colonialism in Africa and the Caribbean up until 1975.

66 See Cohen, "Punks, Bulldaggers, and Welfare Queens."

67 See E. Patrick Johnson, " 'Quare' Studies, or (Almost) Everything I Know About Queer Studies I Learned from My Grandmother," *Text and Performance Quarterly* 21, no. 1 (2001): 1–25.

We are not currently free; we are not currently sovereign. We continue to lose our places as full members of our communities, our lands, and our peoples, and we die young. We die violently. We die because of the fear and hate of others. Our suffering and our deaths are unjust. We have been the smoky mirror against which the human has been defined. In the wake of Christian coloniality, we continue to navigate through the muck of history; the detritus floating on our oceans is but a manifestation of our collective spiritual state: disconnection. Each wave of Christian coloniality has produced fewer and fewer free and sovereign people/lands/structures. Within the conch shell of time,[68] we are moving over palimpsests[69] written into the earth with our blood. There is no return to another place. There is no door to magically go through and become another.[70] This is the world we have received, on loan from future generations, as an inheritance from our ancestors—all of our ancestors, including those yet to come. And so now, we must transform it. Imagine it anew. And imagine it as a place where queer freedom : Black sovereignty is realizable as a consistent and ongoing condition of collective existence that does not replicate the dispossession on which it has too often been predicated.

This ofrenda is not the master's house. It will not look like the master's house. It is not even in the master's field. This text lives in the locus of difference in which the polarities (body/spirit; heaven/earth) that have sustained Christian coloniality will be challenged and undone in order to render new states of being and knowing as possible. When you think you have landed safely in one body of knowledge, it will drop instantly into another. It will argue that within criollo traditions, the alma (soul) is the locus of human being-ness and human being-ness is a constant across different planes of being.[71] When the misterio is known to exist in all living things, the body-land is what incarnates as different kinds of human beings that includes two-legged, one-legged, four-legged, and the winged. Comparable to the concept of orishas among Yoruba practitioners, misterios exist in stark contrast to the Christian

---

68 Thank you to Angela Mictlanxotchil Anderson Guerrero for her articulation of time as a conch shell, unending and expansive.

69 Alexander, *Pedagogies of Crossing*, 190.

70 See Rita Indiana Hernández, *La Mucama de Omicunlé* [*Tentacle*] (Cáceres, Spain: Editorial Periférica, 2015).

71 For a discussion of orisha transmogrification, see Xhercis Méndez, "Transcending Dimorphism: Afro-Cuban Ritual Praxis and the Rematerialization of the Body," *Power* 3, no. 3 (2003): 47–69. I was particularly inspired by her conversation of the orishas as shapeshifters.

colonial concepts of the human, in which the body-land is the locus of human-ness, requiring confirmation of the existence of a soul in order to—through baptism—achieve humanness. Nowhere is this contrast clearer than in the multiple baptisms that a servidora—a person who serves the misterios—receives. The bautizo (initiation) in the criollo tradition serves to enable the body-land to achieve the transformation from one kind of humanness into other kinds of humanness. These transformations enable trans-historical mediation: the collapse of temporality within the corporeal body-land of the servidora. The body-land becomes the altar, the punto, the palo, the poto-mitan, the site of "historiographical practices that generate a distinctive mode of Afro-Atlantic religious subjectivity."[72] That subjectivity is not located in the already-presumed unitary subject of the person. Rather the misterios refer to a context in which "whatever possesses a soul is a subject, and whatever has a soul is capable of having a point of view."[73] Within this conceptualization of the human, spirits "see in the same way as we do different things because their bodies are different from ours. . . . The visible shape of the body is a power-ful sign of these differences in affect."[74] These perspectives, in turn, inform a poetics of relation[75] that undergirds criollo traditions, in which relations are inscribed in body-lands through ritual, through protest, and through desire and where difference is the presumed, welcome outcome of a prayer well said.[76] As Lorde makes clear,

> Difference must be not merely tolerated, but seen as a fund of necessary polarities between which our creativity can spark like a dialectic. Only then does the necessity for interdependency become unthreatening. Only within that interdependency of different strengths, acknowledged and equal, can the power to seek new ways of being in the world generate, as well as the courage and sustenance to act where there are no charters. . . . Within the interdependence of mutual (nondominant) differences lies that security

72 Elizabeth Pérez, "Spiritist Mediumship as Historical Mediation: African-American Pasts, Black Ancestral Presence, and Afro-Cuban Religions," *Journal of Religion in Africa* 41, no. 4 (2011): 333.

73 Eduardo Viveiros De Castro, "Cosmological Deixis and Amerindian Perspectiv-ism," *Journal of the Royal Anthropological Institute* (1998): 476.

74 De Castro, "Cosmological Deixis," 478.

75 See Glissant, *Poetics of Relation*; Katherine McKittrick, ed., *Sylvia Winter: On Be-ing Human as Praxis* (Durham, NC: Duke University Press, 2014).

76 Glissant, *Poetics of Relation*.

which enables us to descend into the chaos of knowledge and return with true visions of our future, along with the concomitant power to effect those changes which can bring that future into being.[77]

Given knowledge and language—not just from books legitimized by academic gatekeepers, but also from elders and communities in ceremonies, also from peers and colleagues in struggles for social justice, also from friends and family who love each other—there is a responsibility to enact that knowledge and that language, and to render with great care the many ways of being that have sustained us and that are the sources of our greatest power. To enact multiple knowledges and languages simultaneously is to embody what I call woven density—that is, a multiplicity of often contradictory registers of being that draw on multiple frameworks to actualize meaning in the everyday. Woven density allows us to visualize how gender, sexuality, and race are interconnected processes that draw on multiple registers and frameworks and, like spirit, shift according to context—shifting from one kind of humanness into other kinds of humanness. When the queerness of time condenses in the production of the Black body-land, then gender is re-articulated along a different space-time axis than that provided by Christian colonial teleology. When the blackness of desire impulses the queer body-land into life, then life is renewed through dance, prayer, sweat, sex, and contact between the immaterial and material worlds. In these moments, our body-lands are at their densest possibilities, and also at their free-est. Aquí, this moment, is when the logics of production, of colonization, of violence, of control no longer matter. The woven density of time itself enables distinct possibilities that redirect our gaze, our being, and our person away from salvation, redemption, and Christian colonial impulses. Decolonization becomes possible.

Queer : Black people manage systems of power that regulate social relations through the mobilization of gender and sexuality as biblical binaries and theological commandments; we manage systems of power that mobilize racial hierarchies lodged within Christian colonial temporal and spatial logics. We manage these systems of power—that excise, that exclude, that concentrate, that discipline, that kill—through the amalgamation of different registers of being that are deeply interdependent and deeply contextual. By deep I mean that the modes of interdependency go beyond the temporal limits of birth/death/living and extend into the realm of ancestors and spirits. By deep I mean

---

77 Lorde, *Sister Outsider*, 111.

that the context goes beyond the seen world into the unseen world where the erotic is born, and where dreams and archives of the imagination are manifest.[78]

This depth is a site of woven density, a space-time compression that produces itself through expressions that do not rest on a fixed punto.[79] The weaving process gives rise to the density of being and zambo consciousness.[80] Zambo consciousness is an epistemic and ontological framework that could enable us to shift our gaze away from the Christian colonial assumptions central to mestizaje and toward Afro-Indigenous solidarities manifest through the erotic, desires, sex, faith, friendships, and through embodied and spiritual struggles for queer freedom : Black sovereignty. Zambo consciousness need not mobilize queer : Indigenous extinction as its requirement. Zambo consciousness could resonate with creolization as a "new and original dimension allowing each person to be there and elsewhere, rooted and open, lost in the mountains and free beneath the sea, in harmony and in errantry."[81] Within zambo consciousness, the subject-object could give way to the infinite subject, capable of multiple enunciations. It could enable us to engage with the shared knowledge of relations and the ways those shared knowledges manifest across sites of worship, struggle, healing, storytelling, protest, and artistic production. These shared knowledges sometimes transit within the waves of Christian coloniality, sometimes in diametric opposition to the ripples produced in its wake. The framework of zambo consciousness enables us to gaze into ethnographic evidence, the evidence that ethnography has indeed taken

---

78 I write about what I call archives of the imagination in Ana Maurine Lara, "I Wanted to Be More of a Person: Conjuring [Afro] [Latinx] [Queer] Futures," *Bilingual Review/Revista Bilingüe* 33, no. 4 (January 2017): 1–14. It is also important to spend time with Audre Lorde's poetry and Alexis Pauline Gumbs, *M Archive: After the End of the World* (Durham, NC: Duke University Press, 2018). Within our imagination there resides an infinite archive of possible worlds.

79 The next section of this ceremony is entirely dedicated to expanding on the concept of altars-puntos, but in short: You are an altar-punto. This book is an altar-punto. Placing a candle by the river creates an altar-punto.

80 *Zambo* is a racial term produced through Spanish colonization. The origins of the term itself—that is, the naming of specific phenotypical admixtures as distinct racial categories—is as violent as the origins of the terms mulato or mestizo, indio and negro. I reappropriate zambo here to signal spaces, histories, and intentional moves toward solidarity and empowerment taken on by Maroons, rebels, protectors, and also everyday people. I don't use zambo as an identity marker but rather as an index for an expansion of particular kinds of consciousness.

81 Glissant, *Poetics of Relation*, 34.

place, to discern the map toward queer freedom : Black sovereignty. It could do so by indexing the interdependent nature of queer : Black subjectivities, that is, interdependence among and between all that exists.

If a new punto appears, it is absorbed into the whole possibility of light. A new body-land incorporates a new density of being. Woven density is rhizomatic: it extends into multiple, simultaneous directions established through relation. Drawing from woven density, I can embody, actualize, and move between what appear to be dimorphic forms but which in actuality are polymorphic, and densely so. We are animate beings within a larger community of animate beings where difference is the norm rather than the exceptionalized exception. Our social understandings of this, however, are still confined by the colonial/modern gender systems—the coloniality of being and knowledge—and we have yet to fully realize that difference.[82]

What I mean is, what would it look like if queer : Black people could fully worship in public the way we do in private?

What I mean is, what would it look like if all people were as fully queer in public as we are in private?

What kind of world would that be, where the structures of power are reconfigured and all beings and desires co-exist without harm?

These questions are my central preoccupation. They inform my creative-intellectual-spiritual work, my relations to other beings, and my relationships to land, history, place, and language. They inform what this ofrenda is and the work this ofrenda will do, in the service of queer freedom : Black sovereignty. The question about worship is not distant from the question about queerness. The source of faith, desire, and creativity is one and the same—no matter how you look at it, what you think, or what you believe. You could look at that source as the erotic. You could call it ashe or voudoun or misterio. You could know that source as rational thought. You could believe that source is the Creator. What matters is how we choose to engage and articulate the truths

82 See María Lugones, "Coloniality and Gender," *Tabula Rasa* 9 (2008): 73–102; María Lugones, "Hacia un feminismo descolonial," *La Manzana de la Discordia* 6, no. 2 (2016): 105–17; María Lugones, "Subjetividad esclava, colonialidad de género, marginalidad y opresiones múltiples," in *Pensando los Feminismos en Bolivia*, ed. Colectiva LESBrujas (La Paz, Bolivia: Conexión Fondo de Emancipación, 2012), 129–40.

about who we love, how we move through the world, how we relate to place, how we relate to other beings, and how we relate to land.

Because of this, this ofrenda at times employs the modal verb form as its rhetorical framework, specifically, what possibility is or can encompass in the present-future-past. I am specifically choosing a form that in English is defined as a polite or weak form of argumentation, knowing full well that the use of words like *could* or *might* in the context of defining possibility generally translates into demure or deferential social posturing. But this is because I am applying a Spanish linguistic assumption to the English grammatical form. I am using the English-language modal form much in the same way I would use the subjunctive in Spanish, a verb tense that is used in desire, emotion, necessity, or uncertainty. This is an exercise in woven density. There is no hesitation in my claims. To be free : sovereign, we could shed our fears of desire, of emotion, of necessity, of uncertainty itself. Echoing Saidiya Hartman's yearning, "by advancing a series of speculative arguments and exploiting the capacities of the subjunctive (a grammatical mood that expresses doubts, wishes, and possibilities), in fashioning a narrative, which is based upon archival research, and by that I mean a critical reading of the archive that mimes the figurative dimensions of history,"[83] I intend here to move into the space of uncertainty, destabilizing what is knowable and undermining the spatio-temporality central to colonial projects.

For some of us, uncertainty could be part of our condition of existence. Collectively, many of us might be negotiating that uncertainty through frameworks that look strangely and simultaneously like movements for de-colonization or, conversely, like ethno-nationalist movements—depending on how one situates oneself within the frameworks of power, corporeality, spirituality, and temporality. As a result of that uncertainty, there may be a great and grave necessity for redefining our relationships. I give valence to desire and emotion as legitimate ontological sources, and I understand that uncertainty is the corporeal and spiritual disposition and locus necessary for creativity, transcendence, and collective social change that is informed by the erotic. In this sense, I articulate desire and emotion distinctly from "affect" or the "impersonal intensities that do not belong to a subject or an object, [which do not] reside in the mediating space between a subject and an object."[84] I

---

83 Saidiya Hartman, "Venus in Two Acts," *Small Axe: A Caribbean Journal of Criticism* 12, no. 2 (2008): 11.

84 Ben Anderson, "Modulating the Excess of Affect: Morale in a State of 'Total

articulate both desire and emotion as elements of the erotic, that illuminate the erotic, and that enable sovereign erotics and erotic autonomy. Part of my desire to enact decolonization is to first draw attention to the ways in which I embody language: having been raised bilingual and knowing—through experiences of learning language, or reaching the limits of my own vocabulary and grammatical expertise in multiple languages—that language shapes an entire worldview, not just in how it is spoken, but also in how, in the process of speech acts, speech is contextualized and re-contextualizes ontological modes.[85] In English, my use of the modal form is always inflected and informed by the Spanish subjunctive. Call it woven density.

For these reasons, this book presents ethnographic evidence as a tool for what I term speculative anthropology, an anthropology that eschews positivism's imperatives and instead attends to the poetics of being: the opinions, thoughts, beliefs, desires, and imaginings of beings as manifested through interviews, themselves an articulation of my opinions, thoughts, beliefs, desires, and imaginings that emerge from my own situated observations.[86] I am choosing to operate within the opacity at the center of knowledge, in that space in between, in the "thought in reality,"[87] a nepantla.[88] It is this "thought in reality [which] spaces itself out into the world. It informs the imaginary of peoples, their varied poetics, which it then transforms, meaning, in them its risks

---

War,' " in *The Affect Theory Reader*, ed. Melissa Gregg and Gregory J. Seigworth (Durham, NC: Duke University Press, 2010), 161.

85 For an extensive engagement with ideas about language, speech, writing, speech acts—i.e., the production of meaning and being through language—see Jacques Derrida, *Of Grammatology* (Baltimore, MD: Johns Hopkins University Press, 1976). If you are interested in thinking about the centrality of race, language, and the construction of the human, see Alexander G. Weheliye, *Habeas viscus: Racializing Assemblages, Biopolitics, and Black Feminist Theories of the Human* (Durham, NC: Duke University Press, 2014).

86 For conversations on the production of situated knowledges within Black feminist intellectual traditions, see Irma McClaurin, ed., *Black Feminist Anthropology: Theory, Politics, Praxis, and Poetics* (New Brunswick, NJ: Rutgers University Press, 2001).

87 Glissant, *Poetics of Relation*, 1.

88 Read Gloria Anzaldúa, *Light in the Dark/Luz en lo oscuro: Rewriting Identity, Spirituality, Reality* (Durham, NC: Duke University Press, 2015), for an extensive conversation on nepantla; also Pat Mora, *Nepantla: Essays from the Land in the Middle* (Albuquerque: University of New Mexico Press, 2008).

become realized."[89] This nepantla "averigua el conflicto. It provides associations and connective tissues. . . . [It] interweaves multiple, superimposed strands of thought."[90] Therefore, this could not be anything but an ofrenda and, as an ofrenda, a potential map to queer freedom : Black sovereignty. By map I mean a reconceptualization of spatio-temporality that centers the woven density of spiritual being-ness as corporeal actualization: including the collapse of time in ceremony, including the manifestation of spirits through bodies and voices and dreams, including the reconfiguration of gender and race through the corporeal-spirit body-land. This map, like all maps, is a combination of embodied experience, observation, and imagination.[91] "The map is never the territory, but if it is well drawn it can help a great deal with the orientation on the ground."[92]

We call out Gracias! We respond . . .

The applications of my own desires, thoughts, and beliefs are informed by my grounded experiences in the abyss of empire; rupture, departure, and integration resulting from migration (of necessity and of privilege); my long-term training in Black feminist theories and praxis; my study of Caribbean and mainland Mexica/Xicana histories, languages, philosophies, and theories; my groundedness in radical always-already transnational Black queer thought;[93] my experiences as an authorial medium for the creation of novels and poetry; my presence and participation in spiritual ceremonies; my presence and participation in marches, protests, and conversations for and about social justice; my tense relationship with the discipline of anthropology and its history; being friends with and personally informed by Xicana, Indigenous/First Nations, and Afro-descendant activists, artists, scholars, and healers; being in community

---

89 Glissant, *Poetics of Relation*, 1.

90 Anzaldúa, *Light in the Dark/Luz en lo oscuro*, 108.

91 See Joy Harjo, *A Map to the Next World: Poems and Tales* (New York: W. W. Norton, 2000).

92 Mats Lundahl and Jan Lundius, *Peasants and Religion: A Socioeconomic Study of Dios Olivorio and the Palma Sola Religion in the Dominican Republic* (London: Routledge, 2012), 7.

93 See Rinaldo Walcott, "Outside in Black Studies: Reading from a Queer Place in the Diaspora," in *Queerly Canadian: An Introductory Reader in Sexuality Studies,* ed. Maureen FitzGerald and Scott Rayter (Toronto: Canadian Scholars' Press, 2012), 23–34.

with so many different people who embody so many distinct understandings of personhood; crossing borders; teaching; expressing my desire/the erotic/my imagination. This ofrenda actualizes my fully embodied experiences, a poetics of relation best expressed in the concept of "compartir"[94]—to be in the presence of, to share, to be with, to be in relation with; it is a concept similar to that of "jazz presence"—an understanding that "our experience, stored in the power of memory's continuum, is what we know."[95]

As we enter into ceremony together, we return to the vêvé presented at the very beginning to articulate the order of events as they may unfold over the remaining text.[96]

To begin, we stand in the center, under the moon and sun, the stars above us guiding us toward something we do not yet know. In that center, we are the *altar-punto*, the poto-mitan, that which connects the world above, the world below, and the world in between. Standing in this world, we move to the eastern horizon, traversing the high and low places, where we ask, what is *body-land*? From there, we go south to the lagoon and its *water-memories*, and with these intact, we head west, where we receive the tools for *war*. Primera vuelta.

And once again, we stand under the sun in the western sky, under the moon in the eastern sky, under the stars pointing us to the five cardinal directions. We become an altar-punto, like each of the stars above us, like the

---

94 See Ana-Maurine Lara et al., "Ra(i)ces: A Black Feminist Encounter," *Asterix. com: A Journal of Literature, Art, Criticism*, spring 2014, http://asterixjournal.com/category/issues/raices.

95 Omi Osun/Joni L. Jones, Lisa L. Moore, and Sharon Bridgforth, *Experiments in a Jazz Aesthetic: Art, Activism, Academia, and the Austin Project*, vol. 23 (Austin: University of Texas Press, 2010), 201.

96 This would be what in most academic texts is understood as the chapter outline.

water-memories below us, like the mountains and valleys to the east, and the blazing horizon tinged red with blood in the west. Standing in the center, we enter history and history enters us. We then walk east to the mountains, to Los Haitises, we travel south to the Agüita de Liborio. We continue west to Haiti and then fly, as if by magic, north to Oregon. When we are satisfied that we have opened up new possibilities, we return. Segunda vuelta.

We stand in the center, altars-puntos, poto-mitans. Before us in the infinite stretch of water-memories is the reflection of the sun, the moon, and the stars. Behind us, a cave into which we cannot see. We turn to the left, where a tree carcass rests on the ground, splayed open like a vessel. We turn to the right, where the serpent has left its unmistakable, all-knowing trail. Tercera vuelta.

We face the center once again.

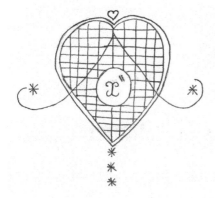

altars-puntos

We are the altars.

We are the puntos.

We are the poto-mitan: the tree that sustains life between the world of the elements and the world of the ancestors. We could expand into space-time, transforming its contours forever. We could weave dreams and yearning into the density of being. The punto is a mystery. It is a crossroad between life and death, between here and there, yesterday-today-tomorrow. We may be that punto traversing seen/unseen geographies. We could be an aquí. We could be all things and nothing all at once. The laws of the erotic are unpredictable, unknowable. What for one is a stone for another is the living home of the elemental forces, and for another, a force of life itself. The erotic impulses us toward action. The altars-puntos transform space-time.

In this story[1] of altars-puntos, we will encounter the altars-puntos Amelia and Veredia and Elizabeth and Junior and Deivis and Manny and Pilar and Gloria and Emeli. We will encounter Canuma and Baby Guede and Santa Marta and Anaisa and Oshun. Those of us in the ceremony together will not

---

1   Stories are central to decolonizing methodologies and praxis. When we tell stories, we broaden the archives and push beyond the Christian colonial, what Linda Tuhiwai Smith calls the Western imperial, ratification of personhood. See Linda Tuhiwai Smith, *Decolonizing Methodologies: Research and Indigenous Peoples* (London: Zed Books, 2013).

be the same at the end of this story. We will speak of greeting altars-puntos. We will speak of reading. We will speak of transforming our relationship to space-time and in that process to Christian colonial ideas of race, gender, and sexuality. We will move around the poto-mitan, greeting each altar-punto in turn, beginning with the spirits and then moving closer and closer to the misterios, until we ourselves are transformed.

Amelia and her husband Javier are both healers and servidores who are well known among middle-class criollo circles for their work with the misterios. Amelia mounts criollo entities (misterios of African and Indigenous descent) and her husband mounts indios (the queer : Indigenous spirits of the water-memories). Amelia embodies the spirit of Canuma. Canuma is different from the indias of the pantheon of La 21 división; she is not an embodiment of an elemental force; she is a spirit. As a spirit, she speaks in Spanish. However, there are things she refers to in gestures because spoken language cannot reach into those places (as she has said). Canuma is beyond time, though she knows—and everybody who has witnessed her concurs—that she is an "old" spirit. Not just in terms of her embodied age (she appears as an elderly woman), but also because of her points of reference, which correspond not to the modern geographies of the arrivant state but to a temporal-spatiality informed by water-memories: "the river along which the people walked to reach the cave in between the pine trees, up the mountain."[2] This geography cannot be mapped outside of the relationships nor the reasons nor the actions that mark its specificity. Canuma regularly heals people by locating them in this distinct temporal-spatiality of water-memory: asking them to recall times when their spirits or ancestors traversed these geographies. She draws their body-lands into movement, through ceremony, so that a lifted hand or closed eyes draws water-memories into the space of consciousness. Once recuperated, they become part of a whole. The person becomes stronger.

Canuma is not necessarily an ancestor to the medium who carries her. For Amelia, ancestors are those who are laid to rest. The spirits that they carried, however, remain. For those who seek spiritual consultation, a spirit may also arrive through a ceremony known as a consulta. In the space of the consulta, any sort of totalizing notion of racial and gender identity is complicated by the woven density produced through the presence of ancestors from "todas partes" (anywhere and everywhere). The spirit could reveal secret knowledge

---

2   This geography was articulated by Canuma in a consulta with Amelia in April 2013.

about those who are present as a way to legitimate their authenticity. Their visit is an avenue for the dispensation of preserved knowledge that the person can use to navigate problems in their life.

One afternoon, I happened to be at Amelia's house when an African American woman, Christine, arrived for a consultation. Christine had come with a Dominican friend. She had never had a consultation with a medium before that day. Amelia, knowing I spoke English, asked me to translate for Christine during the consultation. Having received consent from Christine for me to be present at her reading, and to act as linguistic and emotional go-between, Amelia began the consultation. Over the course of several hours, Amelia received San Miguel, and with San Miguel, she received messages for the visitor. San Miguel told Christine that she had Chinese and Arab ancestors. I translated, and watched as Christine's sense of herself as unequivocally Black American suddenly came apart. She articulated doubt and surprise at the idea that she is anything other than Black American, though eventually, she admitted, "Well, someone once said . . ."

In contrast to the colonial settler states of the northern mainland, where racial formations and political identifications are heavily informed by ideologies of blood quantum and one-drop rules (i.e., hypodescent), thereby configuring racialized subjectivities within either/or frameworks, the problematics of arrivant states rest on discourses of mestizaje so necessary to the eventual whitening of the state.[3] Within the framework of the arrivant state's

---

3   Here I am referring to the voluminous literature on state-articulated/national ist notions of mestizaje in Latin America and the Caribbean (see Peter Wade, *Gente negra, nación mestiza* [Bogotá, Colombia: Siglo del Hombre Editores, 1997] and *Race and Ethnicity in Latin America*, vol. 3 [New York: Pluto Press, 1997]; Juliet Hooker, "Indigenous Inclusion/Black Exclusion: Race, Ethnicity and Multicultural Citizenship in Latin America," *Journal of Latin American Studies* 37, no. 2 [2005]: 285–310; Charles R. Hale, "Between Che Guevara and the Pachamama: Mestizos, Indians and Identity Politics in the Anti-Quincentenary Campaign," *Critique of Anthropology* 14, no. 1 [1994]: 9–39; and "Travel Warning: Elite Appropriations of Hybridity, Mestizaje, Antiracism, Equality, and Other Progressive-Sounding Discourses in Highland Guatemala," *Journal of American Folklore* 112, no. 445 [1999]: 297–315) rooted in white futurities and ideas like that of cosmic races (José Vasconcelos), the triumph of European races/bloods over African and Indigenous races/bloods, and the idea of blanqueamiento as a symbol of development, progress, and superiority. For a broad treatment of this discussion, see the *Journal of Latin American Anthropology* 8, no. 1 (2003), dedicated to a discussion of "Mestizaje, Mulataje, Mestiçagem in Latin American Ideologies of National Identities."

mestizaje, the primary ideological operatives are the logics of an undeniable multiplicity (e.g., "We are of Spanish, Taino, and African descent") and "racial democracies," where structural inequality is rooted in phenotypical traits that obscure the long history of Christian colonial politics of pureza de sangre.[4] The Dominican Republic, as an arrivant state, takes the ideas present within discourses of mestizaje[5] one step further: it roots itself in the superiority of Catholic Hispanidad, explaining away its color through the mythicized figure of the indio,[6] its queerness : blackness in the fictitious narrative of Haitian invasion, and explaining away both in the elevation of Spanish Christian ancestors above all others.

The altars-puntos I speak of here rupture these processes. The woven density that emerges within criollo traditions ruptures Christian colonial blood logics of racial hierarchy and gender binaries. Blood logics—ideas of hypodescent and mestizaje (and its progressive whitening)—fail to take grasp because the presence of multiple, multi-located, and differently geographically, historically, temporally, and socially located spirits and ancestors creates a context in which all are acknowledged and few can be negated, where the arrivant state's temporal-spatiality falls apart. To negate one's ancestors is to negate oneself as their descendant and caretaker. Even so, one's embodied social location and racialized subjectivity is also not negated: Christine did not stop being Black

---

4   What Ginetta EB Candelario refers to as colorism in *Black Behind the Ears: Dominican Racial Identity from Museums to Beauty Shops* (Durham, NC: Duke University Press, 2007).

5   April Mayes discusses the official discourses and policies of the Dominican state as discourses of Latinidad rooted in mulataje. Reading her work opened my own thinking about the ways in which mulatto opponents to Black rule in Haiti and across the island were able to realize the exercise of power through the vehicle of the Dominican arrivant state. What would it mean to conceptualize figures like Ulises Hereaux and Rafael L. Trujillo as figures who realized the mulatto goals that C. L. R. James speaks of in *The Black Jacobins*? Mayes's reading of Latinidad—alongside a conceptualization of mulataje as an outgrowth of the struggles between mulattos and Blacks during and after the Haitian Revolution—could bring new light to the dilemmas present within Haitian-Dominican relations. Outside the scope of this ceremony, I am nonetheless intrigued by this question. See April J. Mayes, *The Mulatto Republic: Class, Race, and Dominican National Identity* (Gainesville: University Press of Florida, 2014).

6   See Doris Sommer's discussions of Galvan's foundational narratives in *Foundational Fictions: The National Romances of Latin America* (Berkeley: University of California Press, 1991).

because she has Chinese or Arab ancestors. Rather, the logics of Christian coloniality are writ large, made visible, in the ways they limit the possibilities for her expression of life. Should she choose to develop herself within the criollo traditions, her ancestral obligations would expand into honoring the Chinese and Arab ancestral forces at play in her familial and communal world—not at the expense of her African ancestors; not for the purposes of whitening her present-future-past. The woven density of Christine's experience unhinged previously coherent worlds and produced new possibilities for her present-future-past. She could choose to love her Arab-ness and Chinese-ness as much as her Blackness. She could choose zambo consciousness, a knowing of solidarity and survival. Or not.[7]

What if queer : Black life and love is the altar-punto
through which our ancestors come to know us?

In some ceremonies, when the spirits are fed, they are first fed with maní and palomitas: peanuts and popcorn. The two are roasted together, and they sit in a large plate on the altar-punto. After the misterios have come down to deliver their messages, the maní is thrown to the four corners of the earth and then into the hands of the revelers. Those who are present stand, or sit, spitting out the roasted popcorn seeds, chewing carefully on the peanuts. In the seeds, one tastes the soil of this island, the maize and peanuts of Abya Yala, the aguas of Ginen. The roasted kernels in our mouths connect us to our ancestors, to those who came before us and also held seeds in their cheeks. This moment and these actions are what give the ceremony its name: maní.

It is a Saturday afternoon and Amelia—the priestess, the servidora—has been embodying misterios, those mysterious forces of life that descend and rise into our space-times in order to balance the world.[8] They arrive to deliv-

---

7   One of the fundamental wounds that we must face is the legacy of rape as an inherent aspect of Christian coloniality. See Andrea Smith, "Christian Conquest and the Sexual Colonization of Native Women," in *Violence Against Women and Children: A Christian Theological Sourcebook*, ed. Carol J. Adams and Marie M. Fortune (New York: Continuum, 1995), 377–403; Angela Y. Davis, *Women, Race & Class* (New York: Vintage, 2011); Heather V. Vermeulen, "Thomas Thistlewood's Libidinal Linnaean Project: Slavery, Ecology, and Knowledge Production," *Small Axe: A Caribbean Journal of Criticism* 22, no. 1 (55) (2018): 18–38.

8   Read Zora Neale Hurston. Visit Zora Neale Hurston's archives at the Library of Congress or at the Beinecke Rare Book and Manuscript Library at Yale University. They are available online. Search for them. Find them. Alice Walker found Zora.

er messages and blessings not because someone has paid them to come, but because they were called. They come because they know they will be received with flowers and perfumes and songs and love. They know, and they come when they see the altar-punto. It is their form of reciprocity.

It is both proper and required to greet the altar-punto of the servidora hosting a ceremony, and the greeting often serves as the moment when a community learns "who you are" and where the priest determines if "who you are" is trustworthy. They, in this moment, "read" you and they "read your head." Reading in the context of criollo traditions can include the actual practice of divination, in which servidores study specific objects such as water-memories, candles, tarot cards, or coffee grounds to ascertain the root of a person's dilemma. Reading, in this instance, is mediated by the interpretation of archetypal signs in relationship to the person. The general assumed belief behind this kind of reading is that the reader has divine access—an ability to see/hear/feel beyond the material/rational/seen world—into the world of spirits and ancestors.

As E. Patrick Johnson has written, reading in African American expressive cultures, particularly African American gay male culture, "has a number of meanings, depending on context. To read someone is to set them 'straight,' to put them in their place, or to reveal a secret about someone in front of others in an indirect way—usually in a way that embarrasses a third party. Reading has two modes [in African American gay male culture]: one is serious and one is playful."[9] Reading as defined by Johnson is a disciplinary process. It can also serve to undermine hierarchies of power, to draw attention to queer : Black agency, and to render truth claims as performative acts.

Yet another mode of reading occurs when a person—a medium, or servidora—embodies a spirit. It is said, then, that the spirit once risen enables the servidora to directly enunciate the signs through their interaction with another person's astralidad (energetic force field). This mode of reading is what occurs in the context of ceremonial greetings, when a servidora "reads your

---

Thank goodness she found Zora. Because Zora found the women in Jamaica, the hoodoo healers in New Orleans, the voodoo drummers in Haiti. She found Kossula. Read Zora Neale Hurston. Read Maya Deren. See Maya Deren's early experimental films. *Divine Horsemen* is a powerful recording. Know how sacred those memories are. There we lay eyes on those Haitian ancestors who now dance among the dead in Ginen. They bring the lwa up through the earth into our world and once again change space-time.

9   E. Patrick Johnson, "SNAP! Culture: A Different Kind of 'Reading," *Text and Performance Quarterly* 15, no. 2: 126.

head." It is a mode of seeing the unseen as manifested through relationship. A person's head is said to carry all of their spirits. Reading your head means a servidora is seeing who you are, in a spiritual sense. Upon greeting a priest or priestess in the context of ceremony, a person is first read in order to, in a public way, establish what the servidora perceives as a person's intentions and place in relationship to those who are present in the ceremony. Reading is a central component of greetings. They, like queer : Black readings, can be carried out in jest or can be forceful and serious. A priest must equally know how to tell the truth directly and through shade,[10] depending on the perceived relationships between the entities riding a person's head.

Greetings exist as their own complex system of belonging. Each altar-punto, each misterio, and each ceremony requires different types of greeting. But what is common across ceremonies is the reading of a person based on their demonstration of respect (or disrespect) to the servidores who keep the altar-punto. Respect, on the one hand, is communicated by correctly following the instructions laid out by the servidores, detecting trampas along the way. Trampas are tricks meant to reveal a person's true intentions. A trampa would state a lie as truth, and it is up to the person listening not to fall into the lie but to respond with its opposite. Servidores who embody a spirit use trampas as tools to prove that they themselves are not lying. Respect in this kind of interaction is demonstrated by avoiding the trampas and by acknowledging the servidora's (and their head's) power to see truth and detect lies. In this moment, both persons enter into an exchange: the priest reads the person, and the person, in turn, presents themselves to the altar-punto, and may or may not present gifts (such as flowers, medicine, and prayers). But it is not the gift itself that reveals the person's intention; rather, it is how they present it. It is how a person responds to being read that confirms the servidora's skill and power.

What does it look like to read queerness : blackness into being?

At a velación, a ceremony for the dead, the servidora Veredia set up a trampa and in this way read the harmful witchcraft that had been sent her way. It was daytime, and the small cement house in the community of Los Guandules was packed. In the main room, the atables—the sacred drums—were gathered

10 See Shaka McGlotten, "Black Data," in *No Tea, No Shade: New Writings in Black Queer Studies*, ed. E. Patrick Johnson (Durham, NC: Duke University Press, 2016), 262–86; Johnson and Henderson, "Queering Black Studies/'Quaring' Queer Studies."

in a corner just opposite the public altar-punto. On the altar-punto, there was a yellow tablecloth, yellow and white flowers, and a cake. There were other details just under the table. We were all inside, some folks dancing, others standing. Suddenly, a young woman dancing in front of me became possessed. As she spun around the room, she made sexual gestures at all of the women in the room. And then she fell on top of me. I gently pushed her away—not having any relationship with her, I did not understand why she had fallen on top of me. Her actions were out of order. She then spun over to the altar-punto and placed a rosary on it. She began to shed her clothes. The priestess hosting the ceremony approached her, stopped her, and asked her who she is (meaning, who was riding her head). The woman responded, "Anaisa." Anaisa is a mis-terio of sexuality, love, and money. She is similar to Oshun in Cuban Lucumí and to Erzili Frida in Haitian Vodoun. Veredia, with the whole room watching, asked for proof. She asked the woman why she had fallen into me. When the woman failed to respond, she asked her to dance like Anaisa. When the woman failed to dance the correct series of steps, Veredia then asked the woman why she had placed a rosary on the altar-punto. Veredia picked the rosary up. She ran the rosary under her nose to see if she could smell witchcraft.[11] Whatever she found in smelling the rosary confirmed her suspicions. Veredia stormed to the front door and threw the rosary out of the house, breaking it against the concrete wall outside. She ordered the young woman out, telling her that she was not Anaisa and that she would not accept trouble in her home. The woman was forced out of the house and onto the street, half-dressed. She was sent "back to where she came from," meaning, to the person who had sent her as a bearer of harm. The priestess turned to everyone in the room and said, "I have been doing this for more than half of my life. No one makes a fool of me. Anaisa loves men, not women."[12] Veredia looked at me as she said this last part, before concluding, "And secondly, she likes to dance." The entire room exploded in laughter, because Veredia was calling attention to the obvious: the woman had failed to demonstrate that she carried the correct embodied knowledge both through her inability to dance correctly and because she fell

---

11   There are specific smells associated with harmful witchcraft. Among these are the smell of gun powder and sulfur, as well as specific herbal preparations.

12   This is in contrast to one of the Santa Martas, who is known for being a female misterio that enjoys the company of women. It's also in contrast to what another servidora de Anaisa shared with me, that Anaisa is bisexual. All possibilities exist—especially if we consider the shape-shifting nature of the elemental forces.

on top of me, a woman. The joke served to discharge the negative energies generated by two female bodies coming into inappropriate contact (the unspoken subtext being "she likes to dance . . . with men") while also setting the stage for a shift in the interactive paradigms. The paleros changed the rhythm to shift the ceremony's vibrations and clear out whatever negative forces had been in the room.

The negotiation between Veredia and the woman contained in its performance the gestures of reading: the priestess read the woman's actions, her gestures, her failures, and her intentions. Because the woman's embodiment did not correspond to Veredia's knowledge—that Anaisa likes men and dancing—the woman's inability to conform to this knowledge made her suspect. So did the placement of a sacred object (the rosary) on the altar-punto, something she did while possessed and without invitation, outside the ritual of greeting. Her inexplicable behavior was explained as a possession that took place with the express purpose of disrupting the celebrations and as an act of spiritual warfare. The object of that war was the dead person's spirit whom the paleros were honoring through their drumming. Changing the drum pattern was necessary to dispel the accumulation of negative energy that had occurred with the woman's possessed presence. That she had fallen on top of me was ambiguous: Was it due to my sexual identity, my gender expression, or the spirit riding my head? I would never know. But through the logics of contamination, my person now needed to be addressed as part of the process of rebalancing the ceremony.

Veredia suddenly became possessed and marched over to me. She placed her forehead against mine and danced me around the room, asking, "Why are you here?" When I told her I had been invited, she leaned back and laughed, slapping my forehead and saying—so that the entire room could hear over the sound of the drums—"This one." In that moment, she had recognized the entity that many other criollo servidores have identified in me. Veredia shook her head, as though suddenly understanding something new. She demanded a song for Ogun and then danced away. Coming back moments later, now out of possession, she made sure I was okay. When I affirmed that I was, she said (in a low voice), "We don't accept that kind of cosa aquí."[13] I nodded, wondering what the cosa was. I was not sure if by cosa she meant witchcraft or the woman's performance of same-sex contact. Later I learned that the issue

---

13 Cosa means "thing" but is used in Spanish to refer to an infinite range of objects, actions, and states of being.

was unauthorized contact: it was the fact of the woman falling into me that was the problem—my body-land became the punto for revealing the woman's intentions. It was the fact of her placement of rosaries on the table. In both instances, she was considered to be stealing a misterio, that is, robbing the ceremony of the mysterious presence of the sacred. At the time, though, Veredia was assuring me that the problem was not me, but rather the other woman. And I noted that *aquí* marked both a physical and ceremonial idea of here/now. Aquí is the here/now that counteracts the presumed horizon of queer : Black possibility.[14] Aquí is the realized, embodied fullness of queer : Black presence; it marks all that is known and unknown in any given punto.

In the instances when I was the unknown person, the guest, or new to a ceremonial circle, by properly greeting the priests and the altars-puntos, I demonstrated respect but also opened myself up to being read. Being read means that my "head" is also presented to the servidora and the spirits on their altar-punto. The servidores, often mounted by misterios, would then speak to me "head to head." So even if I was not embodying the misterios myself, I was expected to respond with the correct bodily and spiritual disposition to the misterio present in the servidora standing before me.[15] Always in this moment of each ceremony the servidora would greet my head by name. This process of naming, like the trampas, served to prove the servidora's powers and to confirm that they are in fact working with their head, who is able to read what the human eye cannot so as to articulate what is unspoken. When I responded in the affirmative, and correctly addressed the servidora with their head's name, I was then greeted with specific body and hand gestures, or asked to present specific body gestures in return. These secret signs of the spirits serve to create an agreement not only between the servidora and me, but also between the misterios.

In the context of ceremony, this story serves as an example of what is considered both acceptable and unacceptable. Reciprocity in this context is not

---

14 For a discussion of horizons, see José Esteban Muñoz, *Disidentifications: Queers of Color and the Performance of Politics* (Minneapolis: University of Minnesota Press, 1999); and Nadia Ellis, *Territories of the Soul: Queered Belonging in the Black Diaspora* (Durham, NC: Duke University Press, 2015).

15 Initiation is a step used to consecrate someone's head in the event that they are able to "mount," carry, hold spirits/luases. However, one does not have to be initiated to "have a head." Someone's head is determined by divination. In some instances, a luas descends into a person's head unexpectedly, at which point they are told who "rides them."

about the gift itself. The mere fact of a gift is not important; rather, it is the intention behind a gift, the acts that lead to its presence within the ceremonial space, and the relationships that give rise to its presentation. Walking between the world of humans and spirits, between spirits and misterios, servidores negotiate the balance of power and the uses of power in communal healing. But they also divert the signs of Christianity, subverting them and mobilizing them for the purposes of activating criollo forces of life and death. Even a rosary loses its sacred qualities when it has been wrapped in harmful spells.

What stories bring us into being?

In my conversations with criollo traditionalists about the theological and ethical frameworks that inform gender and sexuality within ceremony, servidores, iyalorishas, and obas I spoke to responded with moral stories and discussions of how the theo-ethics of these stories translate to general attitudes about sexuality and gender in society as a whole. In all instances, there were stories about queer : Black beings. There were stories that disrupted Christian colonial ideas of gender binaries and hetero-complementarity. In some instances, there was language (adodi and alakuata among the Lucumí santeros, madivines and masisi among Haitian-Dominican practitioners), a sense that our embodied experiences of gender and sexuality are complex and theologically predetermined and/or governed by specific forces of nature. One afternoon, Alba, a self-identified bruja (witch), visited with me. Eventually in our conversation I asked her, casually, "What does Dominican Santería say about sexuality?" She said: "I don't care if the person is gay or a lesbian or whatever. I don't care. In your life, do whatever you want to do [with whomever you want to do it]. That doesn't mean that when you are possessed with a misterio that you can kiss whomever you want to kiss. There are people who do that—they use the misterio to kiss people. But I don't agree with that. Even if you are possessed, you have to respect people." Alba had taken my question to be specifically about sexual identity.[16] But she was also acknowledging that

---

16   For historic discussions and theorizations of sexual identity, see Adrienne Rich's essay "Compulsory Heterosexuality and Lesbian Existence" (*Signs: Journal of Women in Culture and Society* 5, no. 4 [1980]: 631–60) and Ann Ferguson's "Patriarchy, Sexual Identity and the Sexual Revolution" (*Signs: Journal of Women in Culture and Society* 7, no. 1 [1981]: 158–72). Jeffrey Weeks's essay "The Sexual Citizen" (*Theory, Culture & Society* 15, nos. 3–4 [1998]: 35–52) is also an important conversation on US

she understood that this was part of my identity. She was telling me that it was irrelevant to our friendship. And she was generalizing by stating her general distress at people's mobilization of the misterios to justify incorrect behavior—like kissing someone without their consent (or falling into them at a velación). Here, Alba is speaking to generalized ethical sensibilities in which people have the right to exercise their sexual desires or identities however they so choose; *and* that within the world of misterios, people have a responsibility to respect others by not transcending what seem to be implicit codes of conduct. But respect here implies people understanding their role as servidores, too. In other words, there is a liberal sensibility around the idea of the person as an individual who has the right to their own sexual desire, much in the same way they have a right to exercise their religious beliefs, as long as this does not infringe on the body-land of other persons. Alba's liberal stance does not negate the existence of divergent sexualities, even as she exerts a baseline ethical position that no one has the right to kiss someone else just because they are possessed; no one has the right to use the misterio to abuse desire. In other words, in her estimation, these are ethical imperatives that servidores of the religion should uphold, regardless of sexual desire or identity. That in her mind she equates gender transgression with sexual transgression also demonstrates the ways in which "gay" sexual transgressions are explicitly marked, while in the same breath, they are considered irrelevant.

Manny, who is a former Catholic priest and a current Santería oba, is also a friend with whom I spent a lot of time discussing and debating Catholic and Yoruba history and theology. Manny self-identifies as a bisexual man, an adodi, and a son of Obatala. He was crowned in Santería after a severe illness and credits the orisha and the spirits with having saved his life. Manny and I have had many conversations about the overlaps and similarities among Afro-diasporic religions, histories, and practices. He was the one who first shared with me a patakí—a moral story—about the adodi and alakuata (loosely translated into *lesbian*). The patakí he told was about Obatala in the land of Inle. He explained to me that when Obatala was sick, on the verge of death, Inle took him into his kingdom. In this kingdom lived the adodi and alakuata, who had been exiled from their nations. As Obatala was taken to a bed, he noticed "men doing the labor of women, and women doing the labor of

---

conceptualizations of sexual identity that have become salient in contemporary conceptualizations of sexuality.

men." The alakuata were the ones who took care of him, nursing him back to health, while the adodi provided him with nourishment. Because of this, Obatala blessed the alakuata and the adodi—ensuring that the other orisha would respect them. Manny told this story as a way to communicate his own self-worth as an adodi who is also a child of Obatala. This narrative helped him understand himself as a child of Obatala who had, through coronation, conquered illness. Mythologically speaking (and I provide only one interpretation, based on my conversation with Manny), the pataki could establish that one of the forces of creation—Obatala, the orisha who created all humans out of mud (including plants)—maintains a life-and-death connection with the forces that rule over socially transgressive gender and sexuality. The adodi and alakuata were together in Inle's kingdom because they were in exile. However, I later learned that because they were from all of the nations, they became powerful in their ability to transmit information across vast geographies. In their capacity to carry out all kinds of labor, to heal and to nourish, to speak across languages, and to receive and carry information, adodi and alakuata could be understood as central to the balance of the Yoruba world. This pataki also ruptures Christian colonial gender binaries and notions of hetero-complementarity, providing us with a different road map for thinking through theo-ethics. This pataki of Obatala could be understood as a story of queer freedom : Black sovereignty.

When I asked for stories in La 21 división, I encountered two different responses. In one, the story that emerged was of Santa Marta. Among the criollo servidores I spoke with, Santa Marta is characterized by three vueltas (forms). The two most well-known are the French Catholic dragon slayer and the Congo figure (also known as Lubana). The white Santa Marta is benevolent; she is celibate—and this aids her in the process of conquering evil (the dragon). The dark-skinned Santa Marta is hot-headed and can destroy everything in her path; she prefers women. The mulatta Santa Marta (and I have only heard of her from Alba La Bruja) is the seductress and marries both men and women. The story, as told by Alba La Bruja, is that Santa Marta was born in Europe, but when the Europeans (los españoles) went to Africa to start the slave trade, they encountered the Black Santa Marta (Marta la Dominadora, Lubana), who destroyed all of their ships. In retaliation, they killed her and all the women of the Congo village where she was from. She, being a witch and unconquerable, flew across the ocean. Then she appeared in Brazil, as a mulatta. In Brazil, she learned to use her powers to seduce men and women to get what she wants.[17] What the three Martas have in common is their ability to travel over vast distances and their defeat of dragons (blanca/white), serpents (negra/Black), and the colonial phallus (mulata/mulatta). When Santa Marta appears in ceremony, she can appear as any of her vueltas.

In contrast to the pataki about Obatala, in the narrative of Santa Marta, the sacred emerges as body-lands transformed by movement, by water-memories, and by trade. In both narratives, there is no possibility of, or desire for, Christian salvation. The alakuata and adodi live in Inle because they have been exiled from their homes. They will always be at risk as a result, and it is through the mediation of Obatala that possibilities for their protection exist. For Santa Marta, there is no reconciliation, no balance restored; her journey is always marked by the potential to transform and be transformed. This capacity for transformation is central to the ways in which she exercises power over the dragon/serpent/phallus. In the story of her being, she is always marked by the violences enacted against her and by the violences she is capable of carrying out. In Alba La Bruja's story, the sexuality of Santa Marta directly overlaps with the history of the slave trade and New World colonial sexual practices.

We turn back to Anaisa and to a conversation with three women I met within activist circles: Pilar, Gloria, and Emeli. I had met them in my time hanging out with lesbian, bisexual, gay, and trans* activists in the public spaces of Santo Domingo. They had agreed to come together for a group interview. As we sat together in the offices of a national AIDS service organization, we talked about the misterios, also known as santos. I was specific in asking about the role of spirituality in their lives. Their responses extended the geography of the sacred into the space of the political, in this way bringing into sharp relief what Lyndon Gill calls the "perspectival trinity that holds together the political-sensual-spiritual at their most abstract."[18] Anaisa, the figure of erotic feminine sensuality and sexuality, also became a punto in the realization of queer : Black life. Negotiating "the tension between an ideal vision and our lived reality,"[19] Pilar, Gloria, and Emeli became the puntos through which a partial story of Anaisa's complexity came to be expressed.

---

17 Alba, a bruja of La 21 división, told me this story in October 2012.

18 Lyndon K. Gill, *Erotic Islands: Art and Activism in the Queer Caribbean* (Durham, NC: Duke University Press, 2018), 10.

19 P.R. interview, May 23, 2013.

Me: In addition to Christianity, is Dominican Santería part of the ambiente?

Gloria: Yes, of course. You are born with the santas.

Emeli: We are taught about that in our homes. In my home, I am a daughter of Anaisa.

Pilar: In a lot of homes.

Gloria: Yes, in a lot of homes. And you can have any number of powers, too.

Emeli: All the women in my family have the power of visión [sight]. My brother is named Miguel in honor of San Miguel.

Pilar: On the one hand, it's a business. In our country, Catholicism is the primary religion, and since we know here that among the African descendants Vudú and Santería predominate, one way that they [the Catholics] recruit African descendants is by selling them their gods, their beliefs. But we also take care of them, too. San Miguel was a priest when he was sold [into slavery]. And he is very important to us now. In certain moments, I have seen his presence.

Gloria: We have lived it and loved it.

Pilar: Yes, we have, including in your house [points to Gloria].

Gloria: Well, all those who believe in Santería, I respect them. If they ask me for a palo, I will make it. But, personally, I don't believe. I will go with you, and I will even sing [the songs] to you.

Pilar (singing): "Como Belie, como Belie."

Gloria: Well, personally, I don't have seres. Ultimately, if I am invited [to a toque de palos], to compartir [participate], I will go, but you have to respect my way of thinking, my freedom of religion, and that I don't believe. In the same way I respect you. If you invite me to a toque de palos, I will go. If you invite me to the Catholic Church, I will go. Knowing doesn't weigh on me. . . . But don't think I won't accompany you because I don't share your beliefs.

Pilar: Now we are talking about our religious beliefs. . . . We are talking about one God, and we are talking about Santería.

Gloria: Santería is a powerful force in the community.

Me: Is the lesbian, gay, bisexual, and trans* community more open to Santería [than the rest of Dominican society]?

Pilar: In some senses, the two are often associated. I don't know if it's because people say they are. Many gays go in that direction, I don't know if it's because of tradition, or because of the liberties they have in that space. A very high percentage of gays practice it.

Emeli: Near my house there is a young man who gave me my first Anaisa. Like I was saying before, in my family, we have the tradition that the women se montan [carry the spirits].

Me: The women se montan [double entendre of "mounting" as both spiritual and sexual allusion]?

Emeli: Yes [laughing] but not other women.

[Laughter among the women]

Emeli: They carry seres, as we say. So, he gifted me Anaisa. I have her in my house. He is homosexual. I am much older than him, but we were raised together. He knew, he had visited with her and everything.

Gloria: They say that Anaisa is bisexual.[20]

The activists who were in the room—Gloria, Pilar, and Emeli—are all also very active in the Metropolitan Community Church (Iglesia Cristiana Metropolitana), and Pilar, in particular, is very Christian. Their conversation is one story of queer : Black life. For Gloria, Santería is something you are born with. However, she, the darkest person in the room, was also very quick to disassociate herself from the system of beliefs, even though she has hosted ceremonies and healings in her home. In a subtle read, Pilar called out the name of her santo, which Gloria quickly denied—at that time assuming I knew nothing about the traditions at all. This discursive move was a way for her to mediate how I might perceive her, as a darker-skinned person, and to impress upon me the religious freedom that she also associates with her sexual freedom. Earlier in the interview, Gloria had spoken very similarly about her sexual identity. She had been adamant in saying to me, "One time I heard a phrase that impacted me greatly. I consider myself a lesbian because it's the classification that society has created for a woman who loves another woman.

---

20 Group interview, May 23, 2013.

Okay. It is my destiny to fall in love with certain qualities and the person who has all those qualities is a woman, which aside from having my same sex, my same gender, I love her. But since society has already classified women who love other women as lesbians, well then that classification applies to me." In the same way that Gloria articulated lesbian as a social category, she articulated Santería as a tradition that was part of the society, but only part of her insofar as she participates, without believing.

But Emeli, who was raised in the Catholic church, comes from a line of women who maintain the criollo tradition. Her entrance into the tradition came through her interactions with a homosexual friend from her neighborhood. After Emeli told us that she carries Anaisa, in a moment of queer : Black spiritual reading, Gloria responded to Emeli by saying, "They say Anaisa is bisexual," hinting at the knowledge that Emeli is, herself, bisexual. I thought back to the experience at Veredia's house, during the velación. That priestess had been adamant that esa cosa (*that*) was not acceptable in her spiritual home. The young woman's transgression exemplified what Alba La Bruja critiqued: just because someone is possessed by a spirit does not give them the right to kiss (or fall on) anyone else. Anaisa is, after all, the principle of love and eros. She is the one who calls that forth in each of us merely by her presence.

What do queer : Black people call forth through our presence?

Amelia and Javier were initiating a new workspace, and to do so, they invited a group of about twenty people (including me) to come and assist with the ceremony. I arrived a little late, only realizing when we started that they had been waiting for me in order to begin. This was because they had to lock the door in order to maintain the privacy necessary for the rituals. We were meeting in an old house in the zona colonial. It was built in the mid-nineteenth century and is owned by Elizabeth, a longtime feminist activist who is also an Umbanda practitioner. Elizabeth was initiated in Brazil, in Recife. She was introduced to Umbanda during a trip she took for a conference, representing the NGO she worked with for over a decade. She is part of a small circle of Dominicans in the Dominican Republic and Puerto Rico who practice Umbanda. When I asked her why she was initiated in Umbanda, after years as a Communist, she said that she had reached a point in her life where dogma was not sufficient and that Umbanda incorporated African and Indigenous spirits in a way that made sense to her. Her ability to be an Umbanda practitioner is enabled by the fact that she had the income necessary to travel but also to participate in the often-expensive ceremonies of initiation and development within the tradition.

Elizabeth told me, before I arrived at the space, that she had decided to work with Dominican servidores to start an Afro-diasporic healing center, one that recognizes and allows for the connections between the different spiritual branches of African and Indigenous traditions. She was nervous because "there is a lot of hustling." But, she said to me as we walked into the hallway, "I decided to work with Amelia and Javier, and see what happens." The house has the typical colonial architecture with a small courtyard, a big front room, and then a series of smaller rooms that are interconnected with doors, all the way to the back. The courtyard at one time had been open, but the owner had it covered for privacy. They could not open the door once we started because the altars-puntos would be in view, as would the attendants and the servidores, in full possession.

We began in a circle, and another person, Radhames, led everyone in a Catholic "Our Father." To see a man opening the space was unusual for me, as I have most often seen a woman in this role. Radhames continued until Amelia fell into her first possession. Her body-land was overtaken by the spirit of an eighteenth-century enslaved African woman who had been lingering in the house. As Amelia became possessed, her body-land changed. Her height diminished and she stooped over, her voice a meek remnant of her usual boom. The spirit walked into one of the rooms in the back, identifying it as the kitchen and asking for "Pedro." Radhames guided Amelia and the spirit through the process of transmogrification. He explained to her that Pedro was no longer here and that she did not have to stay here anymore, that she could join him "in the light." This conversation continued until the spirit departed, and Amelia fell back into Javier's arms. Radhames cleaned her off with a pañuelo—a satin cloth that is one of the primary implements of criollo traditions. In this first ritual, the medium embodied the spirit in order to "clear" (limpiar) the space. It is believed that the spirit, who was "in pain" and lingering, could be disruptive to Elizabeth's project. Her removal "into the light" was necessary to restore balance.

Amelia and Javier led us all into the second room of the house, where they had an altar-punto set up to the misterios. There were different colored fabrics, different colored sodas, and different kinds of food (cake, peanuts, and corn), and perfume. Save for the lack of the images of Catholic saints, this is a typical altar-punto to the misterios. The minute we walked into the room, Amelia stood at the altar-punto, her head bowed, fingertips on the edge of the table.

She was praying quietly to herself; all we could hear were mumbles. And then she shook and we all knew she was possessed. She picked up a cloth from the altar-punto—a red one—and tied it on her head, lighting a cigar and laughing. Over the course of the next hour, Amelia became possessed with numerous entities, shifting between hot and cold, male and female misterios. The gender of each of the misterios was signaled not just by bodily disposition and changes in voice and gestures, but also by the symbols associated with each of them. In addition to the gender, there were other ways to discern the misterio's contours: whether they are sweet or hot, of a particular lineage, or whether they are indio, blanco, or negro, Dominican or Haitian. The knowledge of the participants themselves was absolutely necessary in order to confirm and maintain the reciprocity required for the healing of individuals, the community, and the space. The entities entering the space could come from any time period and any ethnic/spiritual lineage. The priestess's genealogical bloodline only served to open the way to make different appearances possible. In this way, the misterios entering the room could be queer : Black, they could be queer : Indigenous, they could be Haitian, and they could be male, female, or both or neither. But they were each defined by a series of parameters and material and non-material symbols that helped to make them legible in the contemporary context. After the last misterio departed, Amelia opened the soda bottles, shaking them and spraying everyone in the room. This signaled the ending of this part of the maní.

We then moved into yet another room in the house and into another space-time. By physically moving our bodies, we were also entering different spaces for different kinds of entities. We were led to the back of the house, the very last room, which was also the smallest. There we found an altar-punto for guede—the Fon-Haitian trickster spirits of the dead. As tricksters, the guede are ancestors come back to life as the dead-in-life. They often reveal a person's secrets through jokes. They also offer consejos, which many times are not direct suggestions but complex riddles offering insight into how a person might solve a particular problem.

Amelia and another woman, Cristina, became possessed with guede. Elizabeth leaned over to me and explained that there are two guede—a young one and an old one. Cristina was possessed by the old guede, and Amelia by the young guede. Cristina, possessed with Papa Guede, began to flirt with Amelia. In this way, she was cajoling the energy of the Bebe Guede into the room. Once she took Amelia's hand, Amelia became possessed with Bebe Guede. Bebe Guede pulled on his sunglasses and put on his black handkerchief.

He leaned back, inspecting all the women at the ceremony, and started to flirt with one young woman.

"What a beautiful thing. A precious thing. What do my eyes see? My eyes see beauty, beauty."

In his langage—the Kreyòl term for religious speech—he was pointing out that he could "see" the woman's spirit, because as I sat in front of him, I could see that Amelia had her eyes closed under the guede's sunglasses. Bebe Guede continued: "Girl, you are beautiful. Beautiful. Come here to Bebe."

He gestured to a young Oshun priestess standing by the door. The Oshun initiate is also a very feminine lesbian, and I was observing her macha girlfriend, who was sitting watching everything take place with obvious guarded tension. Her girlfriend sat with her elbow on her knee and did not take her eyes off the guede. I wondered if she might get angry.

In Dominican lesbian sociality, couples jealously guard their boundaries against possible incursions by other women and also by men. The assumption is that one could lose one's girlfriend to someone else at any time. Because of this, the rules of friendship are very strict. One lesbian friend explained to me that when she was single, she could only spend time with other single machas so as to prevent fights with those who were coupled. And now that she has a girlfriend, she is "married" and therefore cannot spend time with "unmarried" women. She also told me how she cannot spend time with another woman alone at all, for fear that other lesbians would spread rumors that she was cheating on her girlfriend. Given this context, the macha woman—behaving in such a guarded way—was responding to the guede's flirtations based on the internal rules of her community, even though she was in a context in which the potential threat was a male spiritual entity embodied by Amelia.

Elizabeth stopped the Oshun priestess from coming over.

"But, Bebe, she has glass."

"She has glass?"

"Yes, she has glass."

"Well tell her to stay over there then. But she's so pretty. I will see her from far. I don't like glass."

I looked quizzically at Elizabeth. She explained, so everyone could hear, "Glass is . . ." and she mouthed the word "water." She pointed to the initiate's head, indicating that the initiate is water embodied (Oshun, the Yoruba force of the river). "Guede is like fire," she said. "He doesn't like water."

Guede's provocation could have led to various transgressions on both the spiritual and material planes. But it was mediated by the theological/

spiritual rules of energy that prevented these two people from coming together, by virtue of the energy in their heads. Amelia, as servidora, challenged the material boundaries of relationship between two women—one embodying a male energy and the other a female energy. But their interactions—had they not been interrupted—could have also provoked a reaction by the woman's girlfriend. Though for Amelia this energy was a temporary state, one that she ritualistically entered and exited, for the Oshun priestess, she is consecrated as the embodiment of Oshun on the earth, and in that way she is always marked as "water." The fluidity of embodiment is a very marked difference between criollo and Lucumí Santería. Elizabeth's knowledge of the spiritual rules, despite the fact that she is initiated in Brazilian Umbanda, generated a social mediation between these two women. The bodies of the two women, as vessels for the spirits (of guede) and the forces (of Oshun), were not materially relevant to the attraction. But the metaphysical rules called for a specific ethical response: an intervention between these forces that assuaged whatever potential conflict might emerge due to the energies that both carry in their heads. The presence of the Oshun priestess's girlfriend in the room, however, also created a crossroads between the spiritual, the social, and the material dimensions of the encounter.

Throughout the day, Amelia moved between the male and female entities/energies seamlessly—not only because she could, but also because she was generating balance by doing so. Embodying the woven density of being, she transformed space-time over and over again. Amelia has been a servidora most of her life (she is in her fifties and was initiated at age twenty-three) and has been actively healing for the last twenty-five years. So her transitions, her work with energy, are highly cultivated and she is deftly trained. For Amelia, maní and other healing ceremonies are part of her actively conscious work to maintain a tradition that, according to her, was born out of the historical "mariage" (union) of Black and Indigenous peoples; it is rooted in a zambo consciousness that draws on a history of solidarity[21] that extends into the aquí. That she uses Kreyòl also speaks to her perhaps implicit work of maintaining a connection born out of exchange between Haitian and Dominican practitioners.

What the maní illustrates are the mobilizations of different spiritual-religious vocabularies (Afro-diasporic and criollo) in the mediation and healing

---

21 Milagros Ricourt provides a beautiful, eloquent discussion of solidarity between Indigenous peoples and African-descendant peoples on the island. To learn about cimarron history, see chapter 4 of *The Dominican Racial Imaginary*, 71–102.

of the material world and human relationships wounded through Christian colonization. Like the ceremony in which the false Anaisa was jettisoned from the room, the interruption between Bebe Guede and the Oshun priestess was mediated by multiple modes of relationality and ethical expectations. All those present were expected to witness and actively exchange with each other in the creation of ceremony, of meaning, of memory, and of the divine order. The disruption of gender binaries through the fluid movement between male and female/hot and cold energies, and the negotiation of spiritual and physical desires, all disrupt the ways in which we have come to understand the body, gender, sex, and sexuality within Christian coloniality. They disrupt the temporal-spacialities of the arrivant state and rupture the idea of colonization as past. Through Amelia's intervention, the colonial wound of an errant spirit's loss was healed. As we traversed the nepantla of space-time in Elizabeth's house, we experienced the collective process of experiencing freedom : sovereignty. The spirit was freed, and in turn, so were we. In criollo traditions varied gender/sexual differences are realized through the presence of both gender- and sexually specific, as well as gender- and sexually fluid, misterios. These ways of knowing, of being, have existed and evolved alongside Christianity since conquest, and they deeply inform the ways in which servidores move through the world.

Take Junior, for example. We were in a small room at the trans* activist organization in Santo Domingo. Outside, a large truck was passing by, rattling the chairs where we were sitting. Junior sat in front of me. Junior was bent over the table, focused on his nails. As I asked him about his faith, his understanding of God, Junior threw his head back in a sharp laugh. Junior is a trans* activist and well-known transvesti performer. Junior is also a priestess of Santa Marta. Before he embarked on the monologue I recount here, Santa Marta entered the room to deliver a message to me. As we spoke, Junior—who up until that moment had been leaning over the table, looking down at his hands as he spoke—leaned back into his chair, swinging his left arm behind him and crossing his legs. He sucked his teeth, and for the first time that hour, his sharp obsidian eyes were clearly visible. Junior—or rather, Santa Marta—looked me up and down. A smile played on his/her/their lips. I listened as the misterio—most visibly present through Junior's change in voice, change in physical gestures, and use of quip and metaphor—"read" me. Junior read me in both the queer : Black sense[22] and the spiritual sense: he/

---

22 Johnson, "Snap!"

she/they could see me and he/she/they could see the forces surrounding me and, in this way, make claims to delivering a particular kind of message and knowledge based on what Santa Marta was seeing and articulating through her servidor, Junior.

As Junior/Santa Marta sat in front of me, reading me, she/he/they was consciously enacting her/his/their agency in order to call attention to my researcher's gaze; she/he/they was also, on a personal level, telling me some things about myself that she/he/they thought I needed to know. In reading me, Junior/Santa Marta exemplified the intersection between the physical-social plane (of a trans* activist) and the spiritual plane (Santa Marta). As in the spaces of ceremony, Junior/Santa Marta was also reading my head.

I let her (Santa Marta) finish speaking and thanked her when it seemed that she was finished. I then gently coaxed Junior back into the conversation. And just as quickly as Santa Marta had arrived, she left and Junior transformed back into the activist who had been speaking to me for well over an hour. As Junior settled back into himself, his body-land relaxed. He returned to his previous posture, bent over the table, studying his nails. I listened.

A while back I was a Christian. Sometimes Christianity and homosexuality don't go hand in hand, but they do influence each other. When I was little, my aunt would tell me that children have to be Christians because that's how God wants them; that is how God makes them. If they told me something was in the Bible, I believed it. Until something inside of me told me, read the Bible. Study it. And I realized that what the Bible says, and what people say are two very different things. . . . One day, I went to church, like a normal day, a regular day. But when I entered, I felt so heavy, as though everyone saw a demon in looking at me. I felt everyone's gaze on me, and I knew they were not acting the same way towards me as they had in the past. Even the pastor stared at me. And every time he spoke, he stared at me. I felt isolated. He was talking about the end of the world, and how we had to ask for forgiveness and speak with God, and communicate with God because Dominicans were sinning, and every time he spoke, he stared at me. And I couldn't shake it off. Why was he looking at me? What did I do? What do I have?

When he finished, I go up to him and I say, "Pastor, with all the respect that you deserve, you were preaching and I couldn't understand what you were saying because every time you said something you looked at me, and so I felt guilty. Since nothing I have said would indicate that I am guilty, I want to know what is going on." He said, back to me, "The problem is that you have a being inside of you, and it is reflected, it is visible through you [se refleja en ti]." He left me with that doubt. I repeated back, "A being? What kind of being?" And I kept asking and he would always leave me with the same doubts. Until I, using my own methods, read the Bible and reached the chapter on the Lost City, which up until that point I had understood was lost as a result of the homosexuals. Well, it wasn't like that. The city was not destroyed by the homosexuals, but rather because the city was already very uncared for. Fathers had problems with their sons; sons had problems with their mothers. The situation was intense. I understood that like in any society, sometimes we homosexuals are promiscuous. I don't think that it is because of homosexuals that the society was burned, but rather that what brought the city down was a result of normal life.

So, [after this encounter] I left the church, and I searched until I found my own spiritual place. I would go to the fiestas de palos [ceremony], but not because I enjoyed them or because they interested me. Since [the pastor] had told me that I had a being inside of me that manifested every time I went to church, I wanted to know what this being was, and what the pastor was trying to tell me. I went to someone recommended to me by a friend. He tells me that Christianity has too rigid a style, and that they have a singular vision, because God created them for that singular purpose. He also explained that for them, those of us who are lesbians, homosexuals, and prostitutes are a sin because we exist, because we think, because we occupy a chair [space]. They don't understand that a person can make a life for themselves. They start to say, you are a lesbian and you are the devil. And that's it. When I used to go, the pastor would tell me I have a being inside of me. And the person I went to said, "The pastor wasn't wrong about that. But he was wrong about the reflection. You have the being Santa Marta [la Dominadora]. You have a santa—all beings have a saint or an ancestor— all of us have guardian spirits. But it's not like the pastor says. You do have a reflection: you don't like people asking you a lot of questions, you don't like to be told what to do, and you don't like to be limited. That spirit that you have, is her. She has control. If she says it's hers, it's hers. If she says it's going to be this way, it will be this way."

For Junior, there was no denying that he is accompanied by a spiritual being, that energies are co-present.[23] But the role of that being is vastly different

23 Aisha Beliso-De Jesús discusses the disintegration of the boundaries of being

in the context of Christianity than it is in the context of criollo traditions. Whereas the pastor generalized from Junior's experience to the broader society ("Dominicans are sinning"), Junior understood—from the pastor's gaze—that the message was for him. But, failing to receive a response that felt adequate to his intellectual and spiritual needs, Junior went to the fiestas de palos, and finally, to "someone recommended by a friend." Not, he insists, out of interest or a sense of joy or belonging, but out of a sense of not-belonging, out of the anguish provoked by the pastor's (and by extension, the congregation's) interpellation, which marked him as a sinner with a demon inside of him.[24] Junior then disrupted this interpolative process by "using [his own] methods [and he] read the Bible." He went yet a step further in search of his "own spiritual place" until finally finding a narrative that rang true to his religious-spiritual subjectivity.

What is left in between the lines is the real possibility that Junior's church community had learned about his transvestite performances or had heard rumors of Junior engaging in homosexual relationships or sex work. This would have been pretext enough for the pastor to justify making a spiritual-moral intervention. But Junior is very careful to leave any such connections out. Instead, this series of events in his church serves as the backdrop for what became a more livable and cohesive sense of his spiritual self: a sense of self in which Junior's being was connected to Santa Marta's being, and vice versa. In the space of criollo traditions, this being is not a reflection of darkness but a reflection of light: of Junior's ancestors and guardian spirits. The answer and possibility of Santa Marta as a saint, a misterio, and not a demon also enabled Junior to explain his transvestite sense of self to his family, who then accommodated Junior's transvestite person as a manifestation of Santa Marta's spiritual presence. For example, Junior's cousin is quick to point out when Junior is not paying sufficient attention to Santa Marta: "My cousin tells me when she is present [la tienes arriba]. She points out to me when I fail to put on accessories or perfume, and she knows it's [Santa Marta] if I get annoyed when someone asks me where I'm going." In response to his cousin's complaints about his occasional neglect of his spiritual power, Junior began

---

within Santería ritual in "Santería Co-presence and the Making of African Diaspora Bodies," *Cultural Anthropology* 29, no. 3 (2014): 503–26.

24 See Louis Althusser, "Ideology and Ideological State Apparatuses (Notes Towards an Investigation)," *The Anthropology of the State: A Reader* 9, no. 1 (2006): 86–98.

to channel Santa Marta into his feminine transvestite self, giving her both a spiritual and a public physical-social space through which to express herself. Junior's status as an already marginalized, dark-skinned trans* person enables the expression of Santa Marta to extend beyond the boundaries of his literal closet and metaphorical enclosures and to legitimize Junior in the realm of both spirits and people.

Marta e, Marta a
Llamo la morena y subio la color'a
En nombre de todo lua en nombre Papa Leba
Te llamo Santa Marta mi morena monta lua
Marta e, Marta a[25]

To be an altar-punto, a poto-mitan, is to walk between worlds, carrying many others with you. Atabales (drums) awaken our being and move us closer to the ground, away from the center, in circles, and in turns. To be an altar-punto *and* an activist is to walk with one's queer : Black dead—including those of us killed by our families, our communities, unknown strangers, and agents of the arrivant state.[26] When servidores call on the atabales, when

---

25 Marta is, Marta ah / I called the morena and the one who came was the color'a / In the name of all the lua, in the name of Papa Leba / I call you Santa Marta, my morena who rides Lua / Marta is, Marta ah.

26 Queer : Black death is a central component of the arrivant state's perpetual quest for Christian colonial hermeticism, a hermeticism in which all those who are not Catholic Hispanic, white, heterosexual, and gender conforming are construed as immoral and excess. The arrivant state's imperatives seep into the fabric of our communities and our families. Here I am thinking about the many ways our families and our communities become the guardians of heterosexual morality and Christian colonial gender binaries rooted in ideas of improving the race by "cleaning the womb." Parents, shamed by their children's queerness : blackness, sometimes see it as a reflection of their own inability to embody the arrivant state's ideals—something must have gone wrong in the womb, a womb that is property of the arrivant state. A virus, an infection, a curse, queerness : blackness makes parents and communities less viable citizens. In an effort to restore their status, these parents exile their queer : Black children, silence them, abandon them, discipline them, kill them. Their queer : Black children must build family elsewhere. Like Junior, they are taken up by the misterios, by LGBT community, by those who are working to claim queer : Black life. Throw maní in the four directions, and from those four directions the queer : Black living and dead may come.

we call on our queer : Black dead, we are working to perpetuate queer : Black life in the face of so many modes of spectacular and quotidian violence. We are working to build a world where queer : Black future beings are rooted in the memory of our celebrations aquí.

One evening in 2013, following the national Lesbian, Gay, Bisexual, Trans* (LGBT) Human Rights Forum, Deivis hosted a celebration at his house and featured atabales from Villa Mella, a historically Congo community. The celebration was for the many volunteers who had helped with the forum, but it was also in honor of Caribbean LGBT activists visiting the island from the Anglophone and Dutch Caribbean. Like in the kingdom of Inle that Manny spoke of, we gathered from many nations and would return to many nations with news of each other's worlds. Deivis's choice to celebrate with atabales was heavily influenced, he told me, by the desire to assert an explicitly clear picture of Afro-Dominicanness in relationship to the queerness : blackness of those from other Caribbean locations. He was not interested in proving Afro-Dominicanness; he was most concerned with differentiating it from other forms of Caribbean queerness : blackness.[27] The atabales were yet another expression of a way of being that is uniquely criollo and Dominican and more broadly Afro-Caribbean and queer : Black. They were a way of bringing us all together, while also marking the space with the specific rhythms rooted in the experiences of queer : Black people on this island. They would be part of the message that all of us would take home.

Though others at the party were perhaps unaware of Deivis's implicit political intentions, many were clearly familiar with the atabales and the music. There, Vivian—a bisexual female activist—spent the evening skirting between laughter and hiding, because, as she told me, "They call me. Then Santa Marta wants to come and ride my head. But I don't like it. When I feel her, I have to relax and stay out of the middle." Vivian covered her head and enjoyed the company, all the while warding off the misterio searching to descend into the crowd through her. At one point, she and I both watched other LGBT activists dance to the call of Anaisa, of Ogun, of San Miguel . . . all misterios.

---

27   When I asked Deivis later about the principles that guide his work and its relationship to his own understanding of his ethnic identity, Deivis responded, "It's about Ubuntu, or Guatiao—say it in Swahili or Taino. The idea is that I am you, you are me." Deivis, like many Dominicans, moved fluidly between a super-local sense of self, an Afro-diasporic sense of self, and one that is publicly Catholic and does not preclude being gay or caring for the misterios.

As articulated by Mirla, a self-identified radical lesbian activist, "My religious identity is grounded in my African descent . . . as well as that which comes from our Indigenous ancestors, the ones who were here before the invasion."[28] This logic—an understanding that struggles for queer freedom : Black sovereignty are informed and strengthened by spiritual rootedness and autonomy—emerged time and time again among LGBT activists. And embodied, it translates into practices of solidarity. As Deivis pointed out, "Others may fight for themselves, but los gays, we fight for everyone." These sentiments were echoed by other LGBT activists, and whether or not it consistently translated into the real and formal structure of the movement, it was often present in the decision-making processes of many of the LGBT movement leaders and activists. These altars-puntos could be found working not just on questions of LGBT human rights, but also within the rank-and-file of movements for fair and equitable education, environmental justice, Dominican-Haitian solidarity, labor movements in the free trade zones, and the struggles against U.S.-led globalization and neoliberal occupation, engaged in a radical queer : Black politics that "seeks to transform the basic fabric and hierarchies that allow systems of oppression to persist and operate efficiently."[29] To be an altar-punto who is also an activist is to work to transform the world aquí, among the living, because it could strengthen the dead among present-future-past generations. The actions of the living could transform the temporal-spatial geographies of the dead, enabling queer : Black life to expand across space-time.

For the feminist and LGBT activists I interviewed—Pilar, Emeli, Gloria, Mirla, Deivis, Junior, and many others—reclaiming a sense of personhood required a collective and individual reclaiming of queer : Black and queer : Indigenous histories and epistemologies repressed by the Catholic church over the last 520 years of conquest. Queer freedom : Black sovereignty could require being self-aware in mobilizing a decolonial politic, one that conceptualizes a modern identity woven densely out of and through zambo consciousness, in which sexuality is but one component of queer : Black life. From this location, the fight for LGBT human rights could be framed as one set out on transforming the whole of society and ending all forms of discrimination. Through their management of their woven density—as queer : Black people—servidores provide us with a lens that enables us to re-conceptualize racial formations, gender, and sexuality in the context of Christian coloniality. For people who

---

28 Personal conversation with Mirla Hernández Núñez, July 20, 2011.
29 Cohen, "Punks, Bulldaggers and Welfare Queens," 437.

fail to conform to biblical notions of personhood, what lies at the heart of their struggle eschews liberal notions of the individual and provides an alternate roadmap for what it means to be both "free" and "sovereign." Zambo consciousness could be about queer freedom : Black sovereignty as an exercise of spiritual autonomy: one's power to make decisions for one's life, without harm to others; it could also be about demanding that of a society born out of an arrivant state that operates through Christian coloniality; it could also be about celebrating queer freedom : Black sovereignty through deep cultural frameworks that recognize the value of preserving one's enemies' lives, as well as one's own. The exercise of an autonomous and sovereign zambo consciousness take place within the very private spaces of ceremony, community labor, and family, despite the threat of violence and repression.[30] In the case of Deivis's party, the atabales could be heard from the rooftops, but the rooftops could not be found.

Who will you call in among your queer : Black ancestors?

Who among the living will remember your dead?

There is an ongoing desire to affirm ancestral memories, histories, and individual and communal healing and regeneration. The ways of being in ceremony prioritize reciprocity based on presence, participation, and relationship. But they also challenge our ideas of gender, sexuality, race, body, and memory. Here, I speak to the exercise of criollo ways of being and knowing that emerge from beyond el ser negro and el ser indio. These ways of being and knowing are rendered visible in the space of ceremony. Even though Christian coloniality altered space-time to the point where Heaven/Earth, man/woman, body/soul, and time/space themselves were divided, it did not fully succeed in this endeavor. Criollo ceremonies demonstrate that it has not, and this centuries-long battle is remembered and reenacted each time there is homage to an altar-punto, with every dance to the misterio, with every celebration with atabales, with each reading done, with each time spirits speak langage. Christian coloniality is ruptured with the existence and life of each

---

30 The Congos de Villa Mella, recognized by UNESCO in 2001 as an Oral and Intangible Heritage of Humanity, is but one example of a family that has maintained its cultural language, memories, dances, rites, rituals, and relationships through multiple church-state formations. They identify as Congo and trace their cultural-linguistic origins to the Congo basin.

altar-punto that brings forth the connection between the misterios, the ancestral dead, and the world of the living.

My work with criollo tradition keepers has pushed me to stretch my own
relationship to decolonial consciousness, to thinking and to feeling, to a concept of self beyond Christian colonial categories of being and knowing. At the
same time, the articulations of freedom : sovereignty that emerge in the space
of ceremony provided insight into how criollo communities honor the rich
legacies of struggle and celebration that mark collective survival in processes
of genocide, slavery, continued Christian repression, invasion and occupation,
multiple authoritarian political regimes, and unjust laws and abuses. It has also
allowed me to see how criollo traditionalists are part of a vast transnational network of Afro-diasporic practitioners, who are actively in conversation
across religious-ethnic groups, in which zambo consciousness upends our
understandings of race, gender, and sexualities.

Simultaneously, my work with servidores who are also LGBT activists
has also allowed me to see that the ways of knowing and being made possible through the space of ceremony also extend into their struggles for social
justice. The zambo consciousness that undergirds continued queer : Black existence makes it possible for altar-punto activists to articulate an embodied
knowledge of acceptance of difference and of complexity. Reading is reading
the person's actions as well as who guards their head. This is a different way of
knowing than the ways of knowing so valued by Christian coloniality and the
arrivant state. This different way of knowing informs a different way of being,
where social transformation is valued when it is for all. The stories of these
altars-puntos can provide us with a different understanding of social justice,
of ethics, and of who/what/where a person is. These are, in essence, lessons
about seeing what is unseen, hearing what is unspoken, and feeling on the
surface of our skin what is well below the surface.

refrain

This is not the Master's house. [*We are the blood in the soil rising up through the cane.*] It is not his field nor his plantation. [*We are the machete.*] This is an ofrenda, a telling of story in conversation with spirit. [*We are the ash rising with la zafra up into the sky.*] This ofrenda is a ceremony where the spirits manifest because they are invited. [*We are the ash turned into rain.*] Because they want to be here. [*We are the rain that feeds the blood that stains the soil that feeds the cane.*] As they traverse the pages of this altar, the world is changed in their wake. [*We are the cane made melasa made azúcar made clerén made rum.*] This ofrenda is the poto-mitan, the enramada, the cenote. [*We are the rum poured on the soil. We are the spirit risen from the wound.*] These words are the vêvé creating roads into the nepantla, guiding us into ceremony.

The drums change rhythm; the spirits gather around us.

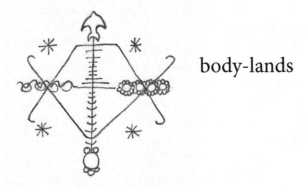

body-lands

> Land remains the common ground for all radical action. But
> land is more than the rocks and trees, the animal, and plant life
> that make up the territory. . . . For immigrant and native alike,
> land is also the factories where we work, the water our children
> drink, and the housing project where we live. For women, lesbi-
> ans and gay men, land is that physical mass called our bodies.
> —CHERRÍE MORAGA, *THE LAST GENERATION*[1]

The concept of body-land indexes the relationships and the simultaneous
co-constructions of bodies and the lands across/through/on which those
bodies exist. Body-lands extend beyond mere flesh-soil[2] into the subjectivities

---

1 Cherríe Moraga, *The Last Generation: Prose and Poetry* (Boston: South End
Press, 1993), 173. For the people of an island divided between two arrivant states,
both surrounded by ocean and sea, land becomes a protagonist and antagonist in
the historical struggle for freedom : sovereignty. It is the "land" where colonization
takes root, transforming peoples, present-future-pasts, temporal-spatiality, water-memories, the terms of war, and where the dispossession of queer : Indigenous
and queer : Black bodies and life is realized. Moraga's statement brings the duality of
islands into sharp relief.

2 Flesh-soil is an engagement with Hortense Spillers's distinctions between "cap-
tive and liberated subject-positions" ("Mama's Baby, Papa's Maybe: An American
Grammar Book," *Diacritics* 17, no. 2 [1987]: 67), and here I seek to rupture the idea of
the unitary, untethered liberal subject—whether that subject is a "body" or "land"—
and, in its stead, ask those of us in this ceremony to consider the implications of us
as body-lands. Conceptualizing body-lands enables us to trace how the tearing and

produced across changing body-lands, whereby the histories, contradictions, absences produced by pillaging, captivity, severance, rape, torture, and development are rendered visible, even if at times illegible. Body-lands "bring into focus a gathering of social realities"[3] that are incommensurate with Occidental conceptualizations of the subject as body, sovereign and boundaried, and corporeal agency as an expression of that sovereign subject—the body.[4] Rather than reproduce the same discourses of land as a subject-object that is phenomenologically distinct from the body as subject-object, we could conceptualize the two as mutually constituting subjects, where both act upon each other to inform the woven density of being.[5]

What does the body-land reveal to us about queer : Black being?

We, the woven, becoming manifest in body-land, what is in our soil?

For criollo traditionalists, "nature [is] analogous with society [and . . .] the forces of the invisible world are often conceived of in analogy with the visible world. . . . 'Impersonal' forces assume human qualities. It then also becomes natural to communicate with the invisible beings. These spiritual entities may be deceased relatives, saints, any kind of supernatural forces, and they are more powerful than living beings, but at the same time they also display human characteristics. Just like your neighbors, they can be both vain and capricious, good or evil."[6] Body-lands are not separate from nature; we are co-constituted bodies and, subsequently, beings. What we have to do to survive as embodied spirits, woven, is always in relation to the body-lands that sustain us. In this context, we do all that is possible to sustain the body-land we have, and

---

destruction of flesh-soil produces new beings across generations that embody and contain previous generations and generations yet to come, while that same tearing and destruction is also transforming the very conditions by which those generations come into being.

3   Spillers, "Mama's Baby, Papa's Maybe," 68.

4   See Michel Foucault, *The History of Sexuality: An Introduction* (New York: Vintage, 1990); Giorgio Agamben, *Homo Sacer: Sovereign Power and Bare Life* (Stanford, CA: Stanford University Press, 1998).

5   Here, I think of the symbiotic relationship between fertilizers (say cow dung, fish bones) or compost and plant health; I also think about our ingestion of plants in the healthy maintenance of the human organism.

6   Lundahl and Lundius, *Peasants and Religion*, 18–19.

if we cannot be sustained through our relations, our spirit could transform. It could transform in multiple directions: we could become a road for the misterios to come to earth (a servidora, a cenote, a poto-mitan, a drumbeat); we could become an ancestor (our body-land's transformation into plant matter actualized through burial, flowers, sand, stone);[7] we could transform into an animal; an animal could transform into us (baka, nahual—there are rumors).[8] There are no fixed boundaries between one state of human-being and another, but rather the always transforming relationship between all.

What is the body-land that does not carry capture, restraint, genocide in its memory? What is that body-land? Who is that body-land?

This is the conjunction of the body-land and subjectivities. A body-land that does not carry the constraining disciplines of colonization is almost impossible to imagine. We are so disciplined into gendered, racialized, sexualized ways of being; we are the product of the colonial imagination. When we say that we are the ones our ancestors prayed for, it is hard to discern who those ancestors might have been. When we actually become a body-land being, we are faced with choices of which ancestors to listen to. How did Christian coloniality land on them? How did it affect their imagination about who the future would be? What is our body-land enabling us to imagine into our present-future-pasts?

The 2010 earthquake that devastated Haiti was the body-land opening into a new era of anti-Haitianism, predicated on the reanimation of Evangelical demonology and neoliberal paternalism.[9] On the eastern part of the island, a reanimation of Catholic Hispanic ethno-nationalism manifested itself through the state- and church-authorized repression of criollo (read: all that are considered Vudú, Vodoun, La 21 división, Santería, Lucumí, Osha, Obeah, Sanse, Gagá, Liborista, Fon, Congo, Bantu, Yoruba, Nago, Igbo, San Juanero, Cristobalsense, Higueyereño, Black, negro, zambo) religious/spiritual

---

7 See Vanessa Agard-Jones, "What the Sands Remember," *GLQ: A Journal of Lesbian and Gay Studies* 18, nos. 2–3 (2012): 325–46.

8 See Méndez, "Transcending Dimorphism."

9 See Claire Payton, "Vodou and Protestantism, Faith and Survival: The Contest Over the Spiritual Meaning of the 2010 Earthquake in Haiti," *Oral History Review* 40, no. 2 (2013): 231–50; Robert Fatton Jr., "Haiti in the Aftermath of the Earthquake: The Politics of Catastrophe," *Journal of Black Studies* 42, no. 2 (2011): 158–85.

expressions; the development of constitutional articles, laws, court judgments, policies, and practices based in anti-Black violence through the vehicle of anti-Haitian xenophobia; and the reanimation of enslaved/exploited people across plantations and in the zonas francas (free trade zones).

No structures settle the same way, not within space across time and not across space at the same time. To have a body-land means that colonization transits differently among us. Crossing different racial imaginaries disciplines our body-lands differently. To be queer : Black in Haiti carries a different meaning than to be queer : Haitian in the Dominican Republic or queer : Caribbean in New York City. Queer : Black is not a universal. Queer : Black body-lands contain specific histories. To be Guajiro in Colombia carries a different meaning than to be Garifuna in Honduras, to be Dougla in Trinidad and Tobago, or to be criollo in the Dominican Republic. Different resistances to colonization generate distinct collectivities, shift relationships between body-lands and to other beings, change language and practice, and enable imagining and embodying new ways of being/knowing. These resistances are rooted in woven density: the amalgamation of different ancestors, spirits, memories, histories, and relationships that produce the grounds for queer freedom : Black sovereignty.

Claims to Indigenous existence, survival, presence in the Caribbean are often met with ridicule, laughter, dismissal. These reactions are products of a Christian coloniality that enables the rhetorics/doctrines of discovery to continue unabated[10] within the continued extirpation of body-lands. They are products of a Christian imperialism, formalizing claims of possession within the structure of the arrivant state that "structures justice and injustice in particular ways, not through the conferral of recognition of the enslaved, but by the conferral of disappearance in subject," and that mobilize extermination as the modus operandi (think: global capital, global Christianity).[11] Across the Caribbean, queer : Indigenous subjects are continuously disappeared within the collective discourse—even as caricatures appear within the collective consciousness as an expression of market interests or ethnonational appropriations.

---

10   As in the discourse that America was discovered. As in the intellectual apparatus sustaining this myth. As in the numerous papal bulls, capitulaciones, requerimientos, and bulas issued by Crown and Catholic church. See Steven T. Newcomb, *Pagans in the Promised Land: Decoding the Doctrine of Christian Discovery* (Golden, CO: Fulcrum, 2008); Maldonado-Torres, "Race, Religion, and Ethics."
11   Audra Simpson, *Mohawk Interruptus: Political Life Across the Borders of Settler States* (Durham, NC: Duke University Press, 2014), 23.

Queer : Indigenous body-lands are supplanted with totalizing plantation (azucarero, hatero) narratives and landscapes that, in order to survive, necessitated the disappearance and subsequent privatization (resorts/free trade zones) of queer : Indigenous body-lands. The revolutionary nation-state—whether Black, criollo, or white—necessitated the same evacuation. In this process, it became an arrivant state, a state in which those brought against their will counter their freedom : sovereignty against the continual dispossession and disappearance of queer : Indigenous beings. Caribbean scholars today are complicit in perpetuating these violent epistemes through our reification of queer : Black essentialism and myths of queer : Indigenous extinctions. The Christian colonial hold on this articulation of being is so powerful that claims to queer : Indigenous survival in the Caribbean are not taken seriously by certain scholarly communities. What to make, then, of the arrivant state that seeks to be validated on colonial settler terms and conditions?

Queer : Indigenous peoples' survival all across the Americas is consistently and constantly threatened by the ongoing brutal forces that destroy body-lands (call it colonization, globalization, neoliberalism, nation-states, militarization, space programs). Among all of the communities that compose the Caribbean, queer : Indigenous collectivities/communities/body-lands are the only ones not permitted to exist outside of a static, unchanging, precolonial state. Queer : Indigenous peoples are not allowed to "exist in time."[12] Unlike the non-Indigenous, in order for them to be valid and legible, queer : Indigenous peoples are often relegated to a colonial, premodern, traditional past.[13] This is Christian colonial violence writ large. As Mark Rifkin articulates,

> The representation of Native peoples as either having disappeared or being remnants on the verge of vanishing constitutes one of the principal

---

12 Rifkin, *Beyond Settler Time*, 5.

13 Read Vine Deloria. For a critique of the anthropological construction of indigeneity and the violence of anthropology and colonial institutions in the perpetuation of American Indian stereotypes, read *Custer Died for Your Sins: An Indian Manifesto* (Norman: University of Oklahoma Press, 1969). But, for your edification and personal well-being, also read *God Is Red: A Native View of Religion* (Golden, CO: Fulcrum, 2003); *The Nations Within: The Past and Future of American Indian Sovereignty*, coauthored with Clifford M. Lytle (Austin: University of Texas Press, 1998); *Red Earth, White Lies: Native Americans and the Myth of Scientific Fact* (Golden, CO: Fulcrum, 1997); *American Indians, American Justice*, coauthored with Clifford M. Lytle (Austin: University of Texas Press, 1983), as well as his abundant list of articles and public commentaries.

means of effacing Indigenous sovereignties. Such a portrayal of Indigenous temporal stasis or absence erases extant forms of occupancy, governance, and opposition to settler encroachments. Moreover, it generates a prism through which any evidence of such survival will be interpreted as either vestigial (and thus on the way to imminent extinction) or hopelessly contaminated (as having lost—or quickly losing—the qualities understood as defining something, someone, or some space as properly "Indian" in the first place).[14]

We can extend this argument into the conflicts and dilemmas of queer : Indigenous existence in the Caribbean. The same logics that we apply to all other peoples—colonial settlers and arrivants—are not applied to the hemisphere's first peoples. Queer : Black people may descend from Africans, but queer : Indigenous peoples cannot descend from extinction. Queer : Indigenous survival is far from silly.[15] We could reorient ourselves to the poto-mitan: the central structure sustaining our existence, in which solidarities are the modes and models of collective survival. This is a call to reimagine queerness : blackness in productive relationship with the truth and the possibilities of continued queer : Indigenous life. To imagine this productive relationship requires a simultaneous and equal valorization of queerness : blackness and queerness : indigeneity. To love being queer : Black and to love being queer : Indigenous and to know what it is to be either and both, and it means accepting ourselves as beautiful and powerful despite intergenerational historical traumas of genocide, slavery, rape, and criminalization.

What is at stake? If one category of peoples can be disappeared, made extinct within discourse and the lenses through which we discern reality, so can another. There is one powerful example we can turn to. The arrivant state we currently articulate as the Dominican Republic seeks the disappearance of the queer : Black subject through policies of blanqueamiento (whitening), denationalization, the fostering of anti-Black, xenophobic violence in the public

---

14 Rifkin, *Beyond Settler Time*, 5.

15 There is an incredibly rich body of scholarship on the complexities of queer : Indigenous personhood and Native identities that we can draw from, including the following collections: Qwo-Li Driskill, Chris Finley, Brian Joseph Gilley, and Scott Lauria Morgenson, eds., *Queer Indigenous Studies: Critical Interventions in Theory, Politics and Literature* (Tucson: University of Arizona Press, 2011); Craig Womack, Daniel Health Justice, and Christopher B. Teuton, *Reasoning Together: The Native Critics Collective* (Norman: University of Oklahoma Press, 2008).

sphere, and the passive and active circulation of homo/transphobic discourse. Because so many queer : Black lives are at stake, and the arrivant state mobilizes such violence, we risk fighting for queer freedom : Black sovereignty on terms not of our own making. But we cannot begin to fully untangle what queer freedom : Black sovereignty requires without considering queer : Indigenous survival. We could admit and deal with our own complicity in the project of Christian coloniality and settler colonialism as queer : Black people (arrivants) who organize ourselves against and through the figure of the mythically extinct india and the erasure of ourselves through colonial misappropriations. We could insist on queer : Indigenous existence—not as a misappropriation of the imagined indio in the consolidation of the Catholic Hispanic arrivant state but as an articulation of ways of being and knowing that are intimately tied into continuous decolonial struggles and ways of relating to body-land, to ancestors, to history, and to memory. By acknowledging the sites and ceremonies and cultural practices and sensibilities and worldviews shaped through resistance to colonization of body-lands, ancestors, histories, and memories, we have another opening into queerness : blackness.[16] This is the application of the and/both—not the and/or of coloniality: this is the basis of criollo resistance. This is not your mother's mestizaje, or even Anzaldúa's new mestizaje. The same body-land that can contain Congo/Fon/Bantu memories can contain queer : Indigenous memories and it can contain Catholicism, too. In a

---

16 This is where historians and anthropologists differ in our relationships to evidence. Milagros Ricourt provides an incredible discussion of the many cultural components of Afro-Indigenous life and solidarity present within the communities she worked with for over a decade, yet she continued to replicate the discourse of Indigenous extinction because the historical evidence is lacking (the census data, the trackable categorizations). Ethnographic evidence is constituted through the constantly shifting ground of the social and the cultural. Again, I ask: Why are queer : Indigenous peoples the only peoples not allowed to change through spacetime? Why does Indigenous descent mean nothing in the face of overwhelming ethnographic evidence that many agricultural, linguistic, cultural, and communal political practices across the Caribbean have queer : Indigenous origins and adaptations? If we were to apply the logics that are used in the Caribbean across the hemispheric mainland, how would we reconcile our own attitudes in relationship to mainland nations and peoples? In the Caribbean, Christian coloniality and the formulation and perpetuation of the arrivant state are predicated on the idea of queer: Indigenous extinction: the simultaneous co-optation of an Indigenous ethnonationalism and evacuation of actual queer: Indigenous people in order to justify its existence.

praxis of relation, the spirits mediate the world of the living through the articulated presence of multiply-located memories, producing a woven density that is zambo consciousness. Zambo consciousness indexes the interdependent nature of queer : Black subjectivities, that is, interdependence among and between (human) beings, spirits, ancestors (queer : Black and otherwise), families, workers, communities, and body-lands.

The reification and instantiation of gender binaries, racial hierarchies, and heteronormativity become dense knots expressing the disciplinary powers of Christian coloniality. Within these dense knots, nothing that is not a Christian soul is legible or legitimized by colonial authorities. Body-lands are conquered and settled for the perpetuation of Christendom. Queer : Indigenous and queer : Black temples are supplanted by churches, forcing those who remain to make the difficult decision of whether to enter the church to pray; they reason it was built with their sacrifices. They reason that the forces of Creation still reside in the body-lands buried beneath them.[17] Some of them enter. Some will refuse—even today.

Other beings are removed from their body-lands, their communities, their temples, and must imagine new sites and relationships. They cross aguas. Agua bendita is placed on their foreheads; words are spoken over their crowns. They are baptized but in a language not their own. They are given new names. Like those around them, they are attempting to understand how the Christian God fits into their pantheons. They don't understand the impulse of Christians to destroy their pantheons through Jesus. Or maybe they understand it too well. Maybe some of them seek that destruction, to be freed of their ancestral relationships and obligations. To enter into obligation with a god that represents a new way of being. The others, who don't wish this to be the case, call on God by other names, names they know in their body-land/water-memory. The others call on Jesus to help Ogun Balendyo, Anaisa Pye, Lubana.

Queerness : blackness is complex. So is queerness : indigeneity. To understand queer : Indigenous survival is to understand queer : Black survival is to understand cimarronaje. Cimarronaje includes the construction of "communities with self-organized economic, political, social, and cultural structures. Some maroons staged armed struggles against white colonial authorities

---

17 Here I am thinking of the Santuario de Nuestras Señoras de las Aguas in Boyá, Monte Plata. I am also thinking of the Basilica in Mexico City's Zocalo, built directly over the Templo Mayor complex. I am thinking of the cathedrals in Lima, where the dead's bones are piled in the catacombs just beneath the sanctuaries.

. . . sabotage or [the depletion of] their masters' workforce[s] through un-authorized temporary absences . . . stole for the runaways . . . murdered their masters."[18] Cimarronaje also includes walking[19] and the unwillingness to be restrained. It exists in relationship to what some would call fugitivity. Fugitivity can also encompass escape and the geographies of escape;[20] it also indexes refusal, like the refusal of liberal subjectivity and colonial logics.[21] Fugitivity can "end with love, exchange, fellowship . . . [ending] as it begins, in motion, in between various modes of being and belonging, and on the way to new economies of giving, taking, being with and for."[22] Fugitivity "include[s] cross-gendered modes of escape,"[23] passing, "the conjoined matters of imagination and theft,"[24] and the making/breaking of linear narratives and temporalities.[25] Cimarronaje includes, but is not just, fugitivity. It is the insistence of being in the face of ongoing efforts to control, dominate, and exterminate queer : Black body-lands. Cimarronaje is a complex articulation of queer freedom : Black sovereignty in a broad and complex field of articulations that also includes drummed prayers for the dead, the transmogrification of spirits through body-lands, and unabashed sexualities that refuse to conform.

My friend Lula makes this complexity visible. Lula is a self-proclaimed servidora and lesbiana. She lives in the campo when she lives with her family. When she lives with her girlfriend, she is usually in the urban outskirts of Santo Domingo. Her practice is familial—she inherited part of it, and the other parts she was initiated into as a young adult. Since I met her in 2011, she has welcomed

---

18 Ricourt, *Dominican Racial Imaginary*, 72.

19 Ricourt, *Dominican Racial Imaginary*, 76.

20 As detailed in slave narratives like those of Frederick Douglass and Harriet Jacobs: Douglass, *Narrative of the Life of Frederick Douglass: An American Slave* (New York: Random House Digital, 2000); Jacobs, *Incidents in the Life of a Slave Girl* (Boston: Self-published, 1861).

21 As discussed in Aimé Césaire's *Discourse* or Simpson's *Mohawk Interruptus*; Aimé Césaire, "From *Discourse on Colonialism*," in *Postcolonialisms: An Anthology of Cultural Theory and Criticism*, ed. Guarav Desai and Supriya Nair (New Brunswick, NJ: Rutgers University Press, 2005), 60–64.

22 Stefano Harney and Fred Moten, *The Undercommons: Fugitive Planning and Black Study* (Brooklyn, NY: Minor Compositions, 2013), 5.

23 Snorton, *Black on Both Sides*, 12.

24 Snorton, *Black on Both Sides*, 12. Also see the in-depth discussion developed in chapter 2.

25 See Alexis Pauline Gumbs, *Spill: Scenes of Black Feminist Fugitivity* (Durham, NC: Duke University Press, 2016).

me into her consultations, "to tell the stories," she says. As a servidora, Lula gives spiritual consultations on Tuesdays and Fridays. At other times, she is attending to her altar-punto or participating in ceremonies in her communities. When in Santo Domingo, she socializes with her friends, her girlfriend, and her girlfriend's friends. She works doing chiripitas—small tasks and day labor—in the city. Since I have known her, Lula has shown me her spirits, Wanga and Naina. Wanga is a Congo spirit. He says he is from 400 years ago and ran away from a plantation. He says he lived in what is now Villa Mella. Naina says she is india, from the charcos—the cenotes that dot the island. The charco she is from is well-known and protected. They both live on Lula's altar-punto; they both pass through her body-land to come to speak with me. Wanga likes to talk politics and queer : Black history. It is from him I learn that treaties are made between chiefdoms and kingdoms. These treaties produce new peoples, consciousness, spatial-temporalities, corporealities, spiritualities. "The Yoruba became wealthy through the sale of enslaved peoples from the outskirts of their empire. At the same time, the enslaved who became first African then negros but were always Mandingo, Bakongo, Bantu, Arara, Fon—they became emissaries of their gods. ¿M'entendiste?" Wanga says. He goes on to tell me that treaties are made between the Indigenous peoples of the island and the Mandingo, Bakongo, Bantu, Arara, Fon, as well as the Yoruba. Their treaties produced new peoples, new relationships to body-lands, new rituals, new altars-puntos, new ways of being and knowing. Over time, I begin to understand what he/she/they mean and why he/she/they tell me these things. It is so it becomes possible to understand what our histories could look like. It is so as to enable the possibilities of queer : Black life across time-space. Wanga and Naina, like Lula, don't conform to Christian colonial space-time. Coming through Lula, Wanga and Naina challenge the boundaries of containability and possessability: their body-lands refuse Christian colonial control. Lula, like other servidores around her, calls on the Christians who came with the Europeans to help animate her queer : Black, queer : Indigenous spirits so that they can be among the living in order to address the conditions affecting our body-lands across space-time.

Since the early 2000s, many campesinos in the Dominican Republic have been involved in struggles to defend the environment and the island's natural resources from international/transnational interests. These include struggles to defend the central mountain region (Loma Miranda) from Canadian mining interests;[26] the fight to stop the arrivant state government's sales of beaches

---

26 Teófilo Bonilla, "Fuego arrasa miles tareas Loma Miranda," *El Nacional*, May

(Bahia de las Aguilas) to foreign investors;[27] and the campaign to prevent the US militarization of the Isla Saona.[28] Some of the campaigns make use of nationalist ideologies (using the flag, for example, as a stand-in for territory), but more frequently, they frame their struggle as one for sovereignty. In this case, the logics of body-land inform the framework of what could be construed as ecological sovereignty. The campesinas, the ecologistas, the activistas, the spiritual and community leaders of Loma Miranda, operate within three distinct registers of discourse: (1) sovereignty as a mode of ecological interdependence, in which local agricultural and mountain-based communities could defend their relationship to body-land, history, and way of life; (2) sovereignty and its exercise as a mode of anti-imperialist resistance rooted in body-lands, in which solidarity with other campesinos, farmers, and laborers around the world transcends national identities; and (3) sovereignty as the rights of the poor against the impositions of the wealthy elites, including wealthy land holders, foreign investors, the arrivant state government, and the local Catholic elite church (what Jesuit priests refer to as the Jerarquía). In this last iteration, their fight is against the continued deterritorialization of campesino (rural/peasant) families from communal body-lands and water-memories by church-sanctioned landowning elites.

8, 2015, https://elnacional.com.do/fuego-arrasa-miles-tareas-loma-miranda; Tony Brito, "Campesinos montan vigilia en demanda de explotación de Loma Miranda," Hoy.com, May 27, 2014, https://hoy.com.do/campesinos-montan-vigilia-en-demanda-de-explotacion-de-loma-miranda.

27 Cristian Natanael Cabrera, "Protesta frente al Palacio por Bahía de las Águilas," Hoy.com, February 20, 2013, https://hoy.com.do/protesta-frente-al-palacio-por-bahiade-las-aguilas.

28 Isla Saona is at the crux of various political interests: the island is located with in a national forest and ecological sanctuary; the presence of a US naval base on Dominican soil presents an affront to Dominican national sovereignty; US military presence in Puerto Rico and Cuba has a long history of land contamination; Isla Saona is a site for major drug trafficking activities. In the US's perpetual war on drugs, it is a strategic location. See "Convocan a dominicanos para protestar contra base naval yanqui en isla Saona," *Juventud Rebelde*, March 13, 2012, http://www.juventudrebelde.cu/internacionales/2012-03-13/convocan-a-dominicanos-para-protestar-contra-base-naval-yanqui-en-isla-saona; Ezra Fieser, "If You Build It, They Won't Come? U.S. Bases in Caribbean Target Drug Trafficking," *Christian Science Monitor*, March 12, 2012, https://www.csmonitor.com/World/Americas/2012/0312/If-you-build-it-they-won-t-come-US-bases-in-Caribbean-target-drug-trafficking.

Relationships to body-land function as mirrors for the struggles over power, resources, and the meaning of queer freedom : Black sovereignty. Struggles over ecological sovereignty coexist with hegemonic mobilizations of sovereignty-as-nationalism. Deep within the discourse of sovereignty-as-nationalism is the idea of body-land as national territory and sovereignty as a liberal national sovereignty within this perceived national territory. This idea is most often mobilized by Dominican ultra-nationalists, who draw from early twentieth-century narratives of latinidad[29] and mid-twentieth-century and Balaguerista theorizations of dominicanidad.[30] The territorial boundary of the Dominican Republic is maritime on three sides of the country; the fourth border—the one it shares with Haiti—is a combination of mountain ranges and bodies of agua (Lake Atibonito, the Massacre River). The Dominican government and media continue to mobilize the Dominican-Haitian border as a multivalent symbol of ultranationalist sentiment deeply embedded with anti-Haitian discourse. Many, in particular the rayanos (border residents) and laborers who work in the binational or multinational free trade zones, know that the border is porous and the movement of people is uncontainable—as are friendships, love, and sex.[31] Yet, from an ultranationalist perspective, the border—like biblical manhood and womanhood, like Dominican Hispanic Catholic ethno-national identity—is a claim that must be defended at all costs.[32] The fabric of ultra-nationalist sovereignty discourses is not silky smooth. When we look more closely at what is taking place in communities throughout

---

29 See Mayes, *Mulatto Republic*.

30 See Joaquín Balaguer, *La isla al revés* (Santo Domingo, DR: Fundación José Antonio Caro, 1983); Ana SQ Liberato, *Joaquín Balaguer, Memory, and Diaspora: The Lasting Political Legacies of an American Protégé* (Lanham, MD: Lexington Books, 2013).

31 Here, in addition to my own experiences, I am also drawing on Lorgia García-Peña's theorization of rayano consciousness as that consciousness that "encompasses the multiplicity of borders—transnational, interethnic, and multilinguistic—that characterize the Dominican experience on and beyond the island" (18). García-Peña's poignant discussion of Manuel Rueda's writings about the 1937 massacre are especially relevant here: "The rayano . . . suffers the great tragedy of having been divided in half, the same way the land was" (135). Lorgia García-Peña, *The Borders of Dominicanidad: Race, Nation, and Archives of Contradiction* (Durham, NC: Duke University Press, 2016).

32 See Eric Roorda, *The Dictator Next Door: The Good Neighbor Policy and the Trujillo Regime in the Dominican Republic, 1930–1945* (Durham, NC: Duke University Press, 1998).

the territory defined as the Dominican Republic, and when we consider the other modes of freedom : sovereignty that emerge within the ruptures produced by Christian colonial violence, we see spaces where communities align themselves with ultra-nationalist politics to produce anti-Haitian violence;[33] we also see where communities undermine these logics through fictive kinship.[34]

Loma Miranda is a strong example of the latter, of a broader understanding of queer : Black life. Campesinos mobilized, understanding that the underground springs contained within the mountains at Loma Miranda feed the rivers of the entire island; understanding that their pollution would poison everyone—including fauna and flora and human communities; understanding that the loss of wildlife, agro-diversity, landscape, forest, and vegetation would result in loss of life across the island; understanding that the mines would produce displacement, land dispossession, and a loss of a sense of place. In 2013, after mobilizing the people, with solidarity from international communities, political parties, local community church leaders and government, labor unions, scientists, and other peoples from other social and economic sectors, the Dominican constitutional court passed a sentence making the destruction of Loma Miranda illegal.[35]

In addition to the mobilization demonstrated by the Loma Miranda camp, there is another dimension to body-land struggles: the idea that body-land and its accompanying ecological integrity are central to campesino spiritual autonomy. Campesinos from small mountain and agricultural communities in various regions throughout the Dominican Republic stand in opposition to the national body-land-owning elites, who are perceived to be colluding with the government and the Jerarquía to desterrar (take away earth from) communities—to remove campesinos from their communal body-lands. The histories of communal land practices are contingent on the kinds of political power being exercised across body-lands at any particular moment. Communal

33 Check out Eddie Paulino's project "Border of Lights": https://www.borderof lights.org/edward-paulino. View Scherezade García's work at https://www.schereza-de.net.

34 See Alaí Reyes-Santos, *Our Caribbean Kin: Race and Nation in the Neoliberal Antilles* (New Brunswick, NJ: Rutgers University Press, 2015).

35 Even though the court decided in favor of ceasing operations, as of 2016 Falconbridge/Barrick Gold resumed their operations unabated. See "Defensores de Loma Miranda dicen energía y minas viola disposiciones legales," *Acción Verde*, May 10, 2016, https://www.accionverde.com/defensores-loma-miranda-dicen-en ergia-minas-viola-disposiciones-legales.

body-land practices have been in place since 1822, when Jean-Pierre Boyer instituted communal land management as part of his agricultural reform in the wake of emancipation.[36] First through the US Occupation (1915–1924), then through the Trujillato (1930–1960) and the Balaguer years (1960–1962, 1966–1978, and 1986–1996), communal land holdings were variously dissolved and reinstated.[37] Even so, campesino communities continue to function through communal land-holding practices. Holding land. Holding body-land. Holding body-land implies a consciousness that emerges from relationships between people and land, people and collective memory, and people and ceremony. Body-land holding mediates the violences of Christian coloniality to produce a different concept of liberation: one grounded in multiple co-constituting discourses of spiritual autonomy.

A strong example of this co-constitution is in the embodied struggles and post-embodiment mobilization of Mamá Tingó. Florinda Soriano Muñoz, also known as Mamá Tingó, was "an elder woman, a proud farmer, a renowned and revered campesina leader and a martyr slain by armed gunmen during the land redistribution campaign she led in 1974."[38] She was a dark-skinned woman. A woman who carried a machete. A woman who knew how to open body-lands, how to nourish them, and how to draw life from them, too. The struggle she led was an intergenerational struggle for body-land that predated the Trujillo regime[39] and could be traced to the period of US occu-

---

36 See Quisqueya H. Lora, *Transición de la esclavitud al trabajo libre en Santo Domingo: El caso de Higüey (1822–1827)* (Santo Domingo, DR: Academia Dominicana de la Historia, 2011).

37 See Michiel Baud, "The Origins of Capitalist Agriculture in the Dominican Republic," *Latin American Research Review* 22, no. 2 (1987): 135–53.

38 Dianne Rocheleau, "Listening to the Landscapes of Mama Tingó: From the 'Woman Question' in Sustainable Development to Feminist Political Ecology in Zambrana-Chacuey, Dominican Republic," in *A Companion to Feminist Geography*, ed. Lise Nelson and Joni Seager (Hoboken, NJ: John Wiley & Sons, 2008), 419.

39 Rafael Trujillo was an authoritarian ruler (i.e., dictator) who installed himself following the period of US occupation. He was trained by the US military. His reign, known as the Trujillato (1930–1961), was characterized by extreme social and political repression; his intellectual author was Joaquin Balaguer, who was in power from 1960 to 1962, 1966 to 1978, and 1986 to 1996. In contemporary times, Trujillo and Balaguer are most remembered for their role in the 1937 massacre of thousands of dark-skinned people—including Haitians and Haitian-Dominicans—in the consolidation of the Dominican-Haitian border. To learn more about Trujillo, see Lauren H. Derby, *The Dictator's Seduction: Politics and the Popular Imagination in the Era*

pation.[40] Mamá Tingó's leadership as a member of the *Federation of Christian Agricultural* Workers Unions (Federación de Ligas Agrarias Cristianas) also exemplified how campesinas took up the spatio-temporal shifts produced through Catholic liberation theology to re-conceptualize their struggles as morally justified. Her work with the international federation provided the language and logics that enabled Mamá Tingó, a devout Catholic lay leader, to mobilize theological resources in the service of her community. As she did this, her leadership and presence challenged the image of light-skinned, Catholic Hispanic campesinos so present in Dominican national ideology.[41] Mamá Tingó's work and presence explicitly brought the history of criolla campesina labor front and center. Women leaders like Mamá Tingó are often conferred power not just because of their political activism but also because of their traditional power as spiritual leaders and healers. The spirit of Mamá Tingó—as well as her life, her struggles, and her death—continues to animate present-day campaigns for campesina autonomy.[42]

One early Thursday morning in 2012, I was with two other social scientists and an elder from one of the local communities. We were on our way to a community at the edges of Los Haitises National Park to assess the impact of the highway and government subsidy projects on subsistence. To get there, we drove on the new highway, a fancy and expensive privatized roadway constructed by a Colombian company in 2008. The tolls on this new

---

of Trujillo (Durham, NC: Duke University Press, 2009); Roorda, *The Dictator Next Door.*

40 The US occupied the DR from 1916 to 1924; the US occupied Haiti from 1915 to 1934. For more information see Richard Lee Turits, *Foundations of Despotism: Peasants, the Trujillo Regime, and Modernity in Dominican History* (Stanford, CA: Stanford University Press, 2003); Derby, *The Dictator's Seduction.*

41 See Light Carruyo, *Producing Knowledge, Protecting Forests: Rural Encounters with Gender, Ecotourism, and International Aid in the Dominican Republic* (University Park, PA: Penn State University Press, 2008); Amelia Hintzen, " 'A Veil of Legality': The Contested History of Anti-Haitian Ideology Under the Trujillo Dictatorship," *New West Indian Guide/Nieuwe West-Indische Gids* 90, nos. 1–2 (2016): 28–54.

42 Light Carruyo discusses the complex landscape of campesina autonomy, including how organizations and community groups navigate the current state of neoliberal development, and the changing geography of labor. See Carruyo, *Producing Knowledge, Protecting Forests*; Hintzen, "A Veil of Legality." CONAMUCA—the Conferederación de Mujeres Campesinas—is one of Mamá Tingó's continuing legacies.

highway exceed two days' minimum wage. As we drove through a high wilderness area, one of the social scientists explained that the local communities that lived within the park had protested the construction of the highway. They were concerned it would destroy their livelihoods and their sources of agua. The government responded by redrawing the boundaries of the park so that construction would fall outside of its area, thereby precluding any context for communities to protest.

We drove past tropical forest. A red spider flew into the car through the lowered windows. We crossed the tollbooth and found ourselves surrounded by rice fields. We turned onto a small dirt road that ran parallel to a river. We followed this all the way to the end, to a stunning blue lake that fed into a delta that, in turn, ran into a bay. To our right were mountains. To our left, small rice fields and fallow plots. We arrived at the main business in the community—a large colmado—and asked for the leader of the women's campesina group. Doña Dulce appeared from behind the colmado. Within thirty minutes she had convened a group of twenty women ready to speak with us about how the highway and the government had affected their livelihood.

Doña Dulce was not only the leader among the women campesinas. She was also the religious (Catholic) lay leader, and she was a successful community businesswoman. Though the entire group was convened, it was primarily Doña Dulce who spoke. Doña Magali, who seemed to be her second-in-command, also led parts of the conversation. Other women chimed in on occasion, but most frequently, they nodded their heads in agreement and stayed silent. Doña Dulce's power as a community leader was reinforced because she was the spiritual leader of the community. In her spiritual role, she was holding space to enable the work of the spirits who protect their community. As a community leader, she was ensuring that the information disseminating was in the community's best interests. Deference to her palabra by the other women was a way to symbolically demonstrate who was with her and who her people are, and to make the presence of the community's women known to us, the researchers. This confluence of both spiritual and community leadership is replicated in many campesino communities throughout the island.

Oftentimes, the power of these leaders is undermined through the political conferral of favors by the arrivant state's institutions and members. Once this occurs, communities are crippled. The arrivant state placates individuals through the disbursement of money, groceries, land parcels, or credit cards. As a result, people turn their backs on the collective body-land and focus on the protection and management of their state-sanctioned goods and properties.

This helps obscure the neglect of basic services, like education and health care, and the privatization and mining of that land for the benefit of wealthy elites, who in turn sustain the local Catholic church through land allocations, the contribution of gold and monies, and the patronization of parishes. These current models are based on those instituted through colonialism, in which Christian landowners privatized body-lands, trading them for increasing possession, all sanctioned and protected by the Catholic church, of which they were patrons.

As Doña Dulce explained to us, wealthy elites who owned large tracts of land lost them to the Trujillato. Trujillo made national parks out of the lands he had taken into government possession.[43] During this entire time, however, campesinos had been farming along the borders of what became the parks. Following the end of the Trujillato, the Dominican government under Balaguer made concessions to the elite families in exchange for political favors, issuing land titles to some of their old land possessions while still keeping those lands as part of the national park system. The Balaguer government, along with subsequent governments, attempted to remove campesinos from the communal land holdings, which overlap with the national park areas, where they grow yucca, yautia, ñame, platano, guandules, and corn. Doña Dulce shared an anecdote from the Balaguer years, when the government sent troops to remove people from the area. "But when they came to move us from the land, they sent soldiers. They sent a whole team of soldiers. And we went and prayed before La Virgen de la Altagracia. And we held her before us as we marched to face those soldiers. And as I stood in front of them, I said to them that they would have to kill me first before taking the land. But they saw us, and they saw that the power of God [and by extension the local Catholic leaders] was with us, and so they left. And we won."

Yo te traje María, Estrella de la luz
Corazón que late, al pie de la cruz

As the conversation with Doña Dulce progressed, we learned that some families had acceded to the government pressure, settling for small private

---

43 For a deeper discussion on the centralization of lands and the economy see Howard J. Wiarda, *Dictatorship and Development: The Methods of Control in Trujillo's Dominican Republic* (Gainesville: University of Florida Press, 1968); Roorda, *The Dictator Next Door*; Derby, *The Dictator's Seduction*; and Emelio Betances, *State and Society in the Dominican Republic* (New York: Routledge, 2018); among others.

farming parcels a bit further from national park boundaries. This latest incarnation of body-land attribution stems from neoliberal economic restructuring policies resulting from various trade agreements over the past three decades.[44] Time and time again, the women emphasized how the parcels were insufficient to sustain their families, or how the soil did not support the crops they needed to eat, or how the narcotraficantes sometimes used the parcels to hide drugs. Some people had sold off their parcels, taking the little money they gained from the sale and moving to the cities. The strongest among the campesinos refused to settle for the parcels. They continue to farm on communal lands, with some concessions—the primary one is giving up slash-and-burn agriculture. Even so, the government continues to perpetuate violence against the community. As Doña Magali explained to me, "We stopped burning the mountains, so why do they keep trying to take our land? We agreed to stop burning in exchange for continuing to use the land to plant our crops."[45] Even so, she said, the Dominican government continues to terrorize the community: "Just when the crops are ready to harvest, the government sends soldiers in to destroy all of the crops. They pull up our harvest and burn it. They bring tractors and destroy the plants."

The arrivant state is starving the community into submission, destroying crops that would sustain their body-lands and those of their children in an attempt to possess those body-lands. Entering the spiral of time, we know this is not the first time these strategies have been enacted against these body-lands. And the people know this, too. They draw on the very tools used against them to reimagine futures where their children and their children's children can plant seeds and harvest food, where they can survive.

The roots of survival are in the spiritual worlds of the communities. As Catholic lay leaders for their communities, Doña Magali and Doña Dulce were able to convene women from their churches, women who are also at the forefront of the struggle for their community. There is a long history and overlap between Catholic lay structures and campesino mobilizations. The Jesuits, and liberation theology, have a strong history in the Dominican campesino

---

44 Charles Geisler, Rees Warne, and Alan Barton, "The Wandering Commons: A Conservation Conundrum in the Dominican Republic," *Agriculture and Human Values* 14, no. 4 (1997): 325–35.

45 Interview with Doña Magali, December 2012.

movement, dating back to the early 1970s.[46] As local priests and nuns became disheartened with the Jerarquía's collusion with the Balaguerista governments, they fanned out into the campesino communities. Once there, they advocated for lay leadership and to decentralize the Catholic church's role in the rural setting. In this way, they hoped to foster an alternative to Communism, which at the time was construed as a real political possibility or threat (depending on your point of view). As Balaguer attempted to establish land reform and to eliminate communal land holdings, cofradias (religious organizations) and other lay groups and organizations within campesino communities were able to mobilize their communities through the networks established and solidified within the liberated Catholic parishes. They were also able to sustain their struggles through the new theological interventions (liberation theologies) provided by the clergy. Criollo traditions were reorganized to accommodate this new interpretation of God. Women were placed at the center.

Forty to fifty years after the liberation of the rural church, the local campesina movement is nationally powerful and connected to global campesina movements like Via Campesina. Like other collectivities, campesinas have been institutionalized through NGO structuring.[47] Alongside suffering NGO-ization, the movement has also embraced the model of buen vivir as a framework to fight for food and ecological sovereignty in particular. Buen vivir is an economic development policy that grew out of Indigenous sovereignty movements in Ecuador and Bolivia. In Ecuador, the term comes from the Quechua phrase sumak kawsay (well living); in Bolivia, the phrase in Aimara is suma qamaña, ñandareko, and as sumak in Guaraní. It offers an alternative to Western development models and prioritizes notions of interculturality between people, society, and Mother Earth, in which basic rights and differences are interdependent rather than schematically hierarchical.

Among campesinas, buen vivir and its attendant interculturalidad have been taken up as a primary strategy by a Jesuit political training center, Centro Bonó, which works with over a hundred campesino communities across the

---

46 Emelio Betances, *The Catholic Church and Power Politics in Latin America: The Dominican Case in Comparative Perspective* (Lanham, MD: Rowman & Littlefield, 2007).

47 See Sonia E. Alvarez, "Beyond NGO-ization? Reflections from Latin America," *Development* 52, no. 2 (2009): 175–84; Lynn Stephen, *Women and Social Movements in Latin America: Power from Below* (Austin: University of Texas Press, 2010).

country. Currently, buen vivir is being disseminated through popular education by the campesino movements, enabling a mirrored reflection of local struggles in conversation with hemispheric ones. This model has served to inform struggles against transnational corporations and wealthy national elites. It mapped onto already extant logics and was re-adapted to amplify those logics. So, in 2018, I walked through a national park with a leader of the Eastern region campesina movement, Lydia, who articulated to me many things: (1) that the national parks were part of campesina ecological and cultural inheritance, (2) that their displacement from these areas were in the interests of transnational corporations, and (3) that "our Haitian brothers and sisters" are central to the struggle against neoliberal displacement by corporations, including mining companies and resort hotels.[48]

Where do queer : Black people stand within these struggles for body-lands?

How do these struggles inform the possibilities of queer freedom : Black sovereignty?

As Naina-Lula tells me, "Who controls the seeds controls the people because we ourselves are seeds."

Naina is different from Wanga. Her presence in Lula's body-land manifests a different temperament, different gestures, different voice inflections. When she comes into the space, there is often a sudden calm. Naina is from the area now known as San Juan de la Maguana. That is what she tells me. When she is present, Lula drinks a lot of water-memory. She douses herself in water-memories. She heals with aguas dulces. Because she is an india.

There are those who are of the indios and those who are not. Lula is of both the indias and the negros. And then there is Migdalia. Her son is HIV positive; some years he fares better than others. He had migrated to the US in the 1980s but ended up as another Black/Latino man in the (transnational) prison industrial complex, which jails 25 percent of African American and Latino men and deports thousands of Dominicans back to the Dominican Republic every year.[49] He was jailed for selling crack in 1991. He served ten years and

48 Interview with Lydia Pereyra, Bayahibe, Padre Nuestro, August 2018.
49 David C. Brotherton and Yolanda Martin, "The War on Drugs and the Case of Dominican Deportees," *Journal of Crime and Justice* 32, no. 2 (2009): 21–48. According to the Department of Homeland Security, the number of removals per year

was deported back to the island in 2001. He received his diagnosis in 2002. Migdalia, his mother, has a US green card and spends six months out of the year in the US working in hotels as a maid. The other six months, she is on the island with her son. With the money she makes in the US, she helps pay for her son's medical care and his medications. She also built her son a house in a barrio on the outskirts of Santo Domingo, where she stays when she is with him. She is a family friend and I have known her all my life, which is how I learned about her son's struggles and, subsequently, her trips back and forth. When we are both on the island together, I visit with her. She is familiar and comforting. She likes to cook for me, and I like to eat her food. I always bring her fruit. This is the basis of our love.

I was visiting with her one day when I saw candles lit throughout her house. There were other things, too.

Ana: "Migdalia, why do you have candles lit?"
Migdalia: "They're prayers."
A: [I pointed with my lips to an object in a corner.] "You have indios?"
M: "Yes, but I don't talk about that."
A: "You have indios?"
M: "Yes, but we don't talk about it!"
A: "Why?"
M: "Because you have to be of that to talk about that."
A: "How can I learn more?"
M: "No. It's not like that. They are of you, and you are of them. There isn't another way."
A: "How did you learn you have indios?"
M: "You just know. From a young age, you know. I got sick, and my mother took me to someone. And I stayed there and since then I have indios."
A: "What are you praying for?"
M: [Laughter] "You ask a lot of questions!"[50]

---

increased from 69,680 in 1997 to 333,341 in 2015. Migdalia's son was deported in 2001, when the US Immigration and Naturalization Services removed 189,026 people. In 2015, the US deported 1,512 people to the Dominican Republic. See "Table 39: Aliens Removed or Returned: Fiscal Years 1892 to 2015," *Department of Homeland Security*, accessed April 10, 2018, https://www.dhs.gov/immigration-statistics/yearbook/2015/table39.
50 Ana: "¿Migdalia, por qué tienes velas puesto?"

She gave me permission to tell this story. But only this far. Even though I have known her all my life, I was an adult before I learned about her beliefs and practice and the way she understands herself. She is of the indios, they are of her. It does not mean she is not negra. It also does not mean we are speaking of the blood logics that inform racial hierarchies or of the blood logics that course through her son's body-land.

Her story is different from Doña Adela's, an herbalist and spiritual healer who lives in a small rural community outside of Santo Domingo. I have known Doña Adela since 2013, when she joined her husband at several toques de palo (drumming ceremonies) that were convened and where I was present. I am sure she knew me before I knew her, if only because she was paying attention to who was in the circle, whereas for a long time, I was just a guest. Also, Doña Adela is not someone who lets herself be known if she doesn't want to be. She, like many folks in her community, is a cimarrona descendant. I was interviewing her a couple of days before the big fiesta to the Virgen de los Remedios, in Jimaní. We had just walked through her herb garden, the small hortaliza she keeps behind her house. Where most people plant tomatoes and eggplant, she plants savila and cundiamor.

Ana: "Doña Adela, do you have indios?"
Adela: "No [waving her finger], no—I'm not about that."
Ana: "Are there indios around here?"
Adela: "Yes, over there—on the other side of the mountain. That's where they are."
Ana: "But you don't have indios?"
Adela: "No."

Migdalia: "Son unos rezos."
A: [I pointed with my lips to an object in a corner.] "¿Tienes indios?"
M: "Si, pero yo no hablo d'eso."
A: "¿Tu tienes indios?"
M: "¡Si, pero no hablamos de eso, muchacha!"
A: "¿Pero por qué?"
M: "Por que uno tiene que ser d'eso pa'hablar d'eso."
A: "¿Y yo, como puedo saber ma'?"
M: "No. No es así. Ellos son de uno, uno es d'ellos. No hay otra forma."
A: "¿Como supiste que tienes indios?"
M: "Uno sabe. Ya de joven, uno sabe."
A: "¿Pa'que 'ta rezando?"
M: [Laughter] "¡Tu si haces preguntas!"

Ana: "Why do all Dominicans want to be indios?"

Adela: "Not me. I'm not [wagging a finger]."

Ana: "Who are your people, Doña Adela?"

Adela: [Laughter] "The Virgen de los Dolores. She is my people."[51]

"Dolores, ay sí mi madre llora	*(Dolores)*
Ay dejanla llorar	*(Dolores)*
Porque nadie sabe	*(Dolores)*
La pena que trae	*(Dolores)*
Ay ay ay dolores	*(Dolores)*
Yo me voy contigo	*(Dolores)*
Ay por dios Dolores	*(Dolores)*
Ay llévame contigo . . ."[52]	

In 2013, my partner—a Yemanya priestess—invited Don Felipe and his drumming group to an Oshun ceremony at the edge of a small river north of Santo Domingo.[53] Don Felipe is Doña Adela's husband. The drumming group arrived in a pickup truck and unloaded next to the altar-punto. The altar-punto was constructed high up in a tree, with flowing yellow and blue fabric cascading down from the potiches (large ceramic containers) onto the ground, covered with fruit and flowers. When Don Felipe first saw the altar-punto to Oshun and Yemanya, he started. We all noticed his face, the way he expressed surprise through his gaze. Abebbe Oshun welcomed him, thanked him for being there.

---

51 Ana: "Doña Ángela, ¿tienes indios?"
    Adela: "No, no—yo no soy d'eso."
    Ana: "¿Y hay indios por aquí?"
    Adela: "Si, por allá—al otro lao de la loma. Ellos están por allá."
    Ana: "¿Pero usted no tiene indios?"
    Adela: "No."
    Ana: "¿Pero por qué todos los dominicanos quieren ser indios?"
    Adela: "Yo no, yo no soy."
    Ana: "¿Quiénes son su gente, Doña Amelia?"
    Adela: "La Virgen de los Remedios. Ella es mi gente."

52 As sung by Atabales Gran Poder de Dios.

53 Alaí Reyes Santos, my partner, tells this story from her perspective in the preface to her book *Our Caribbean Kin.*

"Thank you for being here. This is an altar to mi madre Oshun, and to the orisha of my goddaughter, a daughter of Yemanya. It was my goddaughter's idea to convene a toque de palos for these orisha. In Cuba, we would convene a tambor, but we are not in Cuba. We are in the Dominican Republic, and the drums here are yours. We assure you that Oshun and what you know are the same thing. Under the protection [bajo la mirada] of these great forces, we welcome you."

Don Felipe and the other men chuckled. They spoke softly among themselves and then Don Felipe spoke.

"You welcome us to play for these misterios. You say they are the same thing. I play for the Great Spirit, and I listen to God, because there is only one God. If we are here today, it is because God and the misterios willed it. We are going to play, and then we will see if they are the same."

As the atabales played, calling to Anaisa, Oshun came down to us through the body-land of Abebbe Oshun. Doña Adela went up to her and danced with her. As they danced together, Doña Adela began to cry. Oshun placed honey and sunflowers in her hands and held her head against her body-land. Doña Adela cried and cried. She wailed, calling forth the force of Metre Sili (Erzili Frida) into the presence of Oshun. But as Oshun–Metre Sili danced through the space, the sun peered through the clouds, making the muddy river next to us bright like the color of honey. We all watched, amazed and joyful at the confluence of forces.

After, when Oshun and Metre Sili had left and the drums had stopped and we were all eating, Abebbe Oshun gave Doña Adela a gift of Oshun's ileke— the beaded necklace consecrated with Oshun's strengths/force/energy. Doña Adela was wearing it when I interviewed her in 2016.

Zambo consciousness. We are the poto-mitan. We are the punto. We are the cenote. Zambo consciousness eschews blood logics. We could imagine being without blood logics. We were told we are nothing without blood. One drop. Blood quantums. Blood-borne illnesses. We could imagine queer freedom : Black sovereignty without blood.

One of our options is to turn to water-memories.

refrain

This is not the Master's house. [*How much does memory weigh?*] It is not his field nor his plantation. [*I try to re-member.*] This is an ofrenda, a telling of story in conversation with spirit. [*Forty kilos: the weight of a fifteen-year-old Congo boy. Ten kilos: the weight of a coral block carved to fit the edges of the Cathedral. A half kilo: a stone brought from the river's edge, sucked on in the ship's underpass, cried on in the darkness of the market's stalls.*] This ofrenda is a ceremony where the spirits manifest because they are invited. [*There are no remains to mourn over.*] Because they want to be here. [*Our dead shift among the dead.*] As they traverse the pages of this body-land, the world is changed in their wake. This ofrenda is the poto-mitan, the enramada, the cenote. These words are the vêvê creating roads into the nepantla, guiding us into ceremony. [*In the ocean. In the ash. In the mortar between coral blocks. In the floors of the cathedrals. In the pages of flesh, made paper.*]

The drums change rhythm; the spirits come down and join us.

water-memories

Nana Yvette, Shis-Inday (Mescalero Apache) from the Texas-Mexico borderlands, holds her macaw feathers to the sky. She pulls the clouds down with them, the feathers sweeping toward the earth.

"Water carries all of the memory of our planet. That water—it may have started in an ocean, a river, a spring, but then it evaporates into the sky, and it becomes the clouds and then it rains down onto the earth. It is part of a closed system. It has within it all of the memories of the planet. It is the same water that is inside of us. That is why when we pray to the water, we are praying for all of humanity, too."

We are in the community I will call Palo Blanco, a small rural community of fifty households in the mountains outside of Santo Domingo. Nana Yvette is standing inside a dried creek bed, next to the almost-dry spring. A small trickle of water has appeared under piled, dry leaves that have fallen from the surrounding zapote trees. She clears the leaves from the spring and stands next to it. Nana Yvette is praying for the water to return to the spring, to the community where there is no water. Two days a week, you can see a small truck carrying a large 300-gallon tank in its bed. It wanders along the dirt road, house to house, delivering water. When people have money, they purchase water for cooking and drinking. They use rainwater for their crops, for washing dishes and the floor. In 2008, young men from Palo Blanco and two neighboring communities collaborated to install pipes from a spring deep in the mountains. The spring provided water to over approximately one hundred houses in all three communities. But in 2011, a recently anointed Evangelical minister in the neighboring town—which I will call Chula Vista—made a unilateral decision to cut the pipeline off to Palo Blanco. The water, he decided, would only go to Christian households—not to Catholic ones. Negotiations between the community leaders only further exacerbated the problem: the leaders in Palo Blanco are Catholic. The majority of households in Palo Blanco are Catholic. Many also serve the misterios, what the Evangelical minister calls "demonios" (demons) and which he is attempting to eliminate from the body-lands of the people.

So there we are with Nana Yvette standing in a creek in Palo Blanco, praying for water. She calls on the memory of the water, asks it to return to where it is needed. Space-time collapses and all that is, is water-memory. If water-memory is what sustains us, what makes our life, the life of all plants, animals, and living things possible, then it is our primary alternative to blood logics, that is: the logics of pureza de sangre (blood purity) and of contamination; the logics of enslavement or disappearance; the logics of animal husbandry and chattel breeding; the logics of bad blood and dirty wombs. Blood logics are scripted onto skin logics, rendering the body's color and its features—nose, hair, eyes, lips, hips—as metaphors for blood. These metaphors are dangerous metaphors. They inform narratives of purity. They are used to deterritorialize peoples and to kill them. Blood logics serve violence and the quest for power over all others. The desire to claim mine different from yours. The impulse to draw lines between beings.

What could happen when we upend the logics of blood and in their place we enact the logics of water-memory?

In Loma Miranda, community members created a base camp to defend the mountain, which is the source of the island's primary rivers. Their struggle is against a private multinational mining company, Barrick Gold, which colluded with the Dominican government to extract gold from the mountain region. The extraction of gold destroys local ecosystems and pollutes groundwater. Mercury, a by-product of gold extraction, is particularly poisonous. In 2014, the campesinos found out about a group of people sent to burn down the forest during the night. Someone smelled the smoke. The campesinos, who had organized lookouts around the mountain, mobilized their networks to stop the fires. The Dominican government then sent soldiers to prevent campesinos from putting out the fires. The campesinos confronted the military forces and succeeded in putting out the fires. They also brought national media attention to the negative impacts of the mine. The base camp came into being after this confrontation.

The camp was populated by old and young alike, campesinos and middle-class environmentalists. It was supported by the head of the Dominican Communist Party, and the local priest—Padre Roberto (of the Jesuit order and from one of the Loma Miranda villages)—is the religious voice for the camp. The community's struggle was amplified by the Catholic priest of the Salesian order, Padre Rogelio.[1] In addition to the priests, the community's spiritual caretakers are male and female criollo lay elders who are also leaders of the community's cofradias. This community enacts zambo consciousness in the camp and in their interactions with others outside the camp. As one activist explained to me, "We are all responsible for maintaining harmony in this struggle."[2] While LGBT activists are not necessarily central to the base camp, they are active participants in the public marches and mobilizations and through social media campaigns. As Yesenia, a Black lesbian activist, stated, "If the government can exploit the campesinos, what is to stop them from exploiting us?"[3] By us, Yesenia was simultaneously indexing city dwellers (in particular the urban working poor), women, and LGBT people. Her use of *us* moved simultaneously across these different registers to both express empathy for campesinos and recognize the interdependent nature of the struggle for water-memory and community survival.

The camp is organized to protect the mountain, but more importantly, the water-memories—las aguas, el agua, aguas. Community members from the area report skin lesions, elevated levels of cyanide in their bloodstream, deaths of farm animals, and changes in the colors of the rivers as a result of the run-off from open-pit nickel mines.[4] These reports are similar to re-

---

1 See Emelio Betances, "La ciudadanía y los movimientos populares en la República Dominicana," *Boletín del Archivo General de la Nacion, Año LXXIX (79)* 42, no. 147 (2017), http://www.gettysburg.edu/faculty-pages/betances/pdfs/AGN++Ciudadania+ y+Mov+Soc+AGN+FIINAL.pdf.

2 Interview with R.R., July 6, 2015.

3 Conversation with Y.G., June 2010.

4 See "People Near Gold Mines Test Positive for Cyanide," *Dominican Today*, September 23, 2014, http://www.dominicantoday.com/dr/local/2014/9/23/52803/ People-near-gold-mines-test-positive-for-cyanide; Virginia A. Rodríguez Grullón, "Natural Resource Exploitation in the Caribbean: From Colonialism to

ports from other communities around the continent.[5] If Barrick Gold—and its subsidiary Falconbridge Nickel—were to continue their operations, the results to body-lands and water-memories would be beyond devastating. Eleuterio Martínez, a forest engineer speaking at a 2012 gathering convened by the Dominican Science Academy and the Vega Real Cooperative, a local microfinance cooperative institution, noted that permitting operations of the open-pit mine would destroy

> ninety-eight of the 201 plant species that are endemic to Loma Miranda; 30 acres of cultivated fields (primarily comprised of rice fields), which would be contaminated with runoff waters; the livelihoods of 420,000 people in the surrounding areas who would be directly affected by the chrome and heavy metal runoff, specifically in their capacity to farm; the primary water sources feeding the majority of the island would be contaminated with chrome salt [a derivative of the surface mining process]; an endemic pine forest—and the mixed forests they are a part of (including deciduous forest, gallery forests and cloud forests)—conversely affecting one of the primary conduits for water. Wind distribution would change and, coincidentally, so would the temperature.[6]

Neoliberalism, Case Study of the Pueblo Viejo Gold Mine in Dominican Republic" (master's thesis, University of Sussex, 2011).

5   See Working Group on Mining and Human Rights in Latin America, "The Impact of Canadian Mining in Latin America and Canada's Responsibility: Executive Summary of the Report Submitted to the Inter-American Commission on Human Rights," April 3, 2014, http://www.dplf.org/sites/default/files/report_canadian_mining_executive_summary.pdf. The report culled data from the Pascua Lama project (Argentina and Chile), Bajo de la Alumbrera project (Chile), Marmato project (Colombia), Angostura project (Trinidad/Venezuela), Mina Marlin project (Guatemala), San Martín project (México), Cerro de San Pedro project (México), Caballo Blanco project (México), Wirikuta project (México), San Javier project (México), Blackfire project (México, shut down in 2009), Molejón or Petaquilla project (Panamá), and Lagunas Norte project (Perú). As in the United States, the majority of these mine projects are located on/near/inside the boundaries of Indigenous communities. In the Dominican Republic, the Loma Miranda mine would affect the island as a whole.

6   Eleuterio Martínez, quoted in "Consecuencias Negativas de Explotación de la Loma Miranda," *Acción Verde*, August 13, 2012, http://www.accionverde.com/detallan-consecuencias-negativas-de-explotacion-de-la-loma-miranda. These claims are supported by the scientific assessments carried out by the Observatorio Politico Dominicano and published in their report *Loma Miranda:*

It is 2015 and I am with Nana Yvette. We are visiting the camp at Loma Miranda. She stood up in the enclosure, where about a hundred people were gathered. The local priest, Padre Roberto, was asked to speak, but he developed laryngitis that morning. We, the women, chuckled among ourselves. Another elder who was with us, Tupina, pointed out the irony of a male priest losing his voice on the day that Native women elders came to speak. Nana Yvette spoke. I translated for her.

"The Lakota people have just declared their last war against the United States government. Right now, they are in a war for the water, to protect the water for the people. The US government wants to run a pipeline from Canada all the way down to the border with Mexico. But we know, we Native Americans, know that the pipeline will destroy Mother Earth; it will destroy the waters."

Nana Yvette was talking about the resistances being actualized at Oceti Sakowin, about the courageous youth running from the Black Hills to Washington, DC, elders and people who prayed and set up camp—like those in Loma Miranda had set up camp—to protect the water-memories and to stop the construction of the Dakota Access Pipeline.[7] She was talking about the efforts to stop the Trans-Pecos Pipeline in Texas.[8] The community listened and expressed their listening through nods and muffled murmurs.

"The water is life. Without water, we cannot sustain life on Mother Earth. We stand with you in your struggle for your people. For your water."

After Nana Yvette, the elder Abuela Guadalupe Tonalmitl from Mexico's D.F. (federal district) stood up. She is part of a council of elder Indigenous leaders in Mexico. She is four feet and five inches tall, with a very sweet and

---

Contextualización y protestas, March 23, 2013, http://www.opd.org.do/index.php/analisis-sociedad-civil/1115-loma-miranda-contextualizacion-y-protestas#Consideracionesfinales.

7   See Alexander Sammon, "A History of Native Americans Protesting the Dakota Access Pipeline," *Mother Jones*, September 9, 2016, https://www.motherjones.com/environment/2016/09/dakota-access-pipeline-protest-timeline-sioux-standing-rock-jill-stein; Kyle Powys Whyte, "The Dakota Access Pipeline, Environmental Injustice, and US Colonialism," *Red Ink: An International Journal of Indigenous Literature, Arts, & Humanities* 19, no. 1 (2017): 154–69.

8   See Lorne Matalon, "Displacement on the Border," *ReVista (Cambridge)* 16, no. 2 (2017): 50–52; Amy Hardberger, "Landowners Under Siege in the Big Bend," *San Antonio Express News*, January 24, 2016, http://www.mysanantonio.com/opinion/commentary/article/Landowners-under-siege-in-the-Big-Bend-6777875.php.

soft voice. As trucks passed by on the road, we all strained to listen to her storytelling.

"In Wirikuta, the Huirarica people are fighting the same company you are fighting. They are fighting the gold mines, which has come to take the mountain from them. The mountain is their source of water, it is the heart and life of the Huirarica people. The people offer themselves to protect the mountain, in the lucha to stop the mines from contaminating the water. We will carry back news from here, Loma Miranda, to Mexico. Because we are in the same struggle: a struggle for water, the source of all life."[9]

Then Abuela Bea, a Nahuatl elder from El Paso, stood up. She held on to her staff, leaning into the circle of people as she spoke.

"In El Paso, we have been fighting to preserve Hueco Tanks, our sacred site, from people who climb the rocks. It is our church; it is our place of worship. When the sun rises on the equinoxes, there are things that we see that are not visible at any other time of year. When the moon is full over these stones, there are things we know that we can't in any other way know. But there are people who want to have the right to climb this site, our sacred site. They damage the walls, they leave trash. They desecrate our sacred site."

More than one hundred campesinos received us in the arbor, listening as these Native women elders from Mexico and the US shared their stories, the stories of their people and their homes, and of campesinos and Indigenous people, of gente everywhere. They nodded in agreement. They saw each other. They recognized the similarity of their struggles. This moment of zambo consciousness, of recognition, solidarity, and mutual strengthening, became a new water-memory in the geography of all of our peoples.

We walked from the camp to the center of the mountain. There, in the center, is a large boulder with edges lush with ferns, trees, and other vegetation. Water-memory flows out from cracks in the boulder. It produces a light waterfall, and from that waterfall, the water-memory flows across the rocks, forming the river. That water-memory becomes the river. As we walked, we stopped at each water-memory crossing to offer tobacco and to pray. All of the elders prayed, each and every one of them. They prayed for the water-memory itself. El agua. They prayed for the community defending the water-memory. Las

---

9   Darcy Tetreault, "Sacred Indigenous Site in Mexico Threatened by Canadian Mining Company," *Upside Down World*, April 1, 2011, http://upsidedownworld.org/archives/mexico/sacred-indigenous-site-in-mexico-threatened-by-canadian-mining-company.

aguas. They prayed for the ancestors of those in the community. En el agua. They prayed for wisdom to arrive in the hearts of the leaders in government. Aguas. Along the way, a behike (a criollo healer)—that is what he was called by others in the community—walked next to me. He was quiet, and in low voices, he and I spoke. I showed him a piece of copal that a Mexican elder had given to me. "Do you recognize this?" I asked. He nodded. I placed it in his hands. When we passed by a tall, magnanimous tree he gave me a pod with its seeds. "To plant," he said. That was all.

To plant the seed implies watering it. Providing water-memory for it to grow. Nothing can survive without water-memory. We are more water-memory than blood. Our blood is mostly water-memory. Blood is not denser than water-memory; it is water-memory. When our ancestors died, were killed, when the water-memory took them inside of itself, their blood, their body-lands, became part of the water-memories. Water, of everything, remembers.

Nadie diga, de esta agua no he de beber.
[Nobody can say that they will not drink of this water.]

In 2012, I accompanied a delegation of Nahuatl elders visiting from Mexico and the United States on a trip to various communities around the island. The purpose of the trip was to establish ties between communities on the island and the mainland and to enable the exchange of knowledge and traditions between pueblos—a Spanish word that can simultaneously mean people, community, and town. In this case, pueblos indicate the criollo traditional communities on the island, members of four Nahuatl communities from Mexico and Texas, and a mambo from the Haitian diaspora.

The southern province of San Juan de la Maguana, known to its residents as the historic and contemporary seat of criollo resistance, was a primary destination in the eight-day trip. The mayor of the provincial capital, an architect and part of the urban, new-money business elite of San Juan, designed and built monuments to Taino history throughout the province and was instrumental in advocating for the preservation of Taino archaeological sites. Her grandiose support of queer : Indigenous Taino identity is not without a social cost, however. Part of her efforts were aligned with ultranationalist discourses of Dominican identity as a Catholic Hispanic identity in which ethno-indigeneity is mobilized as a mode of erasing Afro-descent and, more specifically, queerness : blackness. The Catholic Hispanic discourse was also meant to differentiate Dominicans from their neighbors in Haiti. Given this underlying rationale, her reception of the delegation served to buttress her claims to Taino identity, all within a discourse refuting queerness : blackness. The irony of this position was not lost on the members of the delegation, who several times articulated their own zambo consciousness: an awareness that queer : indigeneity and queer : blackness are closely aligned across water-memories.

Bloodlines. Blood as metaphor for a line of people. What connects these people is water-memory. Agua. The water-memory las aguas on which the world was ordered. The water-memory las aguas that invaders crossed. The water-memory las aguas that we crossed. The water-memory las aguas where our bones reside. The water-memory las aguas where our ancestors live. The water-memory las aguas in which we heal. The water-memory las aguas in which we see ourselves. The water-memory las aguas where we pray. The water-memory el agua dulce that we drink. The water-memory el agua dulce that sustains our life. Our lines. All 21 of them.

If water (las aguas) remembers everything,
and we are water-memory,
what are we remembering
when we walk through the world as queer : Black people?

We are more than our fears. More than our blood fears. The fear of Black blood and the fear of queer blood are two interrelated fears. This is most apparent in the context of the HIV pandemic. When the HIV pandemic developed, it transited across the global imagination projected through and across queer : Black bodies. These projections—imagined hauntings—simultaneously manifested as "homosexuals," as "Ugandans," and as "Haitians."[10] This fear—a moral panic—continues to justify policies of exclusion (as in US migration policies prohibiting HIV-positive persons from entering the country—repealed only in 2010),[11] exploitation (such as unilateral agreements by pharmaceutical

---

10   See Wende Elizabeth Marshall, "AIDS, Race and the Limits of Science," *Social Science & Medicine* 60, no. 11 (2005): 2515–25; Catherine Waldby, *AIDS and the Body Politic: Biomedicine and Sexual Difference* (London: Routledge, 2003); Jean Comaroff, "Beyond Bare Life: AIDS, (Bio)Politics, and the Neoliberal Order," *Public Culture* 19, no. 1 (2007): 197–219.

11   See Amy L. Fairchild and Eileen A. Tynan, "Policies of Containment: Immigration in the Era of AIDS," *American Journal of Public Health* 84, no. 12 (1994): 2011–22.

companies in which US companies financially benefit from the exploitation of HIV drug sales);[12] and thousands of murders of queer : Black people every year—both extrajudicial and authorized.[13] This moral panic has also coincided with the ongoing development of discourses of Christian sin and sexual ethics within political arenas (the UN talks in Cairo in 1994, debates around LGBT civil and human rights globally) and international trade (trade agreements negotiated over the terms of US aid, in which aid is constricted to Christian conservative notions of reproductive health).[14] And, as pointed out by Cathy Cohen almost two decades ago, "The forbidden topics regarding AIDS in Black communities—homosexuality and drug use [and prostitution], those 'not so innocent' behaviors—[continue] to be ignored."[15] In the 1980s and 1990s, AIDS was mobilized in public discourse to justify the deaths of Haitian refugees at US maritime borders, to deport Haitians from numerous nation-states across the hemisphere, and to reanimate blood logics that equated queerness : black-ness with animality, curses, and demons.

Following the 2010 earthquake that devastated Haiti and left hundreds of thousands dead, UN peacekeepers infected the water-memories in Haiti with cholera—a waterborne illness that affects the blood.[16] The disease spread

---

12 See Margo A. Bagley, "Legal Movements in Intellectual Property: TRIPS, Unilateral Action, Bilateral Agreements, and HIV/AIDS," *Emory International Law Review* 17 (2003): 781.

13 See A. Marzullo and Alyn J. Libman, "Hate Crimes and Violence Against Lesbian, Gay, Bisexual and Transgender People," *Human Rights Campaign Report*, 2009, https://www.hrc.org/resources/hate-crimes-and-violence-against-lgbt-people; Karel Blondeel, Sofia de Vasconcelos, Claudia García-Moreno, Rob Stephenson, Marleen Temmerman, and Igor Toskin, "Violence Motivated by Perception of Sexual Orientation and Gender Identity: A Systematic Review," *World Health Organization Bulletin*, November 23, 2017, https://www.who.int/bulletin/volumes/96/1/17-197251/en; Calvin Warren, "Onticide: Afro-pessimism, Gay Nigger #1, and Surplus Violence," *GLQ: A Journal of Lesbian and Gay Studies* 23, no. 3 (2017): 391–418.

14 See Barbara B. Crane and Jennifer Dusenberry, "Power and Politics in International Funding for Reproductive Health: The US Global Gag Rule," *Reproductive Health Matters* 12, no. 24 (2004): 128–37.

15 Cathy J. Cohen, *Boundaries of Blackness: AIDS and the Breakdown of Black Politics* (Chicago: University of Chicago Press, 1999), 150.

16 See Jonathan M. Katz, "U.N. Admits Role in Cholera Epidemic in Haiti," *New York Times*, August 17, 2016, https://www.nytimes.com/2016/08/18/world/americas/united-nations-haiti-cholera.html; "Secretary-General Apologizes for United Nations Role in Haiti Cholera Epidemic, Urges International Funding of New Response

through the water-memories, across the island. Since then, hundreds of thousands have become infected, and thousands have died on the western side of the island. Thousands on the eastern side of the island have become infected, and hundreds have died. The disease refuses to stop at the arrivant state borders. It refuses to inhabit one territory and instead permeates the body-land of the island. It spreads through the water-memories. It spreads through food. It spreads across body-lands. Cholera becomes the new metaphor of racial and sexual contamination, spreading fear and violence in its wake. As uncontainable as queerness : blackness, cholera is used to justify the re-inscription of the Dominican-Haitian borders. Now, the river that separated the two countries is itself the site of queer : Black "infection." Public discourses emerge proposing the nationalization of lakes, springs, waterfalls, and rivers like the Artibonito River that floods the Dominican-Haitian border.[17] The Dominican electoral boards (Junta Central Electoral) stripped Dominicans of Haitian descent of their birthright citizenship; the Dominican Constitutional Court upheld these decisions in 2013. Cholera became the influenza, the smallpox, the disease that wiped out those considered excess to Christian colonial capital.

Blood is already water-memory.
Water-memory is already blood.
We cannot deny the water-memory.

Olivorio Mateo, or Liborio, was a resistance leader from the early twentieth century. Liboristas claim that when he died, and because of how he died, Olivorio became a messiah, "a prophet to his followers, a visionary who exposed the root evils of civil society and showed how to expurgate them."[18] Believed to be ushering in a new era of freedom : sovereignty for his people, Olivorio is the promise and certainty of redemption deeply embedded within San Juan's rural community and in a struggle for campesino, specifically Olivorista, rights over sacred commons.[19]

---

to Disease," United Nations SG/SM/18323-GA/11862 (December 1, 2016), https://www.un.org/press/en/2016/sgsm18323.doc.htm.

17 See Arismendy Calderón, "Dialogo con Eleuterio Martínez: Aguas de RD van a parar a Haiti," Hoy.com, July 24, 2019, https://hoy.com.do/el-ambientalista-eleuterio-martinez-enfoca-el-problema-de-agua-en-nuestro-pais-y-critica-que-a-pesar-de-l a-angustiante-situacion-todavia-no-se-aprueba-la-ley-de-agua-en-nuestro-pais-agua.

18 Derby, *The Dictator's Seduction*, 233.

19 Sacred commons encompass sacred knowledge held by communities and

Drawing on criollo cosmologies, Liboristas border on what Catholics consider the heretical. Through the figure of Olivorio Mateo, they simultaneously mobilize Indigenous, Fon, and Catholic logics—all the while facing ecclesiastic opposition from the Jerarquía. Their Catholicism is shaped by their ancestral beliefs, grounded in a sense of themselves as Indigenous and African. Olivorio—and all of those accompanying him—transit through Catholic registers[20] on their way to free the people from the oppressive conditions that produce starvation, illness, and early death. As historian Roberto Cassá states, "Without a doubt, [Olivorismo] expressed a traditional agrarian cosmology, but it was re-elaborated as part of the requirements of a religious and moral message" about spiritual autonomy.[21]

The cenote that bears his name, the Agüita de Liborio, is the place that Liboristas say Olivorio retreated to in his fight against the US Marines. There are numerous Liborista ceremonies that take place here throughout the year, most notably ceremonies to San Juan Bautista—a guede (ancestor spirit) said to be the messenger of Olivorio's arrival. The lagoons are located inside caves. They hold a cenote that many criollos believe have healing powers.[22] People make pilgrimages from all over the country to pray and bathe in Liborio's water-memories, and numerous recorded testimonies speak about how

---

peoples; they also encompass access to sacred sites and shared rights to water-memories and body-lands.

20 See Lundahl and Lundius, *Peasants and Religion*.

21 Roberto Cassá, "Problemas del culto olivorista," in *La ruta hacia Liborio: Mesianismo en el sur profundo dominicano*, ed. Martha Ellen Davis (Santo Domingo, DR: La Ruta Hacia Liborio, 2004), 23. "Podría considerarse el olivorismo como un movimiento herético pasivo, en el sentido de que sus fieles no tenían voluntad de ruptura con la Iglesia. Por el contrario, aunque cayeran en cuenta de la intolerancia eclesiástica, no renunciaban a la certeza de la condición sagrada del Maestro [Olivorio], algo que remitía a claves profundas de la cultura ancestral. De la misma manera, no se encontraban contrapuestos a la Iglesia. . . . Sin duda se expresaba una cosmovisión agraria tradicional, pero era reelaborada como parte de las exigencias de un mensaje religioso y moral."

22 In various visits I made to cenotes around the country, all of them were inside caves, like the cenotes of the Yucatan Peninsula. At each of these sites (Los Tres Ojos, Boca de Yuma, Cueva de las Maravillas), the guides and local community members always spoke to me about the healing powers of the water-memories, and on two occasions, about the indios who live inside water-memory. Community members were also well versed in the archaeological research that had taken place at these sites, as well as the national parks policies pertaining to their use.

individuals have been healed of ailments ranging from madness to physical paralysis.[23] This site, therefore, is imbued with layered meanings that speak to both the individual and the collective well-being of the believers, as well as to their histories of resistance to occupation, to illness, and, explicitly, to their oppression by the Catholic Hispanic state and the wealthy elites. An altar-punto with many altars-puntos—a site of woven density—the water-memory is Olivorio, is the people, is the passageway across time-space. This site is where "Olivoristas have remapped the nation as a dialectic between two spatialized topoi: that of land, state power, and the rich, and that of an invisible realm of arcane powers under the water, a kind of hidden national space accessed through secret portals such as caves."[24] The Agüita de Liborio is a lagoon in-side a cave. Entering the water-memories is entering an altar-punto in the world where the Cartesian logics of space-time hold no meaning, and where body-land is transformed into an island in the midst of a dense sea of wa-ter-memory. The Agüita de Liborio is a nepantla, a space-time where more is unknown than known; we cannot see the source of the cenote, of the aguita, only the aguita itself.

Before arriving at the Aguita de Liborio, one must first greet the guardians. One of the guardians of the Aguita de Liborio is Antonio, a Liborista priest. Antonio inherited his role as the guardian through his family line. He is a fourth-generation guardian and dates his family's role in guarding the sacred water-memories back to a time before the US invasion (which would mean before Liborio was captured and killed). When I asked him directly how long his family has been taking care of the Aguita, he said, "We've been at war for over 100 years." When I asked one of the coordinators, Wendy, who was with us what Antonio might mean by war, she explained,

They are Liboristas. They don't believe that the land can be owned. They resisted the incursions of the Spanish [during the war of the Restoration in 1865], of the gringos [during the US Occupation], and of Trujillo. This

---

23 Martha Ellen Davis and Sobieski De León Lazala, among others, have collect-ed testimonies about the role that both Liborio Mateo and the cenotes bearing his name play in popular understandings of healing and health. Martha Ellen Davis, ed., *La ruta hacia Liborio: Mesianismo en el sur profundo dominicano* (Santo Domingo, DR: La Ruta Hacia Liborio, 2004); José Enrique Méndez, "Sobieski De León Laza-la," *Identidad Sanjuanera* (blog), April 30, 2011, http://identidadsanjuanera.blogspot.com/2011/04/sobieski-de-leon-lazala.html.
24 Derby, *The Dictator's Seduction*, 254.

province is divided between eight [elite] families, and these families say that [the Liboristas] have no right to live and plant on this land. But the Liboristas insist that they do. They are the original peoples of this land. And so, for them, the act of planting and maintaining their ceremonies is part of an ongoing war. It's part of the same war in which Liborio was killed. And in which the community of Palma Sola was massacred [in 1962].[25]

This region is also the site of numerous maroon communities (manieles), uprisings, and the consolidation of rebellion and revolutionary forces against the colonial powers and slavery.[26] The water-memories at play that day in 2012 when we arrived were reanimated in the articulation of a community's place and power.

That same day, our large delegation of Nahuatl elders (Tupina, Guadalupe Tonalmitl, Bea), Haitian Vodoun mambo Dowoti Desir, coordinators, union representatives, local politicians, anthropologists, and the San Juan mayor made our way up to the Agüita de Liborio. We drove in a large caravan, with the mayor and three of the delegates at the head. I was driving a vehicle, and with me were Wendy and three of the delegates, including Dowoti. As the caravan sped by, Liborista community members came out onto the road and flagged us down. We stopped the vehicle. One man wanted to know why we had gone forward without paying our respects at the guardian's altar-punto. We explained that the delegation had been divided and that one half was with the mayor, but that we would go get them and come back. The man pointed to where the guardian, Antonio, was waiting for us. We looked out the window and saw a man dressed in red, standing in a circle of stones, three crosses by his right leg and a group of men with palos—sacred drums—sitting in the shade behind him. It seemed they had been waiting for us.

We made our way to the Agüita de Liborio, where we found the mayor and

25 The War of the Restoration, won in 1865, was between different regional factions: the Spanish, to whom the country had been annexed in 1861, and the Santanistas, the troops and political and religious leaders loyal to Pedro Santana and the Spanish Crown. When Wendy refers to the Spanish, she is not referring to the original colonizers, but rather to the Spanish troops and government that arrived in 1861, at Pedro Santana's invitation of annexation. Palma Sola was a Liborista community that was corralled and gunned down by Balaguer's national army in 1962. Several hundred people were killed. Learn more from Martha Ellen Davis. Or visit San Juan de la Maguana, Dominican Republic.

26 See Ricourt, *Dominican Racial Imaginary*, and her discussion of the manieles during the eighteenth and nineteenth centuries in chapter 4.

a Catholic priest about to guide three of the delegates down to the lagoon. We arrived to inform the eldest of the delegates that the guardian of the Agüita had asked her to stop to pay her respects. What ensued was a heated negotiation between the delegates, the mayor, and the priest. The delegates were angered by the breach in protocol and insisted on paying our respects. The mayor, who had a woman with a rosary at her side, was using her political powers to try to move the party forward, trying to convince us all that this was an unnecessary hassle. The priest quietly pointed to the sign above our heads, which read, "This park is under the protection of the Catholic Church." But in the end, the delegates won out. The priest left the entourage, refusing to participate now that the guardian was going to be acknowledged. The delegates asked the mayor to join them, which made the coordinators chuckle. Voicing her disagreement but ever the politician, the mayor went in the car with them. One coordinator, Sergio, whispered to me, "Antonio doesn't support her campaign, and so she has blackballed him as a witch.[27] This is a coup that she is going to the altar!" This moment established an alliance between pueblos, overturning narratives of nationality and Christian colonial power in favor of spiritual sovereignty.

Dowoti and I joined the rest of the delegation. The other folks remained at the Agüita, awaiting our return. We wandered down the hill and were received by the guardian and the paleros, who led us around three crosses to the entrance of a small wooden shack. The sacred geography of the sanctuary included trees, stone walls, and indoor and outdoor altars-puntos. Our movement through the space mirrored that of a snake's and was meant to highlight our entrance through the puertas leading us into the sacred water-memories. We were asked to wait outside the altar-punto room as Antonio went inside to prepare the altar-punto for our reception. He then pointed to specific people and gave those people permission to enter.

All the delegates were asked in to the altar-punto to greet it. I was invited in as well. When we were inside, the priest simply said, "This is our altar." He then began to play a drum. The Nahuatl delegates responded by dancing a ceremonial dance in their tradition, as a way of asking permission; they danced from eldest to youngest. When they were done, Dowoti also danced, presenting her head to the altar-punto. She explained to me later that she presented herself, as "who she is," because she recognized the spirits on the altar-punto.

27　The exact term she used was *brujo*, which in San Juan means "hechicero," someone who uses magic to do harm.

Antonio acknowledged these forms of greeting and paying respects by sharing the history of the community and of the cenote. The eldest of the Nahuatl delegates responded in kind by sharing a Nahuatl creation story and expressed gratitude for being granted permission to visit. This greeting, this prayer, was the manifestation of zambo consciousness whereby our differences made room for each other and, in so doing, articulated a new possibility for queer freedom : Black sovereignty.

We were then led outside, where the mayor and the coordinators were waiting. Together, we were taken to the other altars-puntos in the sanctuary, and we were asked to greet them. This second step served to confirm that we were drawn into the sacred world of the water-memories and of the ceremonial community. In the first half of the ceremony, the delegates were asked to bring their embodied language forward, and in the second half, they were given knowledge of the embodied language that would grant them access to the Olivoristas' sacred world.

After the brief ceremony, Antonio led the palos up the hill back to the Agüita, where the paleros played music to the spirits of the cenote for the remaining hours of the afternoon. During the afternoon festivities, the delegates were integrated into the community through dance, the sharing of food, and the sharing of rituals: lighting candles, singing to the water-memories, and making offerings and prayers alongside community members doing the same. The arrival of the guardian's palos and the journey to greet the guardian were all an affront to the mayor's political power. She had brought her own palos from the town of San Juan, but in the end the San Juan paleros were incorporated into the Liborista circle—both parties responding to spiritual mandates over and above elite political alliances.

As had happened in many places in the history of Latin America, the Catholic church had taken possession of this sacred site in an attempt to curb the power of the local criollo traditional leaders. This is not a new phenomenon, as the presence of the cathedral built in Mexico City's Zocalo attests. One palero, an assistant to Antonio, told me, "The church is able to do this to us because the [elite] families collude with them to evade national laws, and the government is unable to corral power over the elites." When I asked how the community has responded to the church's incursion, he gestured to the ceremony happening around us. It was clear that despite the church's effort to ban popular expressions of faith at the Agüita de Liborio, the people continued in their practices—as they have for centuries. Recalling the Olivorista worldview, whereby powers that reside in the cenote are mobilized in opposition to the powers of the elite over the body-land, that the guardian and his palos played at the cenote was a powerful symbolic act meant to re-inscribe the memory of Liborio into the public performance of power. For the people involved, el pueblo had won this battle against the state and the landowning elite/church through the powers of Liborio, and specifically the water-memories. When the delegates aligned themselves with the guardians of the water-memories, they acknowledged their connection above and beyond the dictates of the Catholic Hispanic nation-state.

When we descended from the mountain, our parties were once again divided. By the time I caught up to the mayor and the delegation, they were coming out of the San Juan Cathedral, where, as a concession to the priest, the Nahuatl delegates were asked to sing before departing. The delegates—four of whom were raised Catholic and one who was raised as an Evangelical Christian—commented to all of us that the sound inside the cathedral was beautiful; they thanked the mayor for the opportunity to sing their sacred songs inside of it. As one delegate stated, "These churches are always built on top of our Indigenous sacred sites. So what better place to speak to the Creator than in this place where our people have always worshipped?" It was not until we were apart from the mayor and the priest, in the retelling of events, that the delegate articulated "the irony of asking Indigenous people to sing inside of a church." Another delegate was offended, not because of the Christian colonial logic in which they are forced to participate, but because of the imposition of an *elitist* Catholicism. In light of this new knowledge, the claim of "what better place than this" took on new meaning: it was meant to specify the desire to exert an Indigenous authority above that of the elite Catholic church.

In our trip to the Aguita de Liborio, the struggle for criollo spiritual sovereignty ran counter to both the elites' and the Catholic church's claims and propositions. Catholic Hispanic ultra-nationalist discourses—manifestations of Christian coloniality—seek to erase criollo belief systems, histories of resistance, claims to legitimacy, and claims to sites of memory, community, and struggle. This is clearest when community members actively resist government rules and efforts, when communities make explicit and yet indirect declarations about what is at stake. In the case of the Aguita de Liborio, the local guardian of the site exercised his authority through the language of spiritual protocol—a language that was familiar and legible to the Nahuatl delegation and which superseded the authority of the local mayor and the Catholic church.

Colonization is not a distant body-land or a distant past sensation. It is

Christian coloniality held in place by a Catholic Hispanic imaginary. It is a Christian coloniality that emanates from the traces of the colonial past, through contemporary governmental policies and social repression. It is in the political structures that designate sugar cane laborers and their descendants as "in transit," stateless and foreign, all the while configuring dark-skinned Afro-descendant peoples as other and queer : Indigenous people as extinct. The presence of Christian colonial elites is realized through the large plantation fields—owned by a family or a corporation, blessed and protected by the church and state. These fields are planted with the monocrops of peanuts, tobacco, sugar cane, bananas, pineapples, palm oil trees, strawberries. These monocrops are exported to the United States and to Europe, providing wealth to a few families who sustain their plantations using low- or no-wage migrant Haitian and Haitian-Dominican labor. While the landowners smoke their premium cigars, ride their ATVs through small farmers' conucos, invest and reinvest their stocks, attend mass in the cathedral, and travel across the geographies of the global cosmopolitan elite,[28] the laborers who work on those fields go hungry, are stateless, and/or lack basic means to survive. The priests who attempt to protect them are exiled from the country or reassigned. Gangs of Dominican men, goaded or ignored by the local police, circle Haitian migrants and Haitian-Dominicans, enacting lethal violence. Blood logics run thick through the fields.

Employing water-memory logics in the place of blood logics, defeating blood fears, could enable us to confront Christian colonial violences with a new understanding of what is at stake in our collective survival.

We could imagine water-memory in place of blood.
We could constitute our subjectivities through water-memories.
We could remember what it is that water-memory wants us to know.
To understand. To realize.
We could dismantle Christian coloniality by redefining water-memory
as always already inherently sacred.

Christian coloniality is in the Vatican-ratified authoritarian structures realized in the wake of US occupation at the beginning of the twentieth century, when the authoritarian state legitimized itself through Vatican-mediated moral

---

28 For a discussion of global cosmopolitan elites, see Aihwa Ong, *Flexible Citizenship: The Cultural Logics of Transnationality* (Durham, NC: Duke University Press, 1999).

authority. It is central to the US invasion of 1965, when the Jesuits abandoned the campesinos and the political Left in favor of siding with imperial wars against Communism. It is present within the realities of the US in Puerto Rico to the east and of MINUSTAH (a UN stabilization mission) in Haiti to the west and in the ways in which those realities are mobilized as measures of moral personhood. It is inside of the zonas francas (free trade zones), the resorts, the mines that foster large, impoverished communities with small churches with anointed Evangelical ministers (the Catholic priests come once a week). Gold is among the DR's top exports. Gold is what drew the Cristianos to enslave the Indigenous peoples in 1493. Now it draws North American multinational companies. Barrick Gold is killing one of the primary sources of the island's rivers in the Dominican Republic. It is killing the sacred mountains of Wirikuta in Mexico, draining the mountains of water-memories—their life force—and thereby draining the life of the people. Just like Sunoco Logistics and Energy Transfer Partners, who are laying the pipelines across Canada and the US, contaminating our water-memories. When the delegations visited Loma Miranda in 2015, the pueblo learned about the Standing Rock protests in the Dakotas and the Trans-Pecos Pipeline protests in the Southwest, because these stories were shared between all of us.

Years later, I told Lula about Nana Yvette's prayer, about the visit to Loma Miranda in 2015 and to San Juan de la Maguana in 2012. I told her about the privatization of communal lands in Los Haitises. She told me about the families that own a province in the northwest. Lula is friends with servidores everywhere—not just in the Dominican Republic but also in Haiti. She visits with them to learn and to compartir. Alaí Reyes-Santos defines compartir as "a model for exchange across ethnic, class, gender, and sexual differences, that entails learning from one another, sharing resources and experiences, comforting each other, and questioning each other, our privilege, social location, common sense."[29] So, when I tell her about what I am seeing, she is usually familiar with the place. She has traveled all over the country. She had been to San Juan de la Maguana for the ceremony to el Espíritu Santo and San Juan Bautista. She had been to Loma Miranda in support of the camp. And this is not her only way of traveling. She travels, regularly, into the world of the

---

29 For a developed definition/discussion of the concept of compartir, as elaborated by Alaí Reyes-Santos, see "Rubbing Shoulders: A Collective Introduction to the Transnational Black Feminist Retreat," *Asterix: A Journal of Literature, Art, Criticism,* Spring 2014, https://asterixjournal.com/rubbing-shoulders-collective-introduction-transnational-black-feminist-retreat.

spirits. When I tell her stories about my travels, her response is unpredictable. At times in our friendship she gets mad at me for being una gringa, telling me it is the US empire that exports its problems to a country with a corrupt leadership. "Loma Miranda is colonization all over again. They take our gold and leave us with nothing." I ask her if it would be better if Dominicans were compensated for the gold (as suggested by one group of protestors). She stares at me and scoffs. "It would be better if they weren't here at all." When I ask her about the role of the church in all of this, she is clear: "Depends on which church you are talking about. If you are talking about the church of the elites, they will do everything in their power to protect those families. But if you are talking about Padre Rogelio, or of the Belgian nuns, or the Liboristas, or my tío in Higuey..."

Lula often expresses relief at not being a US colonial subject (her comparison is usually Puerto Rico) but usually follows up any expression of relief with anger at the Dominican government's corruption and the rampant xenophobia in the media and on social media. Sometimes she responds to my stories with her own. One evening in late summer 2015, Wanga tells me something. I am trying to understand, but time is not the same when I am with him/her/them. Because we are in what he/she/they calls the infinite, we could be sitting together for one hour or three hours, and I cannot tell the difference. This produces a strange lethargy in my body-land. I am a body-land out of time/inside of ubiquitous time, in "the world of ancestors, spirits and those who are waiting to be born."[30] Wanga does not repeat himself, so I listen carefully.

"The congos and the indios established a treaty that said the indios would take care of the waters and the congos would take care of the land. And that is how it is: the indios live in the water, the negros on the land. That's why in the altars, the santos negros rest on the ground, and the piedras de los indios live in water. That is why los indios play in water. They also live in caves, because that is where they came from. The caves are where the water is born."

Water-memory logics. Wanga tells me there is a treaty between the congo and the indios of the island. He/She/They tells me, and I choose to believe, despite whatever blood evidence others might require. I take his/her/their historical claims as legitimate, despite the lack of archival evidence—proof that history happened. Within this story, there is a legacy of queer freedom

---

30 Ana-Maurine Lara, "'Hay que tener una Fortaleza fuerte': Catholic Coloniality, Sexual Terror and Trans Sobrevivencia in the Dominican Republic," Sargasso 1–2 (2014–2015): 86.

: Black sovereignty. It is a legacy created when a male congo spirit and a lesbian body-land simultaneously transcend Cartesian space-time to creolize temporality, to syncretize being in the woven density of knowing queerness : blackness, to animate the water-memories that traverse ubiquitous time. In that moment, through this story, there was collusion. The spirits—and those who embody them in the present-future-past when our ancestors are imagining us into being—agreed on who would take care of what and ensure it for future generations.

Here, I am only doing what Lula asked: I am "telling the story." It is a story of reconciliation, of solidarity, and also of war.

refrain

This is not the Master's house. [*Fatima said there are no African burial grounds.*]
It is not his rivers or his wells. [*She says the Indigenous peoples were buried
head down into the earth. The Spanish—facing the sun.*] This is an ofrenda, a
telling of story in conversation with spirit. [*But bones have no pigmentation.*]
This ofrenda is a ceremony where the spirits manifest because they are invited. [*So then she said, their bodies bore no evidence of hard labor.*] Because they
want to be here. [*Of the repetition of feeding wood to fire. Of the repetition of
cutting of cutting cane. Of stirring of stirring molasses. Of churning of churning the mill. Of digging of digging for gold.*] As they traverse these waters, the
world is changed in their wake. [*Maybe we are the soil.*] This ofrenda is the
poto-mitan, the enramada, the cenote. [*There was no proof in their bones.*]
These words are the vévé creating roads into the nepantla, guiding us into
ceremony. [*Only the shackles on the wrists and ankles. Only our water-memories, how much they weigh.*]

The drums change rhythm, the spirits dance among us.

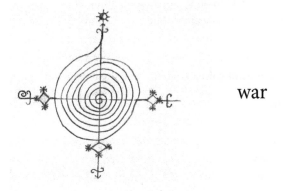

war

Mira San Santiago
Que viene bajando
Con bandera blanca
Montado a caballo

—ATABALES GRAN PODER DE DIOS

Caring for myself is not self-indulgence, it is self-preservation,
and that is an act of political warfare.

—AUDRE LORDE[1]

We are sitting in front of Lula's altar-punto. Two candles are dancing next to
each other: a blue one, a red one. In the backdrop, there are flowers, and two
machetes, crossed over each other, leaning back against the wall, their handles
wrapped in shiny fabric. I don't explore too long. Not because I am not welcome to, but because it is so powerful. Sekou Sundiata once said to me, "You
know what a vibe is? You can sometimes just walk into a room and you feel a
vibe."[2] I knew what he meant. A vibe: that intangible ripple of energy, of some-

1 This quote lives on my office wall, right next to Virginia Grise's book *Your Heal-*
ing is Killing Me (Pittsburgh, PA: Plays Inverse Press, 2017). This chapter takes up
Audre Lorde's declaration and puts it in conversation with some thoughts about
Ogún, epistemic violence, and queer freedom : Black sovereignty.
2 Personal conversation with Sekou Sundiata, November 28, 2006, Austin, Texas. I
had the honor of being in conversation with him and several other authors at Resis-
tencia Bookstore on November 29, 2006.

thing that you can feel in your gut, an awakening of intuition and knowing that is beyond the rational sphere. You *feel* it. In front of Lula's altar-punto, I am feeling a vibe. That vibe pulls me into the room and simultaneously out of time-space. That vibe tells me: those machetes mean something; they are *doing* something. Lula's gruff voice brings me into the nepantla of spirits.

> Because there have always been people who don't accept things, who say, "I would rather die than live under your ideologies, under your control, than be your tribute. I was independent for a long time before you; you aren't going to enslave me. No. I am not interested in being your slave." It is important to know this. To know that strong people—the ones who say "no, I will not allow it"—have always existed . . . Are you willing to defend your existence—just as you are? If you are not willing to do it, who will defend you? Are you willing to defend who you are, the existence you have, and the existence of others who enter into your circles?

Sometimes Wanga says many things while stating very little. At other times, Wanga speaks in parables, metaphors, and questions. In this moment, Wanga, through Lula, was asking me, directly, where I stand and with whom I am standing. He/She/They was asking me if I am courageous enough to live in the world as I truly am, in all of who I am. I am looking down at my notebook, taking notes, avoiding the question while I am also unable to escape it. I bite a nail. I am thinking about the ways I navigate the world. I am not always the person I want to be. Sometimes, I construct walls to hide behind. I retreat behind others' definitions. I contain/constrain my body-land or my water-memories in the presence of certain others. I worry about being too much. Too intense. Too big. Too much. This worry exists because of the internalization of colonization: believing that I am in excess. That my queer : Black existence is beyond what Christian colonial capitalism needs. That I am the unnecessary appendage, just waiting to be cut away. Under the weight of my worry, I silence myself. These mechanisms of self-silencing are a sign that I am navigating violence; they are also a sign of being beholden to the truths of others while silencing my own. But sitting with Lula/Wanga in this moment, this place, this knowing—this is the time-space where my own desire and resistance to the allure of being a modern liberal subject and where other registers of being come into creative conflict.

A flicker of light catches my eye. It is coming from the reflection of the candlelight dancing across the shiny fabric around the machete. Beyond the light there is darkness—shadows, the blackness of iron, dirt, fabric. Within that opacity, there is knowledge and there are tools that are hidden. In these spaces, silence and density bring dissonance into sharp relief. Staring into the darkness beyond the flicker of light, I am reminded that François Makandal did not reveal his strategy before setting fire to the plantations. I am reminded that cimarrones gathered at night, building their manieles within the thickness of forest.[3] The fabric around the machete partially conceals the sharp blade.

Machetes are used for cutting roots, branches, cane; for opening the earth before planting seeds. Machetes are used for many things. They are made of iron or steel. We, on the other hand, are not. The machetes came to this place, these lands, through colonization: with cane and with war.[4] How many of my ancestors were felled with its sharp blade? How many times did my ancestors wield machetes in the cutting of cane? How much did my ancestors tolerate before saying "Basta," before picking up those machetes and hacking through the brush to escape? Before picking up machetes and drawing a line in the earth to define a space for themselves and their loved ones? Before picking up machetes and killing who they had to kill to defend those they love? Before running, hiding, fighting, killing, loving? What were their options and what are ours?

Wanga's questions have everything to do with my embodiment of queerness : blackness and everything to do with the battles I have fought to be able to inhabit queerness : blackness. Coming into queerness : blackness I bucked all social expectations of propriety, of a heterosexual temporality, of all racialized gendered expectations of how my body-land would move through the

---

3   See Ricourt, *Dominican Racial Imaginary*; Julius S. Scott, *The Common Wind: Afro-American Currents in the Age of the Haitian Revolution* (London: Verso, 2018); Stephan Palmié and Francisco A. Scarano, eds., *The Caribbean: A History of the Region and Its Peoples* (Chicago: University of Chicago Press, 2013).

4   In Candice L. Goucher, "African Metallurgy in the Atlantic World," *African Archaeological Review* 11, no. 1 (1993): 197–215, Goucher notes, though there has been some discussion of Ogún, the orisha of iron, in the African diaspora, there has been much less discussion of the proliferation of ironwork. Given this dearth of research, however, Goucher does discuss the relationship between ironworkers and struggles for freedom : sovereignty. She presents several examples, including the examples of Palmares in Brazil and of Winkle Village in Guyana, and the "1796 uprising of slave blacksmiths and leatherworkers [that] led to increased wages and early emancipation" (203). According to Goucher, "transplanted African blacksmiths negotiated positions of leadership in the plantation hierarchy and were presumably instrumental in the exercise of ritual" (203).

world, who I would love, how I would love, and where and when I enter.[5] As a result of my decisions to inhabit the world in ways that fail to conform to biblical gender binaries and to my expected place within Christian colonial racial hierarchies, I am subjected to multiple forms of violence.

This violence is first and foremost epistemic: the reduction of my lineages, and of my being, into the logics of population. As we are reminded by Jodi Byrd, "All who can be made 'Indian' in the transit of empire . . . can be killed without being murdered."[6] Therefore, the genocide of the Caribbean's queer : Indigenous and queer : Black peoples can be thought of as an irreparable crime, one in which the murder of millions of people—to this day—has gone without punishment and, in fact, is justified through the ongoing perpetuation of the subject of the extinct india, of the foreign Haitian, of the criminalized queer. Queer : Indigenous and queer : Black peoples in the Caribbean were made into *populations* not just through war and the discourses of conquest, but through census and the historicization and prioritization of census as a framework for reinterpreting personhood and as a mode of redacting population. Second, it is theological. For with Christian coloniality came "the redaction of custom as crime"[7] and sin, and the articulation of sin as the foundation for establishing a "grammar for whole worlds of meaning."[8] Within the imperatives of Christian coloniality, the unknowability of my experiences requires that I produce the terms by which to make them legible. But the sanctity of my own person and experiences requires that I safeguard them with a cimarron sensibility: a sensibility rooted in an understanding that this world is not constructed to care for queer : Black life, or queer : Indigenous life either. Some of the deepest violence produced by colonization[9] includes this violence, which produces any and all illegible experience as excess or antagonistic to the norm; this violence seeks to know all and everything on terms not of our own making. As excess and antagonism, our personas are excisable. As object, we and all that we know are thought to be possessable. In remedying epistemic violence, I must consistently and repeatedly pass through a door of no return, that place

---

5   See Paula Giddings, *When and Where I Enter: The Impact of Black Women on Race and Sex in America* (New York: W. Morrow, 1984).

6   Byrd, *Transit of Empire*, 227.

7   Rifkin, *Beyond Settler Time*, 63.

8   Snorton, *Black on Both Sides*, 11.

9   Read Frantz Fanon, *Black Skin, White Masks* (New York: Grove Press, 2008), and *The Wretched of the Earth*.

where the unknowable presents itself as both knowable and forever irretrievable; "the door exists as an absence."[10]

Epistemic violence oftentimes manifests, like the spirits, in the material world in both direct and indirect ways: getting called names on the street; being profiled by police; being harassed and interrogated by border agents across all borders; having my legitimate anger reduced to a racial stereotype; being refused service; being told that I just need a good fuck from a man to cure me; being told I do not belong—that I am not, in fact, who I say I am; being told I am so colorful; being asked where I got my tan; being cast as the little Indian girl in the pilgrim plays in US schools; being silenced or not taken seriously; having neighbors call Homeland Security as I enter my home; being told I speak such good English, I am so articulate; being asked to explain my presence;[11] being invisible; being hypervisible; watching my friends die because they can't access medication or doctors, and tending their wounds when they have been stoned or beaten on their way home; being beaten almost to death because I do not conform; being held at gunpoint for my beliefs; being taunted and torn: "queer [: Black] we're still open season."[12]

Some days, I am so exhausted from the barrage of violence that I engage in manielismo. Manielismo is an embodied holistic praxis in which spaces within and beyond the reaches of colonial violence are constituted by being

---

10 Dionne Brand, *A Map to the Door of No Return: Notes to Belonging* (Toronto: Vintage Canada, 2012), 8.

11 This phenomenon could be understood as the confusion produced by cognitive dissonance, what Fanon defines as the discomfort produced by evidence that works against a person's core belief. There are many examples that can illustrate this point, but suffice it to say that the questioning of my presence is rarely ever about inviting me into a space. It is usually a result of people's confusion about their core belief in who they expect me to be and then the evidence of who is standing right in front of them. Fanon, *Black Skin, White Masks*.

12 Reading Chrystos's poem "Against" in her collection *In Her I Am* (Vancouver, CA: Press Gang Publishers, 1993) is like understanding that every time we make love/have sex as queer people, we are resisting 500-plus years of violence—it's like coming to life all over again. Another poem by Chrystos that evokes this deep, erotic connection between sex/love/violence/survival is "I Walk in the History of My People" from the collection *Not Vanishing* (Vancouver, CA: Press Gang Publishers, 1988). Chrystos taught me what it means to enjoy sexuality, despite all of our losses. She also teaches me about the deep, loving relationships between Indigenous women and women of color, and that our experiences bring us closer together, despite all forces attempting to keep us apart.

in community with others seeking freedom : sovereignty. Rooted in zambo consciousness, it is an embodied praxis that requires being with others. From the maniel, I stay silent and observe, or I choose to fight. From the maniel, I gather my strength, my tools, and my people. Within the maniel, I feed my body-lands and spirit and I feed others, too. Within the maniel, the spirits, the elements, the living world, and the world of the ancestors are all interdependent. Within the maniel, there is an interdependent ethic of care. Within the maniel, we love, we laugh, we let our guard down and cry. The maniel is a nepantla—a place between—that is also aquí. Within the maniel, we weave our density into conscious being, unafraid that it will be destroyed because we seek to preserve life in all of its queer : Black forms, queer : Indigenous forms.[13]

And then there is retreat and the uses of silence. On the islands, I often choose to not engage rather than deal with the multiple hostilities produced through Christian colonial ideas about biblical womanhood and neoliberal, post-authoritarian legacies about the performance of respectable femininity. On the mainland, in the north, I traverse the many racially hostile spaces by staying focused just on the integrity of my body-land and by protecting its ample edges. I choose to ignore others' discomfort with my woven density: the multiple registers of being that I inhabit at any one time even as I am aware that both on the islands and the mainland, my body-land reflects back to others their fears about the inherent instabilities of race, gender, sexuality, and citizenship. These fears are what produce violent language and violent interactions because those who produce the violence don't know why I am existing and why I am existing in the same temporal-spatial locations they have constructed as boundaried, knowable, and impenetrable. Colonization was supposed to be complete, total, finished. We were always already supposed to be gone.

Even with their violences, "our roots have proven too deep."[14]

So I understand what Wanga is asking me. She/He/They is asking me to remember who we are and where we come from. We come from people who

13 Since 2015, my partner Alaí and I have been intentionally seeking to live and enable manielismo within our home spaces and in our relations; it is a praxis that we are also thinking through in our work with traditional knowledges and traditions. See "The Caribbean Women Healer's Project—Decolonizing Knowledge within Afro-Indigenous Traditions," UOregon Digital Humanities Project, https://blogs.uoregon.edu/cwhealers.

14 Driskill, "Stolen from our Bodies," 61.

sometimes stayed silent in order to survive. We come from those who know how to say everything while appearing to say nothing at all. We come from people who bore witness to the violences of removal, slavery, and genocide and reacted in many, many ways. We come from people who experienced unfathomable sorrow and loss. We come from people who retreated to forests, who took another being's life to save the lives of those they love. We come from those who said no and who survived the violence that resulted when they said no. We come from those who have survived the dozens of wars—maybe even hundreds—that were fought to ensure their continued oppression, and for which they had to choose where to stand, who to defend, what they would allow.

Where to stand? Who to defend? What would we allow? These questions strike at the heart of the pain of incommensurability that undergirds queerness : blackness. Because there are many queer : Black people who have fought for queer people and Black people (not to mention everyone else), who then suffered violence through the words and actions of those we claimed as our own. Other queer people. Other Black people. Do we then turn our backs on those with whom we have stood, who we have defended, and who now hurt us? Or do we continue to seek possibility, despite the salted wounds? What will we allow? How does negotiating this pain shape us?

Once the external enemies are defeated,
what will grow from the water-memories feeding the ground?
Who among us will take the enemies' places?

War is never realized on just one plane of being. It is a discursive and material realization of specific ideologies used to mobilize changes in relationships of power. Decolonization requires us to examine war as a component of queer freedom : Black sovereignty. In the context of colonization, war produced genocide and chattel slavery as a byproduct of the expansion of European and African empires. The slave trade fed wars of colonial settlement across the Atlantic world. Differing definitions of war and slavery enabled the deterritorialization of Indigenous peoples from multiple body-lands and the production of chattel slavery as a framework for the organization of labor. The religious (ideological) justification for war enables its uninterrupted practice as a central component of Christian coloniality. The violence of colonial warfare is not just in its justification, but also because war was mobilized across multiple planes of being. These wars sought to claim everything in their paths. Wanga speaks:

If you see your enemy sitting there, not doing anything, are you going to decide to dirty your hands? Or are you going to walk away and hide in the forest? You have the right to take whatever action is required to defend your existence. . . . Wars are always occurring on different planes, simultaneously. Military wars are also ideological wars, and they are also cosmological wars. It is a lie to say that wars don't result in deep changes, in death and in damage. They do. . . . War is something that has many implications and is felt for many generations. [For generations we feel] the loss of blood, of culture, of language, of place, of land, of existence, of ways of being, of freedom, of customs, of the freedom to walk, to be able to make decisions as communities and as nations.

The kinds of war Wanga is referring to are not only wars that produce armed conflict between nations, tribes, kingdoms, or peoples. She/He/They is speaking about the "various transformations in space[-time] by which people's lives have been propelled into new and unpredicted terrains" that produce what are new beings in both material and spiritual form.[15] What was once one kind of being without the memory or experience of a particular kind of war becomes fundamentally altered. The body-land that receives the blood of flesh is altered. These new beings are densely woven manifestations of these transformations; across the generations, their density accumulates, shifting individual and collective relationships to space-time. The beings that are transformed include body-lands, water-memories, altars-puntos, ceremonies, and ancestors.

Wanga is not talking about the war of maneuver, "where everything is condensed into one front and one moment of struggle, and there is a single, strategic break in the 'enemy's defences' which, once made, enables the new forces 'to rush in and obtain a definitive (strategic) victory.' "[16] She/He/They is also not talking about war of position, a kind of war "which has to be conducted in a protracted way, across many different and varying fronts of struggle; where there is rarely a single break-through which wins the war once and for all . . . [through and against] the structures and institutions of civil society."[17] She/He/They is also not speaking of Vitoria's justification of war through ius

---

15   Veena Das, *Critical Events: An Anthropological Perspective on Contemporary India* (Delhi: Oxford University Press, 1995), 5.

16   Stuart Hall, "Gramsci's Relevance for the Study of Race and Ethnicity," *Journal of Communication Inquiry* 10, no. 2 (1986): 17.

17   Hall, "Gramsci's Relevance," 17.

predicando,[18] that is the mediation of uncivilized peoples through the rites of baptism, conversion, and the elimination or remediation of mortal and secondary sins—and if need be, the colonial military apparatus that included secular and religious priests, conquistadores, knights, and protectors of the Christian faith, merchants, and government officials. Rather, she/he/they is talking about a war of preservation, a war that extends beyond the boundaries of the state, civil society, and the material world into the nepantla of the erotic, of spirits, ancestors, elemental forces, and Mother Earth herself. This war of preservation is rooted in zambo consciousness, an awareness of present-future-past solidarities in struggles against Christian coloniality. Some wars were started that have not yet ended; they continue through the present-future-past. But they don't look the same in all instances. One such war is made evident through the figure of Ofelia Balendyo, also known as Obatala or Nuestra Señora de las Mercedes.

Two friends and I were in Santo Domingo walking through the zona colonial. We were on our way to the Iglesia de las Mercedes, the church dedicated to the Virgen de las Mercedes. Gabriel, who is crowned with Obatala in the Lucumí tradition of Cuba, is also adodi. Our other friend Elena is a self-defined lesbiana who is baptized with various luases within the criollo tradition. For Gabriel, the Virgen de las Mercedes is Obatala, an orisha. For Elena, las Mercedes is Ofelia Balendyo, a misterio. For both of them, las Mercedes is a colonial tool of the Catholic church and the Catholic Hispanic state that they have to navigate on their way to the orisha and the misterio. She is, in turn, what makes it possible for them to understand each other despite carrying different traditions.

Elena, Gabriel, and I had met in el ambiente of LGBT sociality, and our friendship had deepened when we also discovered each other within a Lucumí community on the island. The bond we shared as a result of the "open secret" of our gayness was strengthened through the "closed secret" of our presence in the space of Lucumí ceremony. Like gayness, participation, presence, and practice in criollo religious ceremonies and spaces in the Dominican Republic

---

18 See Francisco de Vitoria, *Relecciones sobre los indios y el derecho de guerra* (Madrid: Espasa-Calpe, 1975), for a discussion of just war or rather, the debates and justifications for Christian colonial expansion and conquest explained through Christian theology. Because the modes of life and production were not legible on European political economic terms, discursive and military apparatus—justified by theological justifications, that is *ius predicando*—sustained colonial settlement practices.

is stigmatized. The traditions are labeled as brujeria (witchcraft) within hegemonic discourses; the practitioners of these traditions are called brujas (witches) and hechiceras (sorceresses). These terms, like maricón, have negative connotations that have material consequences, like the loss of homes and jobs. While all three of us participate openly in el ambiente, meaning we are visible in the public spaces of LGBT sociality, none of us knew that we knew of, were friends of, or were part of these traditions until we found each other in the Lucumí community. This co-discovery strengthened our friendship and expanded the spaces of our sociality from the parks and bars into the spaces of ritual and offerings—like the one we were carrying out that day. As an aleyo—meaning a non-initiated supporter of the Lucumí tradition—I was often the one to distract police and passersby as flowers were laid down or rum was poured or candles lit. These acts, these offerings, are considered illegal in the United States and its territories, suspect in the Caribbean.[19]

On this afternoon, September 24, 2012, we were going to the church dedicated to La Virgen de las Mercedes in Santo Domingo so that Gabriel could pay his respects to his santo—another term for orisha and for luas or misterio. While both Gabriel and Elena expressed affection for las Mercedes, they were both more directly committed to the orisha and the luas that las Mercedes protects. September 24 is las Mercedes's feast day (el día de La Virgen de las Mercedes). Las Mercedes is one of the two most venerated Virgin Marys in the Dominican Republic (the other being La Virgen de la Altagracia). In the Catholic tradition of Marian processions, the statue of the las Mercedes is removed from her altar-punto inside the church to walk among the people. She is dressed in feast garb and held above the crowd as her figure moves from the peripheries of the community back into the center—the church.

We made our way deeper into the zona colonial, through blocked-off streets and large clumps of people, garlands and bouquets of white flowers in all directions. Once we arrived at the church, the large crowds gave way to small groups of elderly women, dressed for mass and dispersed throughout the neighboring park. I went to stand next to the church entrance while Gabriel and Elena went to purchase flowers. I stood by a metal plaque, from which I learned that the church had been built between 1527 and 1555 and had been

---

19   In the US, leaving offerings in public places could be considered littering. In the Dominican Republic, it is the public exercise of non-Christian beliefs that can often produce violence.

dedicated to the Virgen de las Mercedes in 1844—the year of the first wave of Dominican independence. Something in me bristled at that information.

In the reading room of the Archivo General de la Nación (national archives) there are a series of paintings along each wall. The paintings depict battles between Spaniards and Native peoples. They are a visual story of how in 1495 las Mercedes defended the Spanish in one of the largest military battles against queer : Indigenous peoples, a battle which in the annals of colonial history was depicted as a Spanish victory. Subsequently, when the country suffered a catastrophic earthquake in 1615, the governor of Española, Don Diego Gómez de Sandoval declared las Mercedes the patron of Española. With the declaration of independence in 1844, las Mercedes was named as the Catholic patron of the Dominican Republic. But this was not the whole story. I knew this because on September 24, 2012, I was standing there waiting for two friends initiated in criollo traditions who were about to make offerings to las Mercedes—and not because of this story of conquest.

My friends returned, white zinnias and roses in hand. We leaned against the church walls, waiting. Very soon the procession arrived. First in line was a cadre of soldiers from all branches of the Dominican military (navy, army, and air force), the national police, and special forces, including a cleric wearing a military hat. All of them held church flags and staffs. This procession enacted a very clear symbolic union between the church and the military. Las Mercedes, the one who rules over the celestial armies, ruled over national ones, too. Suddenly, Elena leaned over to me and said, "There's the priest, the one who has been so terrible to the LGBT community."

I stretched to catch a glimpse of the declared local enemy of the LGBT community—by extension, someone who thought little of me, too (*Would I dirty my hands? Would I walk away? Would I hide in the forest?*). In the past three years, this priest had proposed numerous initiatives aimed at causing harm to LGBT people. The first had been through the Junta de Vecinos de la zona [colonial] (the Colonial Zone neighborhood association). In defense of la zona, he had provided a list of names to Dominican newspapers of men and women who were seen at gay clubs in la zona. As a result of this list, those men and women lost their jobs. He had also lobbied local officials to shut down gay clubs, which LGBT activists perceived as both a direct and indirect form of harm to the community. The shutting down of gay clubs harmed gay club owners financially, and it eliminated safe, semi-public spaces for LGBT people to socialize. This priest marched blissfully behind the military cadre, chatting to a television reporter (*I did not dirty my hands. I did not run. I did not hide. I observed. And now I write.*).

As I recovered from the sudden (and overwhelming) military presence, I saw the larger crowd of devotees coming down the street. With them was the las Mercedes, in all her European glory: her hair a golden mane, her skin an alabaster white. The Mercediarian coat of arms was on her chest. In her hands, she held chains and shackles—symbols of enslavement and imprisonment—and the scepter of divine justice.

Among many ultra-nationalist Dominican Catholics, las Mercedes is the guardian of celestial armies; she is the one who presides over ethno-nationalist liberty. She is the force that enabled the military conquest of the island—both in the conquest of the Native peoples and in the establishment of the Dominican Catholic Hispanic arrivant state. She is the protector of the Dominican military, whose primary role today is to guard a constructed and violent border. But, in Gabriel's lineage of Ocha, she is Obatala. She mobilizes her celestial armies in the service of protecting Obatala's children, all of the enslaved and the imprisoned. She holds the chain of creation in her hand, and the sun shines behind her head as she watches over creation. For Elena, she is also known as Ofelia Balendyo, sister to Ogún Balendyo, the warrior, the chief of the Ogún. Ogún is the nación Nago. Ogún Balendyo is Rada. He is the shipmate of Agwe, the ocean/the sea. He is the Ogún of the ships and the navy. He is a horseman and likes to ride his horse. He is syncretized with San Santiago, and on his white horse, he conquers all enemies. In her role as Ogún Balendyo's sister—better understood as an aspect of masculine/feminine duality—Ofelia protects the people from injustice, defending their freedom.

Despite my personal misgivings about the military, ethno-nationalist nature of the celebration, I was moved by the palpable vibe and emotion of the crowd. It was a devotion and love that was directed to both las Mercedes and the people entrusted with her. Just as the statue of las Mercedes was about to enter, the enemy priest rushed over to the church door. As he prayed, devotees continued their singing. People crowded around the entrance to the church, eager to enter. When the procession died down and the mass had begun, Elena and Gabriel disappeared inside the church. I waited outside, observing the dissipating crowds. The soldiers had gone inside. This was their mass, as defenders of the nation-state. They sat in prayer as an adodi and a lesbiana wound their way to the altar-punto to place flowers to Obatala and Ofelia Balendyo. How many others in the crowd experienced las Mercedes in this way? I wondered.

When Elena and Gabriel emerged, we broke away from the church wall to find a place to eat. As we crossed the street, Elena grabbed my arm and directed me to look behind us.

"There goes La Brujita."

I followed her gaze. I saw a woman wearing a yellow scarf on her head and dark sunglasses. She wore a conservative blue cotton dress, and her hair was tucked to the side so that her (straightened, bleached) locks were resting on her shoulder. She was making her way quickly into the church when she was approached by several men, who stopped her. I stared as she adjusted her bangs while talking with them, clutched her purse in front of her, and pressed their shoulders with her manicured hands. It turned out they were plain-clothes police officers; they were trying to prohibit her entrance into the church. Nonetheless, she succeeded in getting inside.

"Who's La Brujita?"

"She's a trans* woman who is very respected here in her neighborhood."

"I take it from her name that she's a bruja?"

"Apparently, she helps a lot of people out. People in this area love her, and she's famous."

I made a mental note to seek her out at some other time, and we continued on our way. The three of us were discussing las Mercedes's alabaster whiteness, her European features and golden hair. A dark-skinned man who was standing on the street overheard us and responded, "Don't be mistaken. She's morena." I turned to him, "Why, then, did they make her blanca?" He gestured with his hands, as though sweeping dust out onto the streets. "That's their racism." This man, a stranger, was letting me know in not so many words what Elena and Gabriel also knew. This was a war of preservation (*Would I dirty my hands? Would I walk away? Would I hide in the forest? Ofelia Balendyo hides in plain sight.*). A war of preservation requires mobilizing all of the available forces of life toward justice. It is a long-term strategy, across generations.

A few days after the las Mercedes procession, I sat at a table with a group of Dominican anthropologists and artists. I shared my experiences with them. They shared more stories about las Mercedes. They reiterated the official state and Catholic church narrative. There was a battle between the Spanish and the island's queer : Indigenous peoples in 1495. The Spaniards, greatly outnumbered, were about to retreat. Suddenly, a monk accompanying the Spanish company brought forth las Mercedes and told the Spanish they would win the battle and conquer the indios. The queer : Indigenous fighters, having retreated, were not prepared for the Spanish counterattack. In the end, the Spaniards defeated the queer : Indigenous fighters, slaughtering hundreds of them, and in the name of the Crown and God were able to establish the Spanish colony. In this version of the narrative, las Mercedes is used as a marker of Christian colonial conquest. Her presence is what enables the success of conquest.

After reiterating the official narrative, Iris told me another story. "The community where this battle took place—known as Las Mercedes—disagrees with this narrative. For many, las Mercedes represents the resistance of the Indigenous peoples, and later Afro-descendant peoples, to Spanish conquest and slavery." In other versions of the narrative, las Mercedes appears in the sky. When she appeared, it was a sign for the Indigenous peoples that the war had ended, that it had been won (*Would I dirty my hands? Would I walk away? Would I hide in the forest?*). I would find this version reiterated in text. The version where retreat is then possible.[20] In this version, there is evidence of another set of cultural logics. As there is when las Mercedes appears standing before a massively enslaved people with broken chains and open shackles in her hands. Subsequently, she also becomes a purveyor of justice for the Afro-descendant people on Española—in particular, those who fight to end slavery on the plantations.[21] In her hands, she loosely holds handcuffs, a metonym for slave shackles, bits, and collars. She intervenes on behalf of those who have known captivity.

Las Mercedes was and is still used by the church to sanctify conquest. In the official narrative, she is the symbol for conquest and the military might that comes with Spanish rule. Yet the pueblo—like the peoples of the historical narrative—understands her presence in a different way. She is the one who enables justice, she is the queer : Black force that mounts the white virgin and, in so doing, mobilizes her in the service of justice. Her golden locks and alabaster skin are also a mask for criollo guardians and forces. Much like La Brujita's blond wig and sunglasses, these masks serve to distract us from other subtler maneuvers of power.

---

20 Read Lynne Guitar, Pedro Ferbel-Azcarate, and Jorge Estevez with a critical eye toward middle-class diaspora adaptations of New Taino Revivalism. Guitar makes important interventions in ethnographic discourses; her claims are refuted by many Afro-Dominicanist scholars. Guitar, Ferbel-Azcarate, and Estevez, "Ocama-Da-ca Taino (Hear Me, I Am Taino): Taino Survival on Hispaniola, Focusing on the Dominican Republic," in *Indigenous Resurgence in the Contemporary Caribbean: Amerindian Survival and Revival*, ed. Maximilian C. Forte (New York: Peter Lang, 2006), 41–67.

21 Conversation with Iris Mondesert, September 29, 2012; interview with E. M., March 25, 2013, Yamasá.

Queer : Black people—our bodies and in particular our nonconformity to the moral and social expectations of how our bodies should behave in the intimate spaces of the arrivant state—are subject to an immense range of violence, from the everyday to the exceptional. In daring to articulate a spiritual autonomy as central to queer freedom : Black sovereignty, our body-lands bring attention to how violence materializes against dark-skinned bodies and those who fail to conform to biblical manhood and womanhood. When we dare to live and to challenge the frameworks of biblical manhood and womanhood, we are remembering that people like us, others, have always existed. We are drawing our water-memories up into our body-lands. They are memories that rest inside of our body-lands, like agua inside the boulders at Loma Miranda, or under the earth in the springs in Palo Blanco, or in the caves guarded over by Papa Liborio. They wait until the time is right, until there are roots and prayers to draw them up. We are redefining what it means to win a war.

Yo soy Ogún Balenyó
y vengo de los Olivos
a darle la mano al enfermo
y levantar a los caídos.[22]

Ogún is one model for thinking about war. Ogún is the primal warrior. And at once forging iron, opening roads, waging war, Ogún is the healer of the sick, the wounded, the bleeding, the shot. Ogún is the setting of bones, the stitching together of flesh. Ogún is the power of life as life itself is being redefined in the processes and wake of war. Ogún retreats into the forest and reminds us that all any of us want is to reduce our suffering and the potential for our suffering. We do not actively seek to be enslaved, imprisoned, exiled, tortured, killed. We do not seek these kinds of suffering, for ourselves or those we love. Social justice, another one of Ogún's qualities, offers a model for the remediation of the forces of suffering through the mobilization of tools for our collective preservation. Ogún is, after all, the tool maker. Ogún, both cutting and sewing together, reorganizes time and space.[23]

---

22 Salve to Ogún Balenyó, made famous by Enerolisa Nuñez and part of the collective song archives of the Atabales Gran Poder de Dios and many other palos groups.
23 Thank you to Solimar Otero for talking with me about Ogún as I worked through a piece on reimagining Ogún in relation to the divine feminine.

Ogún lives in the same space-time as the Catholic Hispanic arrivant state. Even though over 60 percent of the Dominican population identifies as Catholic, and even though Catholicism is the official state religion, the presence of queer : Black body-lands and souls challenges the possibility of any one unifying expression and understanding of Catholicism among the people. (*Ogún opens the ground.*) Inasmuch as Christianity disciplines queer : Indigenous and queer : Black body-lands and water-memories into new modes of being and believing, it and the political economic conditions under which Christian coloniality took root also produce new forms of spiritual expression. Queer freedom : Black sovereignty is mobilized through independent modes of being that emerge from criollo ideas of time, space, and relationship in the everyday. These modes undermine any totalizing Christian colonial narrative of conquest. (*Ogún prepares the furnace to make his tools.*)

The possibility of queer freedom : Black sovereignty directly challenges Christian colonial concepts of freedom : sovereignty stemming from conquest and conversion. This possibility is reflected in the prioritization of and insistence upon the continued practice of criollo beliefs and practices, rather than their destruction, excision, or termination. (*Ogún retreats into the forest.*) In other words, the possibilities of freedom : sovereignty enabled through the continued embodiment of forces like Ofelia Balendyo or Ogún mean that the forces that enabled our ancestors to survive are still alive. They still survive because we still survive. Because we survive, these forces are still alive. There is no teleological progress toward salvation. Rather, survival—freedom : sovereignty—is coterminous, palimpsestic, woefully interdependent across multiple registers of temporal-corporeality.

These multiple registers of temporal-corporeality also undermine Christian colonial articulations of sovereignty, articulations that are fundamentally grounded in wars of conquest. (*Ogún wields her weapons.*) Within Christian colonial epistemologies, "sovereignty resides . . . [not just] in the power and the capacity to dictate who may live and who must die," but also in *how* life and death may be realized.[24] Think: the reorganization of body-lands; think: the poisoning of aguas; think: the marking of flesh; think: the progression toward Heaven or Hell. (*Ogún forges an iron kwa, for Legba, Baron, guede.*) Implicit to the exercise of Christian colonial sovereignty is the exercise of control over the definition of where life begins, what life, death, and after-death are, and how the after-dead are cared for. Christian colonial sovereignty is

---

24 Mbembé, "Necropolitics," 11.

intergenerational in nature: with each generation, queer : Black wombs are cleansed of Ham's sin as the generations progress toward Christian whiteness. Space-time is organized within a unilineal progression toward the conquest of futures, most visibly realized through the figure of the Crown, the church, the modern nation-state leader, and Heaven. Heaven is both inevitable and assumed to be desired. But what if, like Hatuey or the Lemba, we don't want to go to Heaven? What if that is not the present-future-past we imagine for ourselves or those we love? What if this Earth, this time-place-space, is all we have and as a result, we choose to love it? What if we realize that "for the cultures that know that this is the only place to live (for life), we have to care for each flower, each animal, each tree?"[25] The implications of this for queer freedom : Black sovereignty are tremendous.

Criollo traditions could produce ruptures in the realization of Christian colonial sovereignty's expectations. Criollo traditions could reorient our beings toward other possibilities: the figure of the sovereign disappears and, in its place, emerge the misterios, the ancestors and the spirits that preside over the shifting relationships expressed through community; body-lands are not the object of conquest, the reflection of authority or power, but rather the material through which life forces are enabled; death is simply another part of the forces of life. (*Ogún the midwife births life and death.*) Using criollo traditions as a roadmap, queer freedom : Black sovereignty could be manifest through the realization of relation, not domination over temporality-corporeality.

Christian colonial renderings of corporeality configure freedom as the taming of the unclean, animal body through the cultivation of a pure, divine soul. Christian coloniality, in its strictest interpretations, is enacted through conversion, confession, and fear—all aimed at reifying Heaven as the ultimate site of freedom. Queer : Black body-lands are inherently untamed and untamable, therefore irredeemable except through (slow or quick) death, conquest, erasure, silence. (*Ogún stitches together.*) The continual and deepened use of a

---

25 If you can understand Spanish, it is worth listening to Aída Bueno Sarduy in her conversation with Julia Marandeira (curator at the Museo de Arte Contemporaneo, or MACBA, Barcelona); Aída Bueno Sarduy, "Encuentro con Julia Morandeira y Aída Esther Bueno Sarduy," YouTube video, 01:02:10, September 14, 2017, http://youtu.be/eDocYhzXXRs. Her discussion of sacred food of the orisha is embedded within a broader cosmological discussion. The presentation was part of the art exhibition *Santa Comida by Miralda* and on exhibit from 2012 to 2013. The exhibition and performance video are available through MACBA's website: https://www.macba.cat/en/santa-comida-0508.

specific and bound liturgy, over long periods of time, makes and remakes the Christian colonial corporeal. Within criollo traditions, these bound practices of the body, of conversion, of confession, of taming, of liturgy, of knowing are upended. In their place, the shifting expressions of drums and dancing, of spilled rum and flying sweat, mark the aquí as divine, as pure, as life, as abundant. The altars-puntos remake body-lands, water-memories, ceremonial grounds, enabling the realization of continued life and freedom : sovereignty. That which is compressed through the Christian colonial is unbounded. Gone are the lines between the seen and the unseen; this world and others; male and female; race and histories. (*Ogún calls their warriors to the war.*)

Màrìwò yéyéyé. Màrìwò yéyéyé
Èní mob ò ni mo bó. Ogun ení mob ò ni mo bó.[26]

Queer freedom : Black sovereignty coexists alongside and challenges hegemonic mobilizations of Christian colonial arrivant configurations of freedom : sovereignty. In the example of the Dominican Republic, freedom : sovereignty as nationalism relies on the production of discourses and practices that reconfigure Christian colonial ideals of biblical manhood and womanhood, of teleologies of redemption, as Catholic Hispanic ethno-nationalism. Catholic Hispanic ethno-nationalism relies on the consolidation of a racialized biblical manhood and womanhood as measures of national belonging. The disproportionate disciplining of those deemed outside, foreign, or excess to the arrivant nation produces specific targets: specific body-lands deemed incapable of bearing Catholic Hispanic souls; specific water-memories that wear away at the borders; specific altars-puntos that disrupt the death of queer : Black/queer : Indigenous beings.

In the example of the Dominican Republic, the ongoing project of Christian coloniality is further troubled by the way in which the arrivant state has engaged with neoliberal economic and political forces. Through globalized tourism, we see the replication of Christian colonial logics against and through body-lands and water-memories. The already constructed nature of the Caribbean region as feral and uninhabited, where "wild and savage men who ate human flesh (Cannibals) and sexually precocious women (Amazons) who were to be tamed and controlled in the name of God and the Crown,"

---

26 La palma frondosa se agita rápidamente; hoy lo cubriré y seré libre. Prayer to Ogún.

serves as a backdrop to the neoliberal reordering of relationships between global forces as they traverse ethno-national boundaries.[27] Tourism, a large percentage of the gross domestic product (GDP), expands across a landscape that is increasingly restrictive to rural and urban poor queer : Black people.[28] Tourists who go to the Dominican Republic to experience the picturesque tropics,[29] to imbibe rum and partake in the expansive Dominican sex trade, do so in a context in which the Christian churches of all denominations collude with the arrivant nation-state to discipline the imagined lascivious behaviors of its poor (queer: Black) people and to diminish criollo religious practices. In moments when criollo religious practices enter into the public eye, the result can be catastrophic for the communities involved.

Haina, an industrial town on the outskirts of Santo Domingo, is also the location of many deteriorated sugar cane bateyes (plantations) where Dominican-Haitian families and Dominicans of Haitian descent continue to live. On Easter Sunday 2013, Dominican police attacked a gagá procession of revelers as they made their way through Haina. The police attack on the gagá in Haina was unexpected. It was, however, an act of Christian colonial war that contained spiritual, material, and symbolic elements.

I was first introduced to gagá in 1995, when I researched gagás in the plantations of the southeastern Dominican Republic. Gagá is a Dominican-Haitian ceremonial celebration that occurs every year during Catholic Holy Week, observed by hundreds of people in the sugar-growing areas across the Dominican Republic.[30] It is a highly structured ceremony that has deep political knowledge embedded within it.[31] This deep political knowledge is most

---

27 Kamala Kempadoo, *Sexing the Caribbean: Gender, Race and Sexual Labor* (New York: Routledge, 2004), 1.

28 See Nixon, *Resisting Paradise.*

29 See Krista A. Thompson, *An Eye for the Tropics: Tourism, Photography, and Framing the Caribbean Picturesque* (Durham, NC: Duke University Press, 2006); Jamaica Kincaid, *A Small Place* (New York: Farrar, Straus, Giroux, 2000).

30 For a detailed ethnography of gagás, see June C. Rosenberg, *El Gagá: Religión y sociedad de un culto Dominicano: Un estudio comparativo,* no. 37 (Santo Domingo, DR: Universidad Autónoma de Santo Domingo, 1979). Listen to Verna Gillis, *Caribbean Revels: Haitian Rara and Dominican Gagá* (US Library of Congress, 1991).

31 I have drawn from Andrew Apter's concept of "deep knowledge" quite significantly in my own scholarship. Deep knowledge references the hermeneutics of power embedded within ritual/art/praxis. To learn more, see Andrew Apter, *Black Critics and Kings: The Hermeneutics of Power in Yoruba Society* (Chicago: University of Chicago Press, 1992).

evident in its spiritual hierarchy: leaders are identified as the president, generals, sergeants, captains, majors, and queens. There is a mambo, an elder female priestess, who directs the deep ceremonial practices, but the public presentations are led by the male armies. The queens (or metresas) are the energetic balances that guard the edges of the ceremonial spaces and the processions that rule the entrances and protect the altars-puntos, managing the energy from these positions and places.

The public gagá ceremonies begin at sunset on Holy Thursday and end on Easter Sunday. There are two exits (salidas) into larger Dominican society and public space during this time. The first is on Good Friday and the final is on Easter Sunday. The implication is that the gagás are exiting the batey, the sugar cane plantations and the ceremonial center, out into an expanded territory of war: the ethno-national space-time known as the Dominican Republic. These exits have multiple symbolic layers of meaning. Gagá is a staged spiritual war, often against, through, or with the state. As ceremony, it mobilizes the hot earth spirits, the petwo, the spirits born in and after slavery. At different times in Dominican history, gagás have garnered violent responses by the state— much as one did on Easter Sunday 2013. The presence of gagás in Dominican space-time, and outside of the racialized site of Dominican-Haitian labor (the sugar cane plantations), elicits calls to Dominican-Haitian solidarity as much as generating targeted anti-Haitian violence. The history of gagá exits out of plantations begins during the mid-twentieth century.

Beginning in the early twentieth century, Haitian laborers were brought from the occupied western part of the island to work on US-owned/run sugarcane plantations on the occupied eastern part of the island. Following the authoritarian consolidation of the arrivant state in 1930, Haitian laborers (as well as West Indian laborers) were brought as seasonal workers but were also restricted to living on the plantations year-round. The sugar companies, not the state, issued workers their identity documents. This ensured that cane workers could be easily identified within and outside of plantation boundaries. It also ensured a perpetually vulnerable and easily excisable workforce. In the late twentieth century, the Dominican sugar cane industry collapsed. The children, grandchildren, and great-grandchildren of those cane workers were no longer wards of the sugar corporations. They became stateless. Some had succeeded in getting documents for their children born in Dominican hospitals. In the twenty-first century, those same children, grandchildren, and great-grandchildren of cane workers were denationalized. By spring 2013, when the gagá in Haina was exiting the batey, several thousand Dominicans of

Haitian descent had already been denationalized. Later that year, in September, the Dominican Constitutional Court would rescind the nationality of all cane workers and their families—going back to 1929.[32] The mass deportations were now state-sanctioned. To say that Easter 2013 was a difficult time for Dominicans of Haitian descent, and Haitians, in the space-time geography of the Dominican Republic is perhaps an understatement.

During the Christian twentieth century, Holy Week was the only time of the year that people from the bateyes were able to freely circulate outside of the plantations. They could only do so through the public performance of gagá, a manifestation of Haitian-Dominican religiosity. Like its Haitian cousin, rará, gagás are also a site of political protest, though protest is heavily masked within the structures of the ceremony. Gagá has a highly defined military hierarchy, and its performances draw on Haitian revolutionary symbols of war. Gagás can include the placement of flags in a war position (inversely) as they emerge from the sugar cane plantations onto the streets; the purposive use of multiple languages including Kreyòl, Latin, French, Spanish, and English in the ceremonies themselves, which is done to assert hierarchies of power between plantation populations and to mark power over the Christian colonial space-time; the use of Catholic liturgy in the embodied songs and messages of the misterios in the space of Catholic Holy Week; the occupation of public streets by misterios whose existence transcends the political and juridical locations and identities of the body-lands that carry them. The arrivant state cannot document a misterio. For the arrivant state, they are extinct, like other beings. Nor can the church contain a misterio's movements—especially if it dons the guise of a Catholic saint. Gagás represent a decolonial model of time in which the symbols of a Haitian-Dominican ceremony serve to disrupt Christian colonial space-time and to insert ceremonial time into the public space beyond the batey. The interruption of a gagá procession by police forces, and the suffering of gagá priests under the weight of police-church repression hints at the boundaries of Christian coloniality—where it reaches and what it

---

32   See James Ferguson, "Migration in the Caribbean: Haiti, the Dominican Republic and Beyond," Minority Rights Group International, July 2003, https://minorityrights.org/wp-content/uploads/2015/07/MRG_Rep_Caribbean.pdf; Lesley Bartlett, "South-South Migration and Education: The Case of People of Haitian Descent Born in the Dominican Republic," *Compare: A Journal of Comparative and International Education* 42, no. 3 (2012): 393–414; Randal C. Archibold, "Dominicans of Haitian Descent Cast into Legal Limbo by Court," *New York Times*, October 24, 2013.

still cannot touch. Gagás are one cultural-religious site where "Dominicans, Haitian-Dominicans and Haitians subvert national policies of segregation and dominancy by coming together to construct an 'army' of African and criollo deities, cosmologies and identities."[33] During and through gagá, the Catholic resurrection of Christ is re-articulated as a metaphor for the resurrection of criollo, and specifically Haitian-Dominican, life on the island. The narratives embedded within gagá include not only the resurrection but also the story of slavery and emancipation.

Gagás end with a final procession through the public spaces surrounding the batey. This procession is a multilayered public performance that confirms that another war against the forces of death and oppression has been won. The final public procession announces new alliances between gagá communities, new songs that have emerged from the ceremonies, and newly crowned leadership among the gagá hierarchies. It is also the final declaration of victory: the people have succeeded in completing yet another ceremonial cycle, Africa has once again been re-planted (sembrado) in America, and the emancipation of the people has been achieved for yet another year. The final procession is especially important as a form of closure to these processes of celebration and renewal.

On Easter Sunday 2013, in Haina, police attacked a gagá in mid-procession.[34] The gagá had just emerged from the batey. They were making their final round through the broader community before closing. The president of the gagá rode at the front of the procession, followed by the musicians and the other celebrants. As they entered a main street in Haina, the police opened fire using semiautomatic weapons. The procession stopped in its tracks as police arrested all the generals, majors, sergeants, and captains. They shot at the windows of the gagá president's car, destroying the glass. They disbanded the people and confiscated the musicians' instruments. Celebrants dispersed.

The disruption of the spiritual ceremony and the arrest of its leaders shifted the attention of the revelers away from the embodiment and performance of celebration into the embodiment and performance of material warfare. The spiritual war that the gagá processionists were ending, on its symbolic and

33 Ana-Maurine Lara, "Vudú in the Dominican Republic: Resistance and Healing," *Phoebe* 17, no. 1 (spring 2005): 12.

34 Personal observation. For news coverage see Hanobi Delgado, "Balacera interrumpe fiesta de Gagá en Haina," NoticiasSIN.com, March 31, 2013, https://noticiassin.com/balacera-en-gaga-por-oposicion-de-la-policia.

spiritual levels, had not been won. Rather, it devolved into a material reality that generated psychic and physical violence. Not only did the police violate the unspoken cultural agreements and the laws in place that guarantee the right of the people to celebrate gagá, but they arrested the leaders—the president, the generals, etc.—and removed the weapons of war (the instruments). They had declared a social-political-religious war on the people in the exact moment when the people were celebrating their victory in the realm of the spirits.

The symbolism inherent in this act of disrupting the final procession is part and parcel of what drew media attention and led to the resolution of the war. The incident made it onto the news because people began to post footage on social media (making recourse to media and visibility through cellphone video recordings, then posted on social networks). As a result of the attention these postings generated, the director of Santo Domingo's Cultural Commission—the governmental organization that manages folkloric and cultural festivals—learned about the attack. He met with the police in Haina and was able to successfully negotiate the release of the gagá leaders. The incident then drew more media attention. When journalists asked the chief of the national police how this had been allowed to happen, he said he received "orders from above." When asked to clarify whether by "above" he meant the president of the republic or God, he would not respond.[35]

The day of the attack, I was with friends at Ile Abebbe Oshun. We were hanging out and wading through various ceremonies for various people when the news came in. My friend Lourdes and her friend Francisco sat on the sofa across from me. I asked them what they thought. Lourdes responded that it made no difference whether it was the president or the Catholic cardinal (as God's representative); the Catholic church was implicated in this incident because there is no true separation of church and state. She informed me that the cardinal, López Rodríguez, that same morning at the Easter mass, had preached on the need to stop satanic practices in the Dominican Republic. She concluded that his missive, combined with anti-Haitian sentiment, was underlying the police response. At that moment, Abebbe Oshun entered the room. Having overheard us, she pointed out that that is one reason she has a very large framed image of Jesus on her front porch (aside from her belief in the figure of Jesus as one manifestation of God)—because she wanted people around her to know that her house was a house of God. The framing of criollo and Afro-diasporic traditions—including gagá—as satanic has enabled

---

35 Delgado, "Balacera interrumpe fiesta de Gagá en Haina."

the demonization of queer : Black bodies entering into the imagined Catholic Hispanic public space. Gagá was producing a visible rupture in narratives of national, ethno-racial, and Catholic Hispanic purity at a time when the arrivant state was once again mobilizing ultra-nationalist discourses.

An online and TV news agency, SINoticias, directed a poll several days later that revealed that a majority (47 percent) of the 1,513 respondents believed that the incident was provoked by religious intolerance, while only 15 percent thought it had to do with xenophobia.[36] If it is indeed the case that the motivation for the police attack on the gagá in Haina was motivated by religious intolerance, then it would be possible to say that it is this same religious intolerance that underlies the continuing secrecy of ceremonies like manís (ceremonies to spirits) and palos (drum celebrations) and the fact of criollo sacred practices altogether. This form of religious intolerance is undergirded by Christian colonial ideas about sin and evil. It is further substantiated by Dominican Catholic Hispanic discourses, which construct criollo traditions as both satanic and foreign: the media and church leaders continuously inscribe criollo traditions as savage tendencies only tenable through the exercise of queerness : blackness and, specifically, Haitian-ness. The intolerance perpetuated by Cardinal López Rodríguez and the Evangelical leadership—whose discursive violence is directed against queer : Black body-lands, including those of women, poor, dark-skinned, Haitian, and LGBT people—is based on these presumptions. This is in a context in which the majority of Evangelical Christian churches are located in poor communities, and when both the Jesuits and the Evangelical Christians have made concerted efforts to organize, missionize, and incorporate Dominicans of Haitian descent and Haitian migrant laborers; this is despite the fact that on any given day, you will find hundreds of criollos tending to their spirits, their ancestors, and the misterios.[37]

As in other instances, the message that God's representative (the cardinal) released on Easter Sunday in 2013 was acted upon by the rank-and-file of the state's agents: police officers who again and again respond to the cardinal's (and Christians') predications by physically disrupting explicitly criollo public rites of celebration and the public right of assembly, while also imposing

---

36 Delgado, "Balacera interrumpe fiesta de Gagá en Haina."

37 In his dissertation, Brendan Jamal Thornton discusses the contradictions of Evangelical social worlds that are imbued with active beliefs in witchcraft, sorcery, and magic: "The Cultural Politics of Evangelical Christianity in the Dominican Republic" (PhD diss., UC-San Diego, 2011).

Christian colonial space-time.[38] Once the gagá exited the batey and entered the public space-time of the Dominican Republic's geography, they suffered the disciplinary effects of Christian coloniality as imposed by the cardinal's discourses and enacted by state authorities. The violence was spectacular enough to be exceptional.[39]

Until the 1990s, public performances signaling criollo ceremonies were not sanctioned. Though criollo religions are still not officially legitimated, recognized, or sanctioned, some criollo musical and dance forms that have their roots in religious practices have been brought into the tourist publics as folklore. This includes the public performance of palos and criollo dances. These performances take place in museums, universities, international conferences, and European cultural centers. They do not include—at least publicly—the enactment of ritual or prayer. Their purpose is generally folkloric or educational; in many instances, they serve to promote tourism.

Several factors enabled the social opening of public space to criollo practices as folklore performance. The first is the surge of publications and presentations by anthropologists, historians, and other scholars in public forums—including books, museum exhibits, and public talks—that enabled an alternative discourse to emerge. Anthropologists brought drumming and dance troupes into museums to perform. They also published books and films that showed criollo spiritual practitioners enacting rituals.[40] These publications and films circulated through museums, cultural centers, and universities both in the Dominican Republic and abroad.

---

38 On February 7, 2013, police threw tear gas into a crowd of Haitian students in Santiago participating in the Carnival celebrations. The police justified their actions by stating that they were responding to "citizens" complaints about a group of "foreigners" practicing satanic rituals and playing devil's music. "Dominicana Ahoga Vudú Haitiano con Gases Lacrimógenos," *La Prensa FL*, February 7, 2013, http://www.laprensafl.com/policia-dominicana-dispersa-haitianos-vudu.

39 See Deborah A. Thomas, *Exceptional Violence: Embodied Citizenship in Transnational Jamaica* (Durham, NC: Duke University Press, 2011).

40 A small cadre of ethnographers, psychologists, and historians have collected material on criollo traditions in the Dominican Republic. Carlos Andújar Persinal, in his tenure as director of the Museo del Hombre Dominicano, brought much of his research front and center. Carlos Esteban Deive, Soraya Aracena, Fradique Lizardo, June Rosenberg, Martha Ellen Davis, Dagoberto Tejeda Ortiz, and J. Dagoberto provide good insight into criollo traditions. Persinal, *Identidad cultural y religiosidad popular* (Santo Domingo, DR: Editora Cole, 1999), and *La presencia negra en Santo Domingo: Un enfoque etnohistórico* (Santo Domingo, DR: SN Publishing, 1997).

But, aside from the state-approved codification of criollo performance practices, there are many artists who have intentionally integrated traditional criollo beliefs/worldviews/critiques into popular music and visual art. Poets like Manuela Cabral Tavárez (Si con las manos que tienes / sembraste un millón de cañas: / ¿De dónde te sale, di, / una canción tan amarga?), Aida Cartagena Portalatín, and Tomás Hernández Franco in the mid-twentieth century, followed by others such as Norberto James Rawlings, Sherezada Chiqui Vicioso (Entonces la identidad era palmeras / mar, arquitectura / tambores Yemayá y Ochún / y la temporaria paz del agua. / Agua-cero / como el circular origen de la nada. / Y un extraño ulular traía el viento), Mateo Morrison, and Blas Jímenez.[41] Since the 1970s, numerous artists have extensively and consciously reintegrated criollo musical and visual aesthetics into their work, bringing attention to these beliefs in ways that had been unseen for almost a century. This includes musicians like Johnny Ventura, Kinito Méndez, Luis "Terror" Díaz, Rita Indiana Hernández, Xiomara Fortuna, Tony Vicioso, and the Gran Mawon, and painters like Silvano Lora and José Morillo, among others. As a result, criollo values and beliefs disrupt the Catholic Hispanic geography through TV shows featuring these artists, music videos, and public performances. Artists have also made public political claims through their art. The 1992 celebration of Columbus's arrival in the Americas spurred not only great Hispanophilic sentiments but also multiple kinds of cultural protest and dialogue. Many artists, such as Silvano Lora and Kinito Méndez, protested the quincentennial celebration through public acts of defiance or the production of work with criollo motifs, themes, and aesthetics.

Third, the conjunction of state and international interests enabled the revival of a criollo, and specifically Afro-diasporic, geography within the arrivant state. In 1994, UNESCO co-sponsored the Ruta del Esclavo, a public historical and cultural education program which took place in numerous countries in Africa and the Caribbean, including the Dominican Republic. The Ruta del Esclavo initiative provided scholars with an opening to give place to Afro-diasporic memory and create consciousness around the history of African peoples in the Dominican Republic. This was done through the reanimation of plantation geographies, of Maroon geographies, and of the urban geographies of African emancipatory struggles. Similarly, the designation of the Congos of

---

41 Read Manuel Cabral, "Islas de Azúcar Amarga," in *Trópico Negro* (Buenos Aires: Sopena, 1941), 20; Chiqui Vicioso, *Un extraño ulular traía el viento.* (Santo Domingo, DR: Alfa y Omega, 1985).

Villa Mella, a spiritual and cultural community, as a Masterpiece of the Oral and Intangible Heritage of Humanity by UNESCO in 2001 served to legitimize scholarly claims about the ongoing presence of Afro-descendent people in the DR.[42] It also enabled the official recognition of one Afro-descendant community, though only insofar as their practices have contributed to the expansion of tourism.

These factors contributed to the opening of public spaces to specific, secularized, folkloric expression of criollo beliefs. On Easter 2013, these factors enabled the minister of culture to successfully negotiate the release of the gagá leadership: he continuously made recourse to the gagá as an important part of Dominican folklore, and subsequently, of Dominican tourism. The sanctioned presence of these folkloric public expressions stands in contrast to the extreme repression that took place on Easter Sunday 2013. Because gagás are not necessarily politically neutral, because they publicly exercise criollo ceremony as beliefs, and because they bring unashamed criollo, dark-skinned body-lands front and center into the public view of the arrivant state, they are threatening. In these ways, gagás are important sites for the public expression of queer freedom : Black sovereignty.[43]

Queer freedom : Black sovereignty requires defending one's way of life and ways of doing things. Spiritual autonomy at times requires a war of preservation. For queer : Black people, this means that we are often fighting for our lives across various planes: for the right to exist, to live, to maintain our traditions, to enact our cosmologies, to walk through the streets, to not die at the hands of police. All of this fighting requires spiritual resources. The spiritual resistance implicit within the maintenance and exercise of criollo ceremonies provides us with insights into the moral and spiritual resources we can mobilize in response to the dispossession of our body-lands, our water-memories, our altars-puntos. It is in fact a "re-possession" of erotic agency and autonomy, of cultural and spiritual embodiment and movement through ceremony that enables the exercise of queer freedom : Black sovereignty. Queer freedom : Black sovereignty works against the dispossessions and deterritorializations of Christian coloniality.

---

42 See Angelina Maria Tallaj-García, "Performing Blackness in a Mulatto Society: Negotiating Racial Identity through Music in the Dominican Republic" (PhD diss., Graduate Center, City University of New York, 2015).

43 The attack on the gagá that Easter Sunday serves as a powerful mirror from which to examine queer : Black repression more broadly speaking.

The resources used by queer : Black people to survive and reconcile generations of war and the "loss of blood, of culture, of language, of place, of land, of existence, of ways of being, of freedom, of customs, of the freedom to walk, to be able to make decisions as communities and as nations" are many.[44] Oftentimes, we are the first to be killed, to be excised, to be removed. The possibility of our joy is sufficient justification for harm against us. Sometimes, to preserve ourselves, we must leave. Migrants often leave home because they have to. It is because my great-aunt left the island in 1968 and moved to D.C. that my parents met there in 1972. It is because of the experiences I had after my parents left the island that, eventually, I ended up in Oregon. The context (and the stories this context enables) is different, and yet the struggle for queer : Black survival is ever present.

One afternoon, in a gathering of women in Oregon, I was asked to speak about my joy. The gathering was of women healers, the majority of whom were white. I had been invited by an African American friend and she had asked me to bring my friends, elders, people I knew. There we were, in a circle. The question was put to us: to Jannes, a Cuban American Lucumí elder; to Nana Yvette, a Shis-Inday elder; to Josefina Báez, a Dominican York artist; and to me. It seemed like a simple enough question: What gives us joy? I meditated on the question as others answered. I wanted to give an answer that reflected all of who I am and why I was there in the first place. When it was my turn, I spoke (*Are you willing to defend your existence—just as you are? If you are not willing to do it, who will defend you? Are you willing to defend who you are, the existence you have, and the existence of others who enter into your circles?*).

> My joy is in the form of a question. It's a question I ask each of you, and it's a question I ask each of you to take back to your families. My joy is in imagining that gay and trans people can just be ourselves at all times and still be loved by others; my joy is imagining that Black people can walk freely anywhere we want to go without fear of being killed; and my joy is in imagining that the management of this land—this Kalapuya land and all of the land of this continent—has been returned to Indigenous peoples. So in answer to your question about my joy, my question to you is: What can you and your families do so that gay people and trans people are loved and Black people are free and so that land is returned to Indigenous hands? (*Ogún seeks justice.*)

---

44 Wanga/Lula.

There were women in the room who could not contain their fear. Their response was to label my joy anger, to diminish it and silence it with requests for pleasant images and thoughts—as though loving a gay or a trans person is so unbelievably rude; as though imagining a Black person walking freely down the street is somehow unpleasant; as though a Native woman making decisions over the care of body-land and water-memory is somehow violent and wrong. One woman shot up from her chair. She asked us all to stand and to hold each other's hands and imagine joy as light emanating from our hearts. She was so shaken by my question she could not look inward to consider why. I stayed seated. I did not shift from my place of joy, from my vision of queer freedom : Black sovereignty, but instead ensconced myself further in its possibility. Josefina and Jannes stayed seated, too, as Nana Yvette sang a medicine song and walked around the room, looking into each person's eyes, giving love to the other women of color in the room, saying to the white women who could not see her, "See me. We are still here."

Under the moon, under the stars

To exercise queer freedom : Black sovereignty could require making recourse to deep wells of strength, knowledge, joy, and intelligence. Roadmaps to decolonization could require the strength necessary to accept, love, embrace, and stand by our visions, visions born out of the knowledge of what is possible and what is as of yet unimagined. We could reconcile with pasts in which our ancestors may have played multiple roles. Maybe they were queer : Black people "who wanted to continue within the colonial power structures," and maybe they were "those who did not."[45] What, in turn, could their position in our ancestral memories reveal to us about the possibilities for aquí? Will we be ancestors who maintained the colonial power structures, or will we become ancestors who did not? How could we become another possibility within the context of ongoing wars of dispossession?

In criollo traditions, reciprocity is central to the establishment and maintenance of community relationships between living people, between the living and the dead (ancestors), and between the living and the misterios. Reciprocity is both generalized and balanced, requiring in some instances an immediate exchange and, in others, an ongoing presence. What is marked, however, about the space of ceremony is that reciprocity of any sort is rarely quantified by

---

45 Wanga/Lula.

material or symbolic gift exchange; it is instead quantified by the presence of spirits and energies—seen as either desired or unwanted—and the well-being of a community in the wake of ceremony. Because of this, reciprocity is established by one's way of being within the space of community and ceremony, a way of being that is circumscribed by specific ethical expectations, modes of relationality, and bodily dispositions. This is not to say that money or goods are never spent in the preparation of ceremonies or in the context of healings.[46] They are used to purchase all of the necessary ceremonial items in specific instances. Healers, ceremonial leaders, brujos, and others must make ethical decisions about how to provide for the health and well-being of themselves, their communities, and their ancestors, while simultaneously being informed by "global and local religious, economic, and cultural hegemonic forces." But they do so, in general, with an emphasis on the spiritual realm as the primary locus of exchange. As a result of this way of being and of these logics, our body-lands and our water-memories are redefined according to the world of the spirits. But what happens when the Christian colonial war turns us against queer freedom : Black sovereignty? What takes place across the social fabric when these cycles of reciprocity are broken?

Several servidores I met stopped maintaining their altars-puntos or doing healing work once they joined Evangelical Christian congregations. In those instances, they channeled their prior beliefs into a strict relationship with Christian liturgy, and healing work was channeled through the Evangelical church ministries and practices. Take, for example, Wilma, a full-time nurse, and formally a comadrona from a small rural town. Comadronas are rural midwives who also have the church-delegated power to baptize children immediately after birth. They are highly regarded by their communities because of their crucial role in childbirth, but also because of their extensive knowledge of traditional healing methods.

I have known Wilma for about twelve years. Wilma was baptized as a Catholic when she was born. Her mother and aunt are Catholic lay leaders, and her mother was a comadrona who taught Wilma from when she was

---

46 For a discussion on the moral economy of spiritual work, and specifically for an examination of how healers/religious practitioners manage the demands of neoliberal capitalism, see Maarit Forde, "The Moral Economy of Spiritual Work: Money and Rituals in Trinidad and Tobago," in *Obeah and Other Powers: The Politics of Caribbean Religion and Healing*, ed. Diana Paton and Maarit Forde (Durham, NC: Duke University Press, 2012), 198–219; Raquel Romberg, *Witchcraft and Welfare: Spiritual Capital and the Business of Magic in Modern Puerto Rico* (Austin: University of Texas Press, 2003).

very young. Wilma delivered her first baby when she was sixteen years old. As a Catholic, Wilma was also a servidora de misterios. She maintained an altar-punto, and because of her double role as healer and servidora, Wilma has also played a crucial role in baptisms, burial ceremonies, and weddings. In her late twenties, Wilma started a nursing degree in the capital. There she was befriended by a colleague who is a member of an Evangelical Christian church. By the time she finished her degree, at age thirty-two, Wilma had converted to Evangelical Christianity. She took down her altar-punto to San Santiago and channeled all of her healing work into her nursing. People in the community still refer to her as their comadrona, and I spent time with her as she was organizing the preparation of food for a funeral. Aside from cooking, she did not take part in the traditional funeral ceremony.

Wilma's role as a traditional healer in the community was profoundly transformed by her shift from healer to nurse, and from Catholic (criollo servidora) to Christian. In 2016, when I visited the rural clinic where she works, Wilma told me that she starts each and every day preaching the word of Jesus Christ, and it was true. Each morning, weak and wounded people waited outside the clinic while Wilma preached the gospel. Only when she had finished were they allowed inside. As each person filed through the door, Wilma asked them if they accepted Jesus Christ as lord and savior. Several people left before being asked. Others simply mumbled. For Wilma, she was bringing lambs to Christ. This total reorientation to serving Christ and only Christ seemed to have undermined her greater role as both community nurse and servidora of the santos and the people. I was personally startled by this, as the clinic is state-run. In all of the years I had been visiting this community, I had never before seen anything like what Wilma was doing. When I visited Doña Adela, I mentioned what I had witnessed. As I told her the story, she sucked her teeth and crossed her arms in front of her chest.

"I don't go there anymore. They only serve Christians. Can you imagine— one morning I went to get my diabetes medication, and the medication is right there on the counter. Right there! Wilma didn't give it to me. Instead, she told me the medication had run out. But I know it didn't. It was right there on the counter. I could see it with my own eyes. Ever since she found the word of God, she forgot about God. Because God is love, and do you think it's love to deny someone medication?"[47]

---

47 Personal conversation and interview with Doña Adela, September 2016.

Because of that experience, Doña Adela had stopped going to the clinic, even though she suffers from diabetes and the clinic could provide her with free medication. Instead, she started taking the one-hour trip to the pueblo, to visit doctors there. This was not without cost. Trips to the pueblo are expensive, and because of scarce transportation, they require setting aside an entire day for travel and standing in line for longer in the more crowded pueblo clinics. These facts are also indicators that Doña Adela's quality of life is at stake: What will happen to her if she goes into diabetic shock? Will she receive care at the clinic that is one kilometer down the road, or will those around her have to flag down a vehicle and hope she makes it the eleven kilometers into the pueblo? (*Ogún heals the sick.*)

In addition to these drastic changes to her care schedule, other changes have occurred in her life. Doña Adela has dug more deeply into her knowledge as servidora and as curandera. This last decision has served her well. As more and more people are turned away from the clinic, they come to her to seek healing. This upsurge in healing work means that she and her family are receiving sustenance from their fellow community members: in the form of food, of livestock, and of communal help in the fields and in the household. Because of her vast knowledge of healing plants, Doña Adela has started to teach her grandchildren about how to care for medicinal forests, how to identify plants, and how to prepare medicines. This decision she made, she said, because she realized that this was the way "we have always taken care of business [siempre hemos resuelto]."

Wilma's transformation was troubling not only because of the day-to-day violence it produced, but also because it signals the contours of a new spiritual war: over body-lands, over water-memories, over the altars-puntos and the spirit of queer : Black people.

War is something that has many implications and is felt for many generations. What will we feel in the wake of our current wars?

closing
ceremony

Yo tengo un lua que me ilumina
Y me protege de la gente
Por 4 velas de a centavo
Y un poquito de aguardiente
Con un machete en la mano
Con su tabaco en la boca
Y un pañuelo colorảo
—ATABALES GRAN PODER DE DIOS[1]

It was a Saturday afternoon in 2011, and I was making my way to Parque Duarte to hang out with some friends. I got off the bus at Parque Independencia, where the founders of the arrivant state—one white, one mulatto, one Black, all men—are commemorated. I wound down El Conde, the pedestrian walkway that during the day serves as a platform for local artists and artisans and peddlers to sell their wares to tourists and at night is both a cruising scene and an economic zone for sex workers. I arrived at Parque Colón, my stomach turning at the site of the Columbus statue and the cathedral. This camino I have walked is the central axis along which tourism hinges.

---

1   Salve for Candelo and part of the collective song archive of many palos communities. Here it is represented as sung by Atabales Gran Poder de Dios. It says, "I have a lua who enlightens me / and he protects me from people / for four penny candles / and a little bit of rum / with a machete in their hand / with tobacco in their mouth / and a colored scarf."

As I passed the iron gates and the glowing coral walls, I thought about the hands that built this edifice. In 1994, on a visit to the island with a Xicana friend of mine, Veronica, we walked through the zona colonial. We stopped just in front of the cathedral and she asked the dark-skinned state guards standing at the door to the cathedral who had built it. The guards responded as expected, "The Catholic church. The Spanish." But she stood in front of them, waving her finger. "No," she said. "It was the Indigenous peoples and Africans who built it." They laughed at us. The concept of giving credit to the labor of indios and negros was so foreign to anything taught in Dominican history. Not only was Veronica correct in speaking to this invisible history, she was bold to share her view with state guards at a time when the church and official history held such significant social and political power.[2]

A few years after Veronica stood up to the cathedral guards, Jose Luis Sáez recuperated some of the history of enslaved African labor in both the colonial economy and the church's development. He published his findings in a monograph that was later suppressed by the Jerarquía[3] *because* it revealed the church's participation in the slave trade. Sáez writes:

> The license to import negros bozales in the first years of the 16th century, most significantly to assist in the fast construction of temples, materialized with the death of Cardinal Cisneros and the removal of the prohibition (1517), as well as with the appearance of the sugar industry, which had come to substitute the exploitation of the mines as the colony's economic basis. The Church itself would benefit from the new policies, because in 1514, Ferdinand the Catholic "gifted" to the first bishop of La Concepcion 10 black slaves "to more quickly finish the Church" in La Vega, and at the end of the 16th century, the Cathedral of Santo Domingo received 100 slaves of the same race to repair the temple and to build the Hospital of San Andres.[4]

The zona colonial of Santo Domingo was built with encomendado, indentured, and slave labor. The establishment of Christian coloniality through the construction of cathedrals, monasteries, and other church buildings was part and parcel of the extension and seating of church authority on queer : Indigenous

---

2   Balaguer was still in power and the 1992 quincentennial celebrations that his government had sponsored and hosted were still the source of much official pride.

3   Personal conversation with Pablo Mella, November 8, 2012.

4   José Luis Sáez, *Cinco siglos de Iglesia dominicana*, vol. 1 (Santo Domingo, DR: Editora Amigo del Hogar, 1987), 31.

body-lands and into the colonial economy that structured the management of queer : Black body-lands. Nobody knows how much property the Catholic church possesses on the island,[5] but estimates range in the hundreds of thousands of acres and in the millions of dollars.

La Jerarquía, aside from owning vast quantities of body-lands in urban spaces, is also able to determine the use of state-operated body-lands. This power is an extension of both the public, state-granted rights over body-land and the placement of body-land by private elite families into the hands of the local Catholic church. This is done as both a form of tithing and as a result of the Jerarquía's pressure on landowners and the arrivant state. Body-land is yet another way the local Catholic church Jerarquía, as an extension of the worldwide Catholic church, maintains power within local politics, social and civil policies, and the daily lives of people on the island, including those of other faiths and religious practices.[6] Body-land struggles across the arrivant state become extensions of battles for queer freedom : Black sovereignty against the elite landowning interests, the Jerarquía, the arrivant state government, and North American and European transnational corporate interests.

Christian coloniality is enacted not only in the disciplining of body-lands, but also in the interruptions of access to, and the displacement of communities from, body-land and water-memories. It is also enacted through the disruption and dismemberment of altars-puntos.[7] In order for the arrivant

---

5   See Emelio Betances, *Catholic Church and Power Politics*, for a discussion of the local Catholic church's history in the Dominican Republic, as well as local laws and the economic and social impact of the church on Dominican society.

6   For discussions on the role of the global Catholic church, land possession, politics, and power throughout Latin America, see Emelio Betances, *Catholic Church and Power Politics*; Anthony Gill, *Rendering unto Caesar: The Catholic Church and the State in Latin America* (Chicago: University of Chicago Press, 2008); John Frederick Schwaller, *The History of the Catholic Church in Latin America: From Conquest to Revolution and Beyond* (New York: NYU Press, 2011); Madeleine Cousineau Adriance, "The Brazilian Catholic Church and the Struggle for Land in the Amazon," *Journal for the Scientific Study of Religion* 34, no. 3 (1995): 377–82.

7   As I was finishing up this book, I sat down for a conversation with a friend who is a former nun. While revisiting an earlier conversation we had in 2015, the subject of criollo altars-puntos came up. She explained that in the decades when she was a nun, her specific job had been to dismantle altars-puntos in peoples' homes. She explained the entire process, and how women (the majority were women) who refused to take down their altars-puntos were refused communion at church. She outlined from her perspective as a former nun what many servidores had shared with me:

state to continue along its Catholic Hispanic trajectory, there is an implied and actual erasure of queer : Black peoples from the national psyche. For this erasure to take place, the erasure of the places of meaning is also necessary. Simultaneously, to render Catholic Hispanidad visible, physical markers of Christian presence must emerge across the landscape. This manifests in the construction of churches, cathedrals, and crosses, claims to criollo sacred sites by Christian leaders, and the collusion of the Jerarquía with elite land-owners in efforts to displace campesinos—like in the example of the Aguas de Liborio. Queer : Black geographies challenge Christian colonial narratives of conquest and conversion.

Tiene su conuco
Detra del bohío
guarda su machete papa por si arma lio
Candelo tiene un tizon prendi'o
Candelo candelo candelo cedife
Candelo monta lua
o-donde ta papa candelo
Oy mi Candelo colora'o [8]

Criollo traditions exist between being seen and being unseen. Criollo ceremonies occur all over the island and in the island's diasporas.[9] On any given day, there could be any number of ceremonies, healing sessions (consultas), or fiestas taking place around the country. As Brendan Jamal Thornton remarks,

> In . . . towns and cities across the country, the spiritual or supernatural is both hidden and visible. Although spirits, angels, or demons may not be visible to everyone, religious paraphernalia of all kinds can be found in

---

that the churches actively work to suppress and dismantle La 21 división, Liborismo, and other manifestations of criollo spirituality.

8   [The lua] has their garden / behind their home / he hides his machete in case there's trouble / Candelo has kindling lit / Candelo Candelo Candelo cedife / Candelo rides lua / Where are you Papa Candelo / O, my fiery Candelo.

9   See Karen McCarthy Brown and Claudine Michel, *Mama Lola: A vodou priestess in Brooklyn*, vol. 4 (Berkeley: University of California Press, 2011); Peggy Levitt, *God Needs No Passport: Immigrants and the Changing American Religious Landscape* (New York: New Press, 2007); Cristina Sánchez-Carretero, "Santos y Misterios as Channels of Communication in the Diaspora: Afro-Dominican Religious Practices Abroad," *Journal of American Folklore* 118, no. 469 (2005): 308–26.

homes and/or in storefronts. . . . One may encounter mediums or specialists who have a special kind of relationship with the supernatural, or one may speak with a pastor, or a priest, or a witch, or a sorcerer. Much of everyday life for many Dominicans is committed to the spiritual realm.[10]

In other words, there is a worldview and permeated social context in which the unseen and the seen worlds work together, where what is seen is imbued with the unseen and where the unseen includes ancestors, spirits, demons, gods, and the forces of nature. The seen sometimes indexes the unseen world. At other times, it is the unseen world that provokes a new relationship to that which is visible. Rituals, ceremonies, prayers, and dreams mediate these worlds and are part and parcel of everyday life. But the majority of these ceremonies, rites, and rituals are held in secret. In the dark brick homes of the colonial city, with only daylight and candles to light the space. Or in enclosed cement yards of homes in the barrios, tucked away in the maze of streets, or in the enramadas and marquesinas of the countryside, down sloping hills and dirt mountain roads. Coffee grounds are read in the privacy of homes; sacred tools are disguised as household items. Offerings to the orisha and egun are made with the loud music of the television concealing the sounds of prayer. And altars-puntos are sometimes decorated with only candles, soda bottles, and flowers, at other times with pots and wooden vessels.

When I first began my research over twenty years ago, I would ask criollo healers directly if they practiced. I would blunder my way through conversations with Candomblé priestesses and santeras with blunt questions—trying to get to the point. At that time, many would deny any affiliation with La 21 división or similar practices, and would opt to tell me they are Catholic. Others would answer my questions, but with suspicion. Why did I want to know? Time, and my own personal desires to understand my place in the world, changed me. Writing *Erzulie's Skirt* and *Kohnjehr Woman* changed me. Life and graduate school and the development of my own ceremonial practices changed me. Entering the enramada is first and foremost an exercise in love: love for the world, for all of its beings, for our ancestors, for the place on which we stand, and for each other. It is also about mediating envy and harm, chaos and illness, and being humble enough to recognize that one is always susceptible. When I attend a velación, or a maní, or a fiesta de palos—or I am witness to a servidora's healing work—when I demonstrate knowledge and care and

---

10 Thornton, "Cultural Politics of Evangelical Christianity," 52.

thoughtfulness about these traditions, then it is in the opening of our hearts to each other that new conversations emerge. When I acknowledge and validate that there are forces beyond my ability to protect myself from pain, then it is an opening for those who love me to express care. The misterios or the santos or the elementales come to the forefront. The plant and animal medicines reveal themselves. They all enter the room to help me, too. Together, the misterios and their servidores, the orishas, the egun, the iyas, santeras, babalawos and obas who have compartido with me, have only ever demonstrated love for me, as a child of the African diaspora, as—in their own words—"una morena con muchos indios," and as a "daughter" of Ogún. Despite my own personal sentiments about Christianity's role in perpetuating colonialism and harm to queer : Indigenous and queer : Black people, criollo traditionalists remind me that they are Catholic. As a result, I have had to deepen my own understanding of how the Catholic saints are honored for the work they do in service to the forces of nature that are the misterios—a process that has been mislabeled syncretism but could be better understood as transmogrification. As J. Lorand Matory reminds us,

> Throughout Yorubaland, initiates of the *orisa* priesthoods (*olórìṣa*) have always been a small minority of the population. So the fact that most contemporary Yoruba identify themselves as Muslims and Christians is not the reversal of an earlier situation. . . . *Orisa*-worship retains a central place in the towns and quarters that most Yoruba Muslims and Christians consider their ancestral homes. That is not to affirm the standard, and often racist, claim that Christianity and Islam are but superficial elements of African culture and personal identity. On the contrary, the interaction among these religions is a constituting dynamic in Oyo-Yoruba culture, which resists being classified as fixed and bounded.[11]

As a people whose ancestors suffered the bindings of iron on their wrists, their heads, their legs, being "unbounded" and resisting classification and fixity are central to our collective survival and sense of place. We are the woven density that ruptures expectation and, instead, produces spiritual autonomy—the root of zambo consciousness: Catholic saints are known for working both hands. They can open the road to healing, but they can also open the road to great repression. They allowed the misterios to come to the islands from Africa, but

---

11 J. Lorand Matory, *Sex and the Empire That Is No More: Gender and the Politics of Metaphor in Oyo Yoruba Religion* (New York: Berghahn, 2005), 67.

they came on slave ships and they ushered in genocide. Catholic saints work both hands. San Santiago (Saint James the Greater) rides in on a white horse, a sword in his hand—the knight behind him riding in with a white flag. That white flag has a cross, and the Muslim dead lie under their feet, trampled over by the horse. San Santiago tells the story of the Reconquista, the inciting events that produced colonialism: the unification of the Spanish Crown, the invasion of Abya Yala,[12] and the subsequent capture and enslavement of peoples from the islands of Abya Yala, Iberia, and the African continent. San Santiago is also known as Ogún Balenyo, who is the conqueror of all ills. Disguised as a Christian conqueror, he is the figure that tells the story that allows the memories of conquest, invasion and slavery to be remembered. In Ogún Balenyo's world, it is not the Muslim who lies at the feet of the horse, but rather the ills of slavery and colonization, of injustice and illness, of poverty and early death. Catholic colonial expectations are inverted, and the criollo warrior takes over the reins to stage a war against true evil.[13] This process of inversion is a mode of zambo consciousness.

Zambo consciousness is present in the multiple ways in which Christian colonial logics are appropriated and inverted. It is reflected in relationships between people, the forces of life (misterios), and the land that those forces traverse. These relationships are inscribed onto place through the marking of sacred space-time through ceremony and through the presence of symbols of criollo traditions in the landscape. They are also inscribed through agricultural practices including the planting of diverse food crops, instead of monocultural crops like sugar cane or timber; planting in traditional forms such as the conuco (diversified plots of vegetable, root, herbal, and medicinal plants) instead of in large monocultural plots; the incorporation of criollo beliefs and practices in processes and forms of planting and harvesting; and the mobilization of criollo forces in the service of campesina struggle. By examining how zambo consciousness is expressed through ceremony, we begin to

---

12 Abya Yala is the Kuna name for the earth, and most directly the part that has come to be known as América. The earth is also known by many other names. Many of the activists and community members I worked with refer to the earth as "El Caribe," "la tierra," "Madre Tierra," "América," "Abya Yala." The Nahuatl delegates also refer to the earth as "Anahuac." Many also refer to other spiritual geographies like "Ginen," "el cielo," and "el mar," and distinct political geographies like "Haiti," "República Dominicana," "Cuba," "Puerto Rico," and "los países."

13 See Emilie M. Townes, *Womanist Ethics and the Cultural Production of Evil* (New York: Springer, 2006).

understand the centrality of body-land and water-memory for the production of meaning, specifically as manifested through the altars-puntos, the poto-mitan, the cenote, the nepantla.

Candelo fuma
Candelo bebe
El no le teme a la distancia
Ni tampoco los problemas
El no le tema al agua
Ni tampoco la candela
Oy candelo
General candelo Oye
General candelo[14]

From the twentieth century to the present day, campesinas have continued to struggle against large multinational companies like Monsanto, Dole, and Barrick Gold.[15] These battles, led by cultural guardians who are both political and spiritual leaders, are not illogical and ill-fated battles against a teleological neoliberal development. They are struggles informed by deep, intergenerational relationship to place and to body-land itself. By exploring the tensions that emerge when campesinas exert their authority and claims to body-land—through protest and through ceremony—it is possible to further elaborate upon the extension of Christian colonial logics in elite attempts to consolidate power through land ownership and resource extraction.

Through waves of neoliberal economic restructuring, Christian coloniality further constrains criollo claims to body-land, livelihoods, and the exercise of spiritual autonomy. This is the case of Los Haitises and Loma Miranda. The ongoing struggles between the Jerarquía (usually in support of land-owning elites) and local communities over physical sites of criollo spiritual significance also provide insight into the material and cultural conditions that continue to relegate criollo beliefs to the margins and literal shadows of legitimized, respectable society. Such is the reality of those who protect El Agüita de Liborio. Each articulation of criollo belief is an affront to the Christian colonial project. This

---

14 Candelo smokes / Candelo drinks / He is not scared of distance / He is not scared of problems / He does not fear water / He does not fear candles / Oy Candelo / General Candelo Hear me / General Candelo.
15 Rocheleau, "Listening to the Landscapes of Mama Tingó," 427.

affront to the violent epistemic conductions of Christian coloniality, as exercised through the arrivant state, is met with church- and state-sanctioned material violence against dark-skinned people in public spaces. We see this with La Bruja and Junior and the gagá in Haina. The many disciplinary modes of Christian colonial violence affect the exercise of freedom : sovereignty among queer : Black people and yet, we are in the campos, we are in the barrios, we are in the enramada, we are in the velaciones, we are on the border, and we are in Oregon. We are always in unexpected places, and we know things. So it is that Lula/Wanga/Naina, Amelia, Doña Adela, Veredia, Abebbe Oshun, Don Felipe, Nana Yvette, Jannes, and Josefina Báez teach us; so it is that Elizabeth and Junior and Deivis and Manny and Pilar and Gloria and Evelyn teach us; so it is that Doña Dulce, Doña Magali, Migdalia, Abuela Tonalmitl, Abuela Bea, Dowoti Desir, Antonio, Elena, Gabriel, Lourdes, Francisco, and a random stranger on the street teach us; so it is that Legba, Guede, Liborio, Yemanya, Anaisa Pye, Ogún, Santa Marta, Oshun, Mamá Tingó, Las Mercedes, Obatala, Ofelia Balendyo, Virgen de los Dolores, and Candelo teach us. In turn, I must ask, what have we learned?

Candelo tiene su tizón prendi'o
O-yo llame a candelo que venga al bohío
Donde ta candelo papá con tizón prendi'o
Candelo tiene un tizón prendi'o (x2)
Donde ta candelo donde ta metio
Oy papá boko candelo papá ven a tu bohío
Candelo tiene un tizón prendi'o (x2)[16]

The Master's house is falling into ruins. Some choose to preserve its walls, its decaying floors. For posterity they say. For history they say. For tourism. Others turn away. We search the woods for almaciga, the oily tree that is used to light fires, to build boats that take people out to sea in a middle passage to Puerto Rico, the tree nicknamed "gringo" by some.[17] The almaciga references

---

16 Candelo has lit kindling / Listen, call Candelo to come here / Where is Candelo with his lit kindling? / Where is Candelo, where is he hiding? / Listen Papa Boko Candelo, come to your home / Candelo has a lit kindling.

17 Interview with Lydia Pereyra, August 2018, Bayahibe, Padre Nuestro. Lydia shared how in the 1980s, almaciga was the preferred wood in the building of yolas— small wooden boats—used by those seeking to cross the Mona Channel to Puerto Rico. She also told us that locals had nicknamed the trees "gringos" because they lose their red skin like foreigners do when they are sunburnt.

so many different kinds of freedom and possibilities. It is the wood that keeps us warm. It is the wood that makes our boats. It is the wood that peels to reveal new bark. We splinter its branches and place them carefully around the edges of the field. We carefully pile on dried cane palm and wood. We tell the guards we are building a fence. On a new moon we strike a match. A mosquito crosses the fields and lands at Candelo's feet. Candelo descends and walks among the humans, who now resemble dragonflies and cats.[18] Candelo walks among us. When we are asked, we will be able to tell the truth: we were nowhere near the house. We were down by the river.

There are some who will build new master's houses. They will look like us. They will not. They will resemble pigs and goats and unknown beasts.[19] They will pocket monies from the state's coffers. They will pilfer the body-lands and the water-memories, sea and rivers. They will continue to guard the gates. They will change the rules so as to amass riches in the form of gold. They will do all they can so that we stay far from them. They will call the priest and he will walk their land with myrrh and a Bible. They will claim, "We have arrived." We will walk among them, wearing clothes and skins so they will not notice.

This book is not the Master's house. It is not his field nor his plantation.

This book is an ofrenda, a telling of story in conversation with spirit. This book is a ceremony where the spirits manifest because they are invited to do so as they see fit. Because they want to be here. As they traverse the pages of this body-land, the world is changed in their wake. They weave us into being. We are made and unmade.

This book is the poto-mitan, the enramada, the cenote. These words are the vêvê scattered across the roads inside the nepantla. The corn flour turns to sand and dust. The red earth stains our feet. Gently, gently, the servidores are guided out of ceremony. Tcha-tcha-tcha-tcha. A rattle marks the four directions. The sun is to our right. The moon is to our left. Above us are the stars. Beneath us are the cenotes. The serpent crosses our path. The machete opens the soil.

As I write, I meditate on how we are fueled to seek justice.
I realized that I have been facing quickly shifting punches for a long time.
But what ties all of those punches together is deep suffering.

---

18 See Nalo Hopkinson, *The Salt Roads* (New York: Grand Central, 2004).
19 J. Achille Mbembé, "Provisional Notes on the Postcolony," *Africa* 62, no. 1 (1992): 3–37.

None of us want to suffer.
We don't want suffering for ourselves and all that we love.
I do not speak about normal human suffering.
I speak of the suffering that comes from feeling, in our body-lands and water-
memory, the weight of shackles, the suffocation of prisons, camps, and slave
ships, the suffering of watching all those we love killed in one fell swoop, the
pain of exile and being forced to leave and to suffer in that leaving, the deep
suffering of unannounced and swift,
dehumanizing violence, the asphyxiation of cement.
So many of us—our people, our communities, our collectivities—suffer,
every single day.
And we seek remedy in action, in art, in prayer, in healing,
in working the soil, in thought, in being with others.
We who know suffering know so much about remedy.[20]
As we actualize our remedies, we sit one moment with the suffering
we remember,
the suffering we know and the suffering we seek to end or prevent.
We sit and search those memories and knowings for a roadmap
to our present and future liberation.
In each of those memories of suffering,
we know and trust that we will also find breath,
a dance, a word, a morsel of sweetness, a hand extended,
a root seeking the deep warmth of our Mother the Earth.

As we open we close. The ceremony has allowed us to traverse new possibilities, to imagine queer freedom : Black sovereignty. To reflect upon the magic of the world, across time, across space, within time-space and spirit. We are imagining queer freedom : Black sovereignty. We are calling ourselves down to Earth to walk among ourselves—as divine power, ashe, misterio, the erotic. Upon our encounter, we will know. We will know and in the knowing, we will not be able to un-know.

The drums change rhythm; the spirits rise above us. The spirits call.

---

20 Read Aurora Levins Morales, *Remedios: Stories of Earth and Iron from the History of Puertorriqueñas* (Boston: South End Press, 2001).

Adriance, Madeleine Cousineau. "The Brazilian Catholic Church and the Struggle for Land in the Amazon." *Journal for the Scientific Study of Religion* 34, no. 3 (1995): 377–82.

Agamben, Giorgio. *Homo Sacer: Sovereign Power and Bare Life*. Stanford, CA: Stanford University Press, 1998.

Agard-Jones, Vanessa. "What the Sands Remember." *GLQ: A Journal of Lesbian and Gay Studies* 18, nos. 2–3 (2012): 325–46.

Alexander, M. Jacqui. "Erotic Autonomy as a Politics of Decolonization: An Anatomy of Feminist and State Practice in the Bahamas Tourist Industry." In *Feminist Genealogies, Colonial Legacies, Democratic Futures*, edited by M. Jacqui Alexander and Chandra Talpade Mohanty, 63–100. New York: Routledge, 1997.

———. "Not Just (Any) Body Can Be a Citizen: The Politics of Law, Sexuality and Postcoloniality in Trinidad and Tobago and the Bahamas." *Feminist Review* 48, no. 1 (1994): 5–23.

———. *Pedagogies of Crossing: Meditations on Feminism, Sexual Politics, Memory, and the Sacred*. Durham, NC: Duke University Press, 2005.

Allen, Jafari S. "Black/Queer/Diaspora at the Current Conjuncture." *GLQ: A Journal of Lesbian and Gay Studies* 18, no. 2–3 (2012): 211–48.

———. *¡Venceremos? The Erotics of Black Self-making in Cuba*. Durham, NC: Duke University Press, 2011.

Althusser, Louis. "Ideology and Ideological State Apparatuses (Notes Towards an Investigation)." *The Anthropology of the State: A Reader* 9, no. 1 (2006): 86–98.

Alvarez, Sonia E. "Beyond NGO-ization? Reflections from Latin America." *Development* 52, no. 2 (2009): 175–84.

Anderson, Ben. "Modulating the Excess of Affect: Morale in a State of 'Total War.'" In *The Affect Theory Reader*, edited by Melissa Gregg and Gregory J. Seigworth, 161–85. Durham, NC: Duke University Press, 2010.

Andújar Persinal, Carlos. *Identidad cultural y religiosidad popular*. Santo Domingo, DR: Editora Cole, 1999.

———. *La presencia negra en Santo Domingo: Un enfoque etnohistórico*. Santo Domingo, DR: SN Publishing, 1997.

Anzaldúa, Gloria. *The Gloria Anzaldúa Reader*. Durham, NC: Duke University Press, 2009.

———. *Light in the Dark/Luz en lo oscuro: Rewriting Identity, Spirituality, Reality*. Durham, NC: Duke University Press, 2015.

Apter, Andrew. *Black Critics and Kings: The Hermeneutics of Power in Yoruba Society*. Chicago: University of Chicago Press, 1992.

Aracena, Soraya. *Apuntes sobre la negritud en República Dominicana*. Santo Domingo, DR: Helvetas, 1999.

Archibold, Randal C. "Dominicans of Haitian Descent Cast into Legal Limbo by Court." *New York Times*, October 24, 2013. https://www.nytimes.com/2013/10/24/world/americas/dominicans-of-haitian-descent-cast-in to-legal-limbo-by-court.html.

Atluri, Tara L. *When the Closet Is a Region: Homophobia, Heterosexism and Nationalism in the Commonwealth Caribbean*. Cave Hill, Barbados: Centre for Gender and Development Studies, University of the West Indies, 2001.

Bagley, Margo A. "Legal Movements in Intellectual Property: TRIPS, Unilateral Action, Bilateral Agreements, and HIV/AIDS." *Emory International Law Review* 17 (2003): 781–98.

Balaguer, Joaquín. *La isla al revés*. Santo Domingo, DR: Fundación José Antonio Caro, 1983.

Bambara, Toni Cade. *The Salt Eaters*. New York: Vintage, 1992.

Banks, Taunya Lovell. "Mestizaje and the Mexican Mestizo Self: No Hay Sangre Negra, so There Is No Blackness." *Southern California Interdisciplinary Law Journal* 15 (2005): 199–233.

Bartlett, Lesley. "South-South Migration and Education: The Case of People of Haitian Descent Born in the Dominican Republic." *Compare: A Journal of Comparative and International Education* 42, no. 3 (2012): 393–414.

Batista, Celsa Albert. *Mujer y esclavitud en Santo Domingo*. Santo Domingo, DR: Ediciones CEDEE, 1993.

Baud, Michiel. "The Origins of Capitalist Agriculture in the Dominican Republic." *Latin American Research Review* 22, no. 2 (1987): 135–53.

Beliso-De Jesús, Aisha. "Santería Co-presence and the Making of African Diaspora Bodies." *Cultural Anthropology* 29, no. 3 (2014): 503–26.

Beltrame, Sara. "Aída Bueno Sarduy: 'Las afrodescendientes no somos feministas de habitación propia, sino de barracón.'" *El Salto*, December 12, 2018. https://

www.elsaltodiario.com/feminismos/aida-bueno-sarduy-antropologa-no-s
omos-feministas-de-habitacion-propia-sino-de-barracon.

Betances, Emelio. *The Catholic Church and Power Politics in Latin America: The
Dominican Case in Comparative Perspective*. Lanham, MD: Rowman &
Littlefield, 2007.

———. "La ciudadanía y los movimientos populares en la República Dominicana."
Boletín del Archivo General de la Nación, Año LXXIX (79) 42, no. 147 (2017).
http://www.gettysburg.edu/faculty-pages/betances/pdfs/AGN++Ciudadania+
y+Mov+Soc+AGN+FIINAL.pdf.

———. *State and Society in the Dominican Republic*. New York: Routledge, 2018.

Blas, Zach. "Opacities: An Introduction." *Camera Obscura: Feminism, Culture, and
Media Studies* 31, no. 2 (92) (2016): 149–53.

Blondeel, Karel, Sofia de Vasconcelos, Claudia García-Moreno, Rob Stephenson,
Marleen Temmerman, and Igor Toskin. "Violence Motivated by Perception of
Sexual Orientation and Gender Identity: A Systematic Review." *World Health
Organization Bulletin*, November 23, 2017. https://www.who.int/bulletin/vo
lumes/96/1/17-197251/en.

Bonilla, Teófilo. "Fuego arrasa miles tareas Loma Miranda." *El Nacional*, May 8, 2015.
https://elnacional.com.do/fuego-arrasa-miles-tareas-loma-miranda.

Bonilla, Yarimar. "Unsettling Sovereignty." *Cultural Anthropology* 32, no. 3 (2017):
330–39.

Boyce Taylor, Cheryl. *Convincing the Body*. New York: Vintage Entity Press, 2005.

Brand, Dionne. *A Map to the Door of No Return: Notes to Belonging*. Toronto:
Vintage Canada, 2012.

Bridgforth, Sharon. The Bull-Jean Stories. Washington, DC: RedBone Press, 1998.

———. *Love/Conjure Blues*. Washington, DC: RedBone Press, 2004.

Brito, Tony. "Campesinos montan vigilia en demanda de explotación de Loma
Miranda." Hoy.com, May 27, 2014. https://hoy.com.do/campesinos-mo
ntan-vigilia-en-demanda-de-explotacion-de-loma-miranda.

Brotherton, David C., and Yolanda Martin. "The War on Drugs and the Case of
Dominican Deportees." *Journal of Crime and Justice* 32, no. 2 (2009): 21–48.

Brown, Karen McCarthy, and Claudine Michel. *Mama Lola: A Vodou Priestess in
Brooklyn*. Berkeley: University of California Press, 2011.

Bueno Saudy, Aída Esther. "Encuentro con Julia Morandeira y Aída Esther Bueno
Saudy." Barcelona, Spain. YouTube video, 01:02:10, September 14, 2017. http://
youtu.be/eDocYhzXXRs.

Byrd, Jodi A. *The Transit of Empire: Indigenous Critiques of Colonialism*.
Minneapolis: University of Minnesota Press, 2011.

Cabrera, Cristian Natanael. "Protesta frente al Palacio por Bahía de las Águilas."
Hoy.com, February 20, 2013. https://hoy.com.do/protesta-frente-al-pal
acio-por-bahiade-las-aguilas.

Cabrera, Lydia. *Anagó: Vocabulario Lucumí*. Miami: Ediciones Universal, 1996.

Calderón, Arismendy. "Dialogo con Eleuterio Martínez: Aguas de RD van a parar a Haiti." Hoy.com, July 24, 2019. https://hoy.com.do/el-ambientalista-eleute-rio-martinez-enfoca-el-problema-de-agua-en-nuestr o-pais-y-critica-que-a-pesar-de-la-angustiante-situacion-todavia-no-s e-aprueba-la-ley-de-agua-en-nuestro-pais-agua.

Call, Charles T. "The Fallacy of the 'Failed State.'" *Third World Quarterly* 29, no. 8 (2008): 1491–1507.

Candelario, Ginetta EB. *Black Behind the Ears: Dominican Racial Identity from Museums to Beauty Shops*. Durham, NC: Duke University Press, 2007.

———. "La ciguapa y el ciguapeo: Dominican Myth, Metaphor, and Method." *Small Axe: A Caribbean Journal of Criticism* 20, no. 3 (51) (2016): 100–12.

Carruyo, Light. *Producing Knowledge, Protecting Forests: Rural Encounters with Gender, Ecotourism, and International Aid in the Dominican Republic*. University Park, PA: Penn State University Press, 2008.

Cassá, Roberto. "Problemas del culto olivorista." In *La ruta hacia Liborio: Mesianismo en el sur profundo dominicano*, edited by Martha Ellen Davis, 3–44. Santo Domingo, DR: Secretaría de Estado de Cultura, United Nations Educational, Scientific, and Cultural Organization, 2004.

Césaire, Aimé. "From *Discourse on Colonialism*." In *Postcolonialisms: An Anthology of Cultural Theory and Criticism*, edited by Guarav Desai and Supriya Nair, 60–64. New Brunswick, NJ: Rutgers University Press, 2005.

Chrystos. *In Her I Am*. Vancouver, CA: Press Gang Publishers, 1993.

———. *Not Vanishing*. Vancouver, CA: Press Gang Publishers, 1988.

Clarke, Kamari Maxine. "Assemblages of Experts: The Caribbean Court of Justice and the Modernity of Caribbean Postcoloniality." *Small Axe: A Caribbean Journal of Criticism* 17, no. 2 (41) (2013): 88–107.

Cohen, Cathy J. *Boundaries of Blackness: AIDS and the Breakdown of Black Politics*. Chicago: University of Chicago Press, 1999.

———. "Punks, Bulldaggers, and Welfare Queens: The Radical Potential of Queer Politics?" *GLQ: A Journal of Lesbian and Gay Studies* 3, no. 4 (1997): 437–65.

Comaroff, Jean. "Beyond Bare Life: AIDS, (Bio)Politics, and the Neoliberal Order." *Public Culture* 19, no. 1 (2007): 197–219.

"Consecuencias Negativas de Explotación de la Loma Miranda." *Acción Verde*, August 13, 2012. http://www.accionverde.com/detallan-consecuencias-negat ivas-de-explotacion-de-la-loma-miranda.

"Convocan a dominicanos para protestar contra base naval yanqui en isla Saona." *Juventud Rebelde*, March 13, 2012. http://www.juventudrebelde.cu/internacio nales/2012-03-13/convocan-a-dominicanos-para-protestar-co ntra-base-naval-yanqui-en-isla-saona.

Crane, Barbara B., and Jennifer Dusenberry. "Power and Politics in International Funding for Reproductive Health: The US Global Gag Rule." *Reproductive Health Matters* 12, no. 24 (2004): 128–37.

Crenshaw, Kimberlé. "Mapping the Margins: Intersectionality, Identity Politics, and Violence Against Women of Color." *Stanford Law Review* 43 (1990): 1241–99.

Cruz, Angie. *Let It Rain Coffee: A Novel*. New York: Simon & Schuster, 2006.

Curiel, Ochy. "Crítica poscolonial desde las prácticas políticas del feminismo antir-racista." *Nómadas (Col)* 26 (2007): 92–101.

———. "Identidades esencialistas o construcción de identidades políticas: El dilema de las feministas negras." *Otras miradas* 2, no. 2 (2002): 96–113.

Das, Veena. *Critical Events: An Anthropological Perspective on Contemporary India*. Delhi: Oxford University Press, 1995.

———. *Life and Words: Violence and the Descent into the Ordinary*. Berkeley: University of California Press, 2007.

Davis, Angela Y. *Women, Race & Class*. New York: Vintage, 2011.

Davis, Martha Ellen, ed. *La ruta hacia Liborio: Mesianismo en el sur profundo domin-icano*. Santo Domingo, DR: Secretaría de Estado de Cultura, United Nations Educational, Scientific, and Cultural Organization, 2004.

Davis, Martha Ellen, Jovanny Guzmán, and Norma Urraca de Martínez. "Vodú of the Dominican Republic: Devotion to 'La Veintiuna División.'" *Afro-Hispanic Review* (2007): 75–90.

De Castro, Eduardo Viveiros. "Cosmological Deixis and Amerindian Perspectivism." *Journal of the Royal Anthropological Institute* 4, no. 3 (1998): 469–88.

Decena, Carlos Ulises. *Tacit Subjects: Belonging and Same-Sex Desire Among Dominican Immigrant Men*. Durham, NC: Duke University Press, 2011.

"Defensores de Loma Miranda dicen energía y minas viola disposiciones legales." *Acción Verde*, May 10, 2016. https://www.accionverde.com/defensores-l oma-miranda-dicen-energia-minas-viola-disposiciones-legales.

Deive, Carlos Esteban. *La esclavitud del negro en Santo Domingo, 1492–1844*. Vol. 2. Santo Domingo, DR: Museo del Hombre Dominicano, 1980.

———. *Los guerrilleros negros: Esclavos fugitivos y cimarrones en Santo Domingo*. Santo Domingo, DR: Fundación Cultural Dominicana, 1989.

———. *Vodú y magia en Santo Domingo*. Vol. 2. Santo Domingo, DR: Fundación Cultural Dominicana, 1992.

Delgado, Hanobi. "Balacera interrumpe fiesta de Gagá en Haina." NoticiasSIN.com, March 31, 2013. https://noticiassin.com/balacera-en-gaga-por-oposicion-d e-la-policia.

Deloria, Vine. *Custer Died for Your Sins: An Indian Manifesto*. Norman: University of Oklahoma Press, 1969.

———. *God Is Red: A Native View of Religion*. Golden, CO: Fulcrum, 2003.

———. *Red Earth, White Lies: Native Americans and the Myth of Scientific Fact*. Golden, CO: Fulcrum, 1997.

Deloria, Vine, and Clifford M. Lytle. *American Indians, American Justice*. Austin: University of Texas Press, 1983.

———. *The Nations Within: The Past and Future of American Indian Sovereignty*. Austin: University of Texas Press, 1998.

Derby, Lauren H. *The Dictator's Seduction: Politics and the Popular Imagination in the Era of Trujillo*. Durham, NC: Duke University Press, 2009.

Deren, Maya. *Divine Horsemen: The Living Gods of Haiti*. London: Thames & Hudson, 1953.

Derrida, Jacques. *Of Grammatology*. Baltimore, MD: Johns Hopkins University Press, 1976.

Dipp, Hugo Tolentino. *Gregorio Luperón: Biografía Política*. Havana: Casa de las Américas, 1979.

"Dominicana Ahoga Vudú Haitiano con Gases Lacrimógenos." *La Prensa FL*, February 7, 2013. http://www.laprensafl.com/policia-dominicana-dispersa-haitianos-vudu.

Douglass, Frederick. *Narrative of the Life of Frederick Douglass: An American Slave*. New York: Random House Digital, 2000.

Driskill, Qwo-Li. "Stolen from Our Bodies: First Nations Two-Spirits/Queers and the Journey to a Sovereign Erotic." *Studies in American Indian Literatures* 16, no. 2 (2004): 50–64.

Driskill, Qwo-Li, Chris Finley, Brian Joseph Gilley, and Scott Lauria Morgensen, eds. *Queer Indigenous Studies: Critical Interventions in Theory, Politics, and Literature*. Tucson: University of Arizona Press, 2011.

Duggan, Lisa. "The Discipline Problem: Queer Theory Meets Lesbian and Gay History." *GLQ: A Journal of Lesbian and Gay Studies* 2 (1995): 179–91.

Ellis, Nadia. *Territories of the Soul: Queered Belonging in the Black Diaspora*. Durham, NC: Duke University Press, 2015.

Espinosa Miñoso, Yuderkys, Diana Gómez Correal, and Karina Ochoa Muñoz, eds. *Tejiendo de otro modo: Feminismo, epistemología y apuestas descoloniales en Abya Yala*. Popayán, Colombia: Universidad del Cauca, 2014.

Facio, Elisa, and Irene Lara, eds. *Fleshing the Spirit: Spirituality and Activism in Chicana, Latina, and Indigenous Women's Lives*. Tucson: University of Arizona Press, 2014.

Fairchild, Amy L., and Eileen A. Tynan. "Policies of Containment: Immigration in the Era of AIDS." *American Journal of Public Health* 84, no. 12 (1994): 2011–22.

Fanon, Frantz. *Black Skin, White Masks*. New York: Grove Press, 2008.

———. *Wretched of the Earth*. New York: Penguin, 1995.

Fatton, Robert Jr. "Haiti in the Aftermath of the Earthquake: The Politics of Catastrophe." *Journal of Black Studies* 42, no. 2 (2011): 158–85.

Ferguson, Ann. "Patriarchy, Sexual Identity, and the Sexual Revolution." *Signs: Journal of Women in Culture and Society* 7, no. 1 (1981): 158–72.

Ferguson, James. "Migration in the Caribbean: Haiti, the Dominican Republic and Beyond." Minority Rights Group International, July 2003. https://minorityrights.org/wp-content/uploads/2015/07/MRG_Rep_Caribbean.pdf.

Fieser, Ezra. "If You Build It, They Won't Come? U.S. Bases in Caribbean Target Drug Trafficking." *Christian Science Monitor*, March 12, 2012. https://www.csmonitor.com/World/Americas/2012/0312/If-you-build-it-they-won-t-come-US-bases-in-Caribbean-target-drug-trafficking.

Finley, Chris. "Decolonizing the Queer Native Body (and Recovering the Native Bull-Dyke: Bringing 'Sexy Back' and Out of Native Studies' Closet." In *Queer*

Indigenous Studies: Critical Interventions in Theory, Politics, and Literature, edited by Qwo-Li Driskill, Chris Finley, Brian Joseph Gilley and Scott Lauria Morgensen, 31–42. Tucson, AZ: University of Arizona Press, 2011.

Forde, Maarit. "The Moral Economy of Spiritual Work: Money and Rituals in Trinidad and Tobago." In *Obeah and Other Powers: The Politics of Caribbean Religion and Healing*, edited by Diana Paton and Maarit Forde, 198–219. Durham, NC: Duke University Press, 2012.

Foucault, Michel. *The History of Sexuality: An Introduction*. New York: Vintage, 1990.

García-Peña, Lorgia. *The Borders of Dominicanidad: Race, Nation, and Archives of Contradiction*. Durham, NC: Duke University Press, 2016.

Gaskins, Joseph. " 'Buggery' and the Commonwealth Caribbean: A Comparative Examination of the Bahamas, Jamaica, and Trinidad and Tobago." In *Human Rights, Sexual Orientation and Gender Identity in the Commonwealth: Struggles for Decriminalisation and Change*, edited by Corinne Lennox and Matthew Waites, 429–54. London: Institute of Commonwealth Studies, 2013.

Geisler, Charles, Rees Warne, and Alan Barton. "The Wandering Commons: A Conservation Conundrum in the Dominican Republic." *Agriculture and Human Values* 14, no. 4 (1997): 325–35.

Giddings, Paula. *When and Where I Enter: The Impact of Black Women on Race and Sex in America*. New York: W. Morrow, 1984.

Gill, Anthony. *Rendering Unto Caesar: The Catholic Church and the State in Latin America*. Chicago: University of Chicago Press, 2008.

Gill, Lyndon K. *Erotic Islands: Art and Activism in the Queer Caribbean*. Durham, NC: Duke University Press, 2018.

Gillis, Verna. *Caribbean Revels: Haitian Rara and Dominican Gagá*. Recorded by Verna Gillis, notes by Verna Gillis and Gage Averill. Smithsonian/Folkways SF 40402, 1991.

Glave, Thomas, ed. *Our Caribbean: A Gathering of Lesbian and Gay Writing from the Antilles*. Durham, NC: Duke University Press, 2008.

———. *Words to Our Now: Imagination and Dissent*. Minneapolis: University of Minnesota Press, 2005.

Glissant, Édouard. *Poetics of Relation*. Ann Arbor: University of Michigan Press, 1997.

Gordon, Avery F. *Ghostly Matters: Haunting and the Sociological Imagination*. Minneapolis: University of Minnesota Press, 2008.

Goucher, Candice L. "African Metallurgy in the Atlantic World." *African Archaeological Review* 11, no. 1 (1993): 197–215.

Gramsci, Antonio. *Prison Notebooks*. Vol. 2. New York: Columbia University Press, 1992.

Gudynas, Eduardo, and Alberto Acosta. "El buen vivir más allá del desarrollo." *Revista Qué Hacer* 181 (2011): 70–81.

———. "La renovación de la crítica al desarrollo y el buen vivir como alternativa." *Utopía y praxis latinoamericana* 16, no. 53 (2011): 71–83.

Guitar, Lynne, Pedro Ferbel-Azcarate, and Jorge Estevez. "Ocama-Daca Taino (Hear Me, I Am Taino): Taino Survival on Hispaniola, Focusing on the Dominican Republic." In *Indigenous Resurgence in the Contemporary Caribbean: Amerindian Survival and Revival*, edited by Maximilian C. Forte, 41–67. New York: Peter Lang, 2006.

Gumbs, Alexis Pauline. "Don't Touch My Crown: The Failure of Decapitation and the Power of Black Women's Resistance." Bitch Media, April 27, 2017. https://www.bitchmedia.org/article/dont-touch-my-crown/failure-decapitation-and-power-black-womens-resistance.

———. *M Archive: After the End of the World*. Durham, NC: Duke University Press, 2018.

———. *Spill: Scenes of Black Feminist Fugitivity*. Durham, NC: Duke University Press, 2016.

Gunn Allen, Paula. *Off the Reservation: Reflections on Boundary-Busting Border-Crossing Loose Cannons*. Boston: Beacon Press, 1999.

Hackett, Conrad, and David McClendon. "Christians Remain World's Largest Religious Group, but They Are Declining in Europe." *Pew Research Center*, April 5, 2017, http://www.pewresearch.org/fact-tank/2017/04/05/christians-remain-worlds-largest-religious-group-but-they-are-declining-in-europe.

Hale, Charles R. "Between Che Guevara and the Pachamama: Mestizos, Indians and Identity Politics in the Anti-Quincentenary Campaign." *Critique of Anthropology* 14, no. 1 (1994): 9–39.

———. "Travel Warning: Elite Appropriations of Hybridity, Mestizaje, Antiracism, Equality, and Other Progressive-Sounding Discourses in Highland Guatemala." *Journal of American Folklore* 112, no. 445 (1999): 297–315.

Hall, Stuart. "Gramsci's Relevance for the Study of Race and Ethnicity." *Journal of Communication Inquiry* 10, no. 2 (1986): 5–27.

Hardberger, Amy. "Landowners Under Siege in the Big Bend." *San Antonio Express News*, January 24, 2016, http://www.mysanantonio.com/opinion/commentary/article/Landowners-under-siege-in-the-Big-Bend-6777875.php.

Harjo, Joy. *A Map to the Next World: Poems and Tales*. New York: W. W. Norton, 2000.

Harney, Stefano, and Fred Moten. *The Undercommons: Fugitive Planning and Black Study*. Brooklyn, NY: Minor Compositions, 2013.

Hartman, Saidiya. "Venus in Two Acts." *Small Axe: A Caribbean Journal of Criticism* 12, no. 2 (2008): 1–14.

Hemphill, Essex, and Charles I. Nero. *Ceremonies: Prose and Poetry*. New York: Plume, 1992.

Hernández, Rita Indiana. *La Mucama de Omicunlé [Tentacle]*. Cáceres, Spain: Editorial Periférica, 2015.

Hintzen, Amelia. "'A Veil of Legality': The Contested History of Anti-Haitian Ideology Under the Trujillo Dictatorship." *New West Indian Guide/Nieuwe West-Indische Gids* 90, nos. 1–2 (2016): 28–54.

Hooker, Juliet. "Indigenous Inclusion/Black Exclusion: Race, Ethnicity and Multicultural Citizenship in Latin America." *Journal of Latin American Studies* 37, no. 2 (2005): 285–310.

Hopkinson, Nalo. *The Salt Roads*. New York: Grand Central, 2004.

Hurston, Zora Neale. *I Love Myself When I Am Laughing . . . and Then Again When I Am Looking Mean and Impressive: A Zora Neale Hurston Reader*. New York: Feminist Press at CUNY, 1979.

———. *Mules and Men*. New York: Perennial Library, 1990.

———. *Tell My Horse: Voodoo and Life in Haiti and Jamaica*. New York: Harper & Row, 1990.

Jacobs, Harriet. *Incidents in the Life of a Slave Girl*. Boston: Self-published, 1861.

Johnson, E. Patrick. " 'Quare' Studies, or (Almost) Everything I Know About Queer Studies I Learned from My Grandmother." *Text and Performance Quarterly* 21, no. 1 (2001): 1–25.

———. "SNAP! Culture: A Different Kind of 'Reading.' " *Text and Performance Quarterly* 15, no. 2 (1995): 122–42.

Johnson, E. Patrick, and Mae G. Henderson. "Queering Black Studies/'Quaring' Queer Studies." In *Black Queer Studies: A Critical Anthology*, edited by E. Patrick Johnson and Mae G. Henderson, 1–17. Durham, NC: Duke University Press, 2005.

Jones, Joni L./Omi Osun, Lisa L. Moore, and Sharon Bridgforth. *Experiments in a Jazz Aesthetic: Art, Activism, Academia, and the Austin Project*. Vol. 23. Austin: University of Texas Press, 2010.

Katz, Jonathan M. "U.N. Admits Role in Cholera Epidemic in Haiti." *New York Times*, August 17, 2016. https://www.nytimes.com/2016/08/18/world/americas/united-nations-haiti-cholera.html.

Keene, John. *Counternarratives*. New York: New Directions, 2016.

Kempadoo, Kamala. *Sexing the Caribbean: Gender, Race and Sexual Labor*. New York: Routledge, 2004.

Kincaid, Jamaica. *A Small Place*. New York: Farrar, Straus and Giroux, 2000.

King, Rosamond S. *Island Bodies: Transgressive Sexualities in the Caribbean Imagination*. Gainesville: University Press of Florida, 2014.

King, Tiffany Lethabo. *The Black Shoals: Offshore Formations of Black and Native Studies*. Durham, NC: Duke University Press, 2019.

La Fountain-Stokes, Lawrence Martin. *Queer Ricans: Cultures and Sexualities in the Diaspora*. Vol. 23. Minneapolis: University of Minnesota Press, 2009.

Lara, Ana-Maurine. " '*Hay que tener una Fortaleza fuerte*': Catholic Coloniality, Sexual Terror and Trans *Sobrevivencia* in the Dominican Republic." *Sargasso* 1–2 (2014–2015): 75–92.

———. "I Think I Might Be Broken: The Reconstitution of Black Atlantic Bodies and Memories in Sharon Bridgforth's *Delta Dandi*." In *Diasporic Women's Writing of the Black Atlantic: (En)gendering Literature and Performance*, edited by Emilia María Duran-Almarza and Esther Álvarez López, 34–51. New York: Routledge, 2013.

———. "I Wanted to Be More of a Person: Conjuring [Afro] [Latinx] [Queer] Futures." *Bilingual Review* 33, no. 4 (January 2017): 1–14.

———. "Vudú in the Dominican Republic: Resistance and Healing." *Phoebe* 17, no. 1 (spring 2005): 1–20.

Lara, Ana-Maurine, et al. "Ra(i)ces: A Black Feminist Encounter." *Asterix.com: A Journal of Literature, Art, Criticism*, spring 2014. http://asterixjournal.com/ca tegory/issues/raices.

Levitt, Peggy. *God Needs No Passport: Immigrants and the Changing American Religious Landscape*. New York: New Press, 2007.

Liberato, Ana SQ. *Joaquín Balaguer, Memory, and Diaspora: The Lasting Political Legacies of an American Protégé*. Lanham, MD: Lexington Books, 2013.

Lizardo, Fradique. *Apuntes: Investigación de campo para el montaje del espectáculo Religiosidad popular dominicana*. Santo Domingo, DR: Dirección General de Bellas Artes, 1982.

———. *Cultura africana en Santo Domingo*. Santo Domingo, DR: Taller, 1979.

Lora, Quisqueya H. *Transición de la esclavitud al trabajo libre en Santo Domingo: El caso de Higüey (1822–1827)*. Santo Domingo, DR: Academia Dominicana de la Historia, 2011.

Lorde, Audre. *Sister Outsider*. Freedom, CA: Crossing Press, 1984.

Lowe, Lisa. *The Intimacies of Four Continents*. Durham, NC: Duke University Press, 2015.

Lugones, María. "Coloniality and Gender." *Tabula Rasa* 9 (2008): 73–102.

———. "Hacia un feminismo descolonial." *La Manzana de la Discordia* 6, no. 2 (2016): 105–17.

———. "Subjetividad esclava, colonialidad de género, marginalidad y opresiones múltiples." In *Pensando los Feminismos en Bolivia*, edited by Colectiva LESBrujas, 129–40. La Paz, Bolivia: Conexión Fondo de Emancipación, 2012.

———. "Toward a Decolonial Feminism." *Hypatia* 25, no. 4 (2010): 742–59.

Lundahl, Mats, and Jan Lundius. *Peasants and Religion: A Socioeconomic Study of Dios Olivorio and the Palma Sola Religion in the Dominican Republic*. London: Routledge, 2012.

Lundschein Conner, Randy P. *Queering Creole Spiritual Traditions: Lesbian, Gay, Bisexual and Transgender Participation in African-Inspired Traditions in the Americas*. London: Routledge, 2004.

Maldonado-Torres, Nelson. "Race, Religion, and Ethics in the Modern/Colonial World." *Journal of Religious Ethics* 42, no. 4 (2014): 691–711.

———. "The Topology of Being and the Geopolitics of Knowledge: Modernity, Empire, Coloniality." *City* 8, no. 1 (2004): 29–56.

Marshall, Wende Elizabeth. "AIDS, Race and the Limits of Science." *Social Science & Medicine* 60, no. 11 (2005): 2515–25.

Martínez-San Miguel, Yolanda. "Más allá de la homonormatividad: Intimidades alternativas en el Caribe hispano." *Revista Iberoamericana* 74, no. 225 (2008): 1039–57.

Marzullo, A., and Alyn J. Libman. "Hate Crimes and Violence Against Lesbian, Gay, Bisexual and Transgender People." *Human Rights Campaign Report*, 2009. https://www.hrc.org/resources/hate-crimes-and-violence-against-lgbt-people.

Matalon, Lorne. "Displacement on the Border." *ReVista (Cambridge)* 16, no. 2 (2017): 50–52.

Matory, J. Lorand. *Sex and the Empire That Is No More: Gender and the Politics of Metaphor in Oyo Yoruba Religion.* New York: Berghahn, 2005.

Mayes, April J. *The Mulatto Republic: Class, Race, and Dominican National Identity.* Gainesville: University Press of Florida, 2014.

Mbembé, J. Achille. "The Banality of Power and the Aesthetics of Vulgarity in the Postcolony." *Public Culture* 4, no. 2 (1992): 1–30.

———. "Necropolitics." *Public Culture* 15, no. 1 (2003): 11–40.

———. "Provisional Notes on the Postcolony." *Africa* 62, no. 1 (1992): 3–37.

McClaurin, Irma, ed. *Black Feminist Anthropology: Theory, Politics, Praxis, and Poetics.* New Brunswick, NJ: Rutgers University Press, 2001.

McGlotten, Shaka. "Black Data." In *No Tea, No Shade: New Writings in Black Queer Studies*, edited by E. Patrick Johnson, 262–86. Durham, NC: Duke University Press, 2016.

McKittrick, Katherine. *Demonic Grounds: Black Women and the Cartographies of Struggle.* Minneapolis: University of Minnesota Press, 2006.

———, ed. *Sylvia Wynter: On Being Human as Praxis.* Durham, NC: Duke University Press, 2014.

Méndez, José Enrique. "Sobieski De León Lazala." *Identidad Sanjuanera* (blog), April 30, 2011. http://identidadsanjuanera.blogspot.com/2011/04/sobieski-de-l eon-lazala.html.

Méndez, Xhercis. "Transcending Dimorphism: Afro-Cuban Ritual Praxis and the Rematerialization of the Body." *Power* 3, no. 3 (2003): 47–69.

Mootoo, Shani. *Cereus Blooms at Night.* New York: Grove Press, 2009.

Mora, Pat. *Nepantla: Essays from the Land in the Middle.* Albuquerque: University of New Mexico Press, 2008.

Morad, Moshe. *Fiesta de diez pesos: Music and Gay Identity in Special Period Cuba.* Aldershot, UK: Ashgate, 2015.

Moraga, Cherríe. *The Last Generation: Prose and Poetry.* Boston: South End Press, 1993.

———. *A Xicana Codex of Changing Consciousness: Writings, 2000–2010.* Durham, NC: Duke University Press, 2011.

Morales, Aurora Levins. *Remedios: Stories of Earth and Iron from the History of Puertorriqueñas.* Boston: South End Press, 2001.

Muñoz, José Esteban. *Cruising Utopia: The Then and There of Queer Futurity.* New York: NYU Press, 2009.

———. *Disidentifications: Queers of Color and the Performance of Politics.* Minneapolis: University of Minnesota Press, 2013.

Naylor, Gloria. *Mama Day.* New York: Vintage, 1989.

Newcomb, Steven T. *Pagans in the Promised Land: Decoding the Doctrine of Christian Discovery.* Golden, CO: Fulcrum, 2008.

Nixon, Angelique V. *Resisting Paradise: Tourism, Diaspora, and Sexuality in Caribbean Culture.* Jackson: University Press of Mississippi, 2015.

Nixon, Angelique V., and Rosamond S. King. "Embodied Theories: Local Knowledge(s), Community Organizing, and Feminist Methodologies in Caribbean Sexuality Studies." *Caribbean Review of Gender Studies* 7 (2013): 1–16.

Nyong'o, Tavia. *Afro-Fabulations: The Queer Drama of Black Life.* New York: NYU Press, 2019.

Obejas, Achy. *Memory Mambo: A Novel.* San Francisco: Cleis, 2016.

———. *We Came All the Way from Cuba So You Could Dress Like This? Stories.* San Francisco: Cleis, 1998.

Observatorio Politico Dominicano. *Loma Miranda: Contextualización y protestas.* March 23, 2013. http://www.opd.org.do/index.php/analisis-soc iedad-civil/1115-loma-miranda-contextualizacion-y-protest as#Consid eracionesfinales.

Ong, Aihwa. *Flexible Citizenship: The Cultural Logics of Transnationality.* Durham, NC: Duke University Press, 1999.

Otero, Solimar. *Afro-Cuban Diasporas in the Atlantic World.* Rochester, NY: University of Rochester Press, 2010.

Otero, Solimar, and Toyin Falola, eds. *Yemoja: Gender, Sexuality, and Creativity in the Latina/o and Afro-Atlantic Diasporas.* Albany: SUNY Press, 2013.

Padilla, Mark. *Caribbean Pleasure Industry: Tourism, Sexuality, and AIDS in the Dominican Republic.* Chicago: University of Chicago Press, 2008.

Palmié, Stephan, and Francisco A. Scarano, eds. *The Caribbean: A History of the Region and Its Peoples.* Chicago: University of Chicago Press, 2013.

Paulino, Edward. "Anti-Haitianism, Historical Memory, and the Potential for Genocidal Violence in the Dominican Republic." *Genocide Studies and Prevention* 1, no. 3 (2006): 265–88.

Payton, Claire. "Vodou and Protestantism, Faith and Survival: The Contest Over the Spiritual Meaning of the 2010 Earthquake in Haiti." *Oral History Review* 40, no. 2 (2013): 231–50.

"People Near Gold Mines Test Positive for Cyanide." *Dominican Today*, September 23, 2014. http://www.dominicantoday.com/dr/local/2014/9/23/52803/Peo ple-near-gold-mines-test-positive-for-cyanide.

Pérez, Elizabeth. "Spiritist Mediumship as Historical Mediation: African-American Pasts, Black Ancestral Presence, and Afro-Cuban Religions." *Journal of Religion in Africa* 41, no. 4 (2011): 330–65.

Pérez, Loida Maritza. *Geographies of Home*. New York: Penguin, 2000.

Portorreal Liriano, Fátima. *Plantas medicinales en el Este dominicano: estudio etnobotánico en las provincias de Monte Plata, Hato Mayor y El Seibo de la República Dominicana*. Instituto de Investigaciones Científicas, Universidad Central del Este, 2011.

Puri, Shalini. *The Caribbean Postcolonial: Social Equality, Post/Nationalism, and Cultural Hybridity*. New York: Springer, 2004.

Quijano, Anibal. "Coloniality of Power and Eurocentrism in Latin America." *International Sociology* 15, no. 2 (2000): 215–32.

Reyes-Santos, Alaí. *Our Caribbean Kin: Race and Nation in the Neoliberal Antilles*. New Brunswick, NJ: Rutgers University Press, 2015.

Rich, Adrienne. "Compulsory Heterosexuality and Lesbian Existence." *Signs: Journal of Women in Culture and Society* 5, no. 4 (1980): 631–60.

Ricourt, Milagros. *The Dominican Racial Imaginary: Surveying the Landscape of Race and Nation in Hispaniola*. New Brunswick, NJ: Rutgers University Press, 2016.

Rifkin, Mark. *Beyond Settler Time: Temporal Sovereignty and Indigenous Self-Determination*. Durham, NC: Duke University Press, 2017.

Robinson, Tracy. "A Loving Freedom: A Caribbean Feminist Ethic." *Small Axe: A Caribbean Journal of Criticism* 11, no. 3 (2007): 118–29.

Rocheleau, Dianne. "Listening to the Landscapes of Mama Tingó: From the 'Woman Question' in Sustainable Development to Feminist Political Ecology in Zambrana-Chacuey, Dominican Republic." In *A Companion to Feminist Geography*, edited by Lise Nelson and Joni Seager, 419–33. Hoboken, NJ: John Wiley & Sons, 2008.

Rodríguez, Ileana. "Hegemonía y dominio: Subalternidad, un significado flotante." In *Teorías sin disciplina (latinoamericanismo, poscolonialidad y globalización en debates)*, edited by Santiago Castro-Gómez and Eduardo Mendieta. Mexico: Miguel Ángel Porrúa, 1998. https://www.ensayistas.org/critica/teoria/castro.

Rodríguez, Juana María. *Queer Latinidad: Identity Practices, Discursive Spaces*. Vol. 24. New York: NYU Press, 2003.

———. *Sexual Futures, Queer Gestures, and Other Latina Longings*. New York: NYU Press, 2014.

Rodríguez Grullón, Virginia A. "Natural Resource Exploitation in the Caribbean: From Colonialism to Neoliberalism, Case Study of the Pueblo Viejo Gold Mine in the Dominican Republic." Master's thesis, University of Sussex, 2011.

Rollefson, J. Griffith. "The 'Robot Voodoo Power' Thesis: Afrofuturism and Anti-Anti-Essentialism from Sun Ra to Kool Keith." *Black Music Research Journal* 28, no. 1 (2008): 83–109.

Romberg, Raquel. *Healing Dramas: Divination and Magic in Modern Puerto Rico*. Austin: University of Texas Press, 2010.

———. *Witchcraft and Welfare: Spiritual Capital and the Business of Magic in Modern Puerto Rico*. Austin: University of Texas Press, 2003.

Roorda, Eric. *The Dictator Next Door: The Good Neighbor Policy and the Trujillo Regime in the Dominican Republic, 1930–1945*. Durham, NC: Duke University Press, 1998.

Rosario, Nelly. *Song of the Water Saints: A Novel*. New York: Vintage, 2007.

Rosenberg, June C. *El Gagá: Religión y sociedad de un culto Dominicano: Un estudio comparativo*. No. 37. Santo Domingo, DR: Universidad Autónoma de Santo Domingo, 1979.

Sáez, José Luis. *Cinco siglos de Iglesia dominicana*. Vol. 1. Santo Domingo, DR: Editora Amigo del Hogar, 1987.

———. *La Iglesia y el negro esclavo en Santo Domingo: Una historia de tres siglos*. Vol. 3. Santo Domingo, DR: Patronato de la ciudad colonial de Santo Domingo, 1994.

Sammon, Alexander. "A History of Native Americans Protesting the Dakota Access Pipeline." *Mother Jones*, September 9, 2016. https://www.motherjones.com/environment/2016/09/dakota-access-pipeline-protest-timeline-sioux-standing-rock-jill-stein.

Sánchez-Carretero, Cristina. "Santos y Misterios as Channels of Communication in the Diaspora: Afro-Dominican Religious Practices Abroad." *Journal of American Folklore* 118, no. 469 (2005): 308–26.

Sandoval, Chela. *Methodology of the Oppressed*. Minneapolis: University of Minnesota Press, 2000.

Schwaller, John Frederick. *The History of the Catholic Church in Latin America: From Conquest to Revolution and Beyond*. New York: NYU Press, 2011.

Scott, Julius S. *The Common Wind: Afro-American Currents in the Age of the Haitian Revolution*. London: Verso, 2018.

"Secretary-General Apologizes for United Nations Role in Haiti Cholera Epidemic, Urges International Funding of New Response to Disease." United Nations SG/SM/18323-GA/11862 (December 1, 2016). https://www.un.org/press/en/2016/sgsm18323.doc.htm.

Silié Valdéz, Rubén. "El hato y el conuco: contexto para el surgimiento de la cultura criolla." In *Ensayos sobre cultura dominicana*, edited by Bernardo Vega, 143–67 (Santo Domingo, DR: Museo del Hombre Dominicano, 1988).

Simpson, Audra. *Mohawk Interruptus: Political Life Across the Borders of Settler States*. Durham, NC: Duke University Press, 2014.

———. "On Ethnographic Refusal: Indigeneity, 'Voice' and Colonial Citizenship." *Junctures: The Journal for Thematic Dialogue* 9 (2007).

Simpson, Leanne Betasamosake. "Land as Pedagogy: Nishnaabeg Intelligence and Rebellious Transformation." *Decolonization: Indigeneity, Education & Society* 3, no. 3 (2014): 1–25.

Smith, Andrea. "Christian Conquest and the Sexual Colonization of Native Women." In *Violence Against Women and Children: A Christian Theological Sourcebook*, edited by Carol J. Adams and Marie M. Fortune, 377–403. New York: Continuum, 1995.

———. "Heteropatriarchy and the Three Pillars of White Supremacy: Rethinking Women of Color Organizing." In *Color of Violence: The INCITE! Anthology*, edited by INCITE! Women of Color Against Violence, 66–73. Durham, NC: Duke University Press, 2016.

———. "Queer Theory and Native Studies: The Heteronormativity of Settler Colonialism." *GLQ: A Journal of Lesbian and Gay Studies* 16, nos. 1–2 (2010): 41–68.

———. "Social-Justice Activism in the Academic Industrial Complex." *Journal of Feminist Studies in Religion* 23, no. 2 (2007): 140–45.

Smith, Barbara, ed. *Home Girls: A Black Feminist Anthology*. New Brunswick, NJ: Rutgers University Press, 2000.

Smith, Linda Tuhiwai. *Decolonizing Methodologies: Research and Indigenous Peoples*. London: Zed Books, 2013.

Snorton, C. Riley. *Black on Both Sides: A Racial History of Trans Identity*. Minneapolis: University of Minnesota Press, 2017.

Sommer, Doris. *Foundational Fictions: The National Romances of Latin America*. Berkeley: University of California Press, 1991.

Spillers, Hortense J. "Mama's Baby, Papa's Maybe: An American Grammar Book." *Diacritics* 17, no. 2 (1987): 65–81.

Stephen, Lynn. *Women and Social Movements in Latin America: Power from Below*. Austin: University of Texas Press, 2010.

Tallaj-García, Angelina Maria. "Performing Blackness in a Mulatto Society: Negotiating Racial Identity through Music in the Dominican Republic." PhD diss., Graduate Center, City University of New York, 2015.

Tatonetti, Lisa. "Indigenous Fantasies and Sovereign Erotics: Outland Cherokees Write Two-Spirit Nations." *In Queer Indigenous Studies: Critical Interventions in Theory, Politics, and Literature*, edited by Qwo-Li Driskill, Chris Finley, Brian Joseph Gilley and Scott Lauria Morgensen, 155-171. Tucson, AZ: University of Arizona Press, 2011..

Tejeda Ortiz, J. Dagoberto. *Religiosidad popular dominicana y psiquiatría*. Santo Domingo, DR: Editora Corripio, 1993.

Tetreault, Darcy. "Sacred Indigenous Site in Mexico Threatened by Canadian Mining Company." *Upside Down World*, April 1, 2011. http://upsidedownworld.org/archives/mexico/sacred-indigenous-site-in-mexico-threatened-by-canadian-mining-company.

Thomas, Deborah A. *Exceptional Violence: Embodied Citizenship in Transnational Jamaica*. Durham, NC: Duke University Press, 2011.

———. *Modern Blackness: Nationalism, Globalization, and the Politics of Culture in Jamaica*. Durham, NC: Duke University Press, 2004.

Thompson, Krista A. *An Eye for the Tropics: Tourism, Photography, and Framing the Caribbean Picturesque*. Durham, NC: Duke University Press, 2006.

Thornton, Brendan Jamal. "The Cultural Politics of Evangelical Christianity in the Dominican Republic." PhD diss., UC-San Diego, 2011.

————. *Negotiating Respect: Pentecostalism, Masculinity, and the Politics of Spiritual Authority in the Dominican Republic*. Gainesville: University Press of Florida, 2016.

Tinsley, Omise'eke Natasha. "Black Atlantic, Queer Atlantic: Queer Imaginings of the Middle Passage." *GLQ: A Journal of Lesbian and Gay Studies* 14, nos. 2–3 (2008): 191–215.

————. *Ezili's Mirrors: Imagining Black Queer Genders*. Durham, NC: Duke University Press, 2018.

Torres-Saillant, Silvio. *An Intellectual History of the Caribbean*. New York: Springer, 2006.

————. "The Tribulations of Blackness: Stages in Dominican Racial Identity." *Latin American Perspectives* 25, no. 3 (1998): 126–46.

Townes, Emilie M. *Womanist Ethics and the Cultural Production of Evil*. New York: Springer, 2006.

Trouillot, Michel-Rolph. *Silencing the Past: Power and the Production of History*. Boston: Beacon, 1995.

Tuck, Eve, and K. Wayne Yang. "Decolonization Is Not a Metaphor." *Decolonization: Indigeneity, Education & Society* 1, no. 1 (2012): 1–40.

Turits, Richard Lee. *Foundations of Despotism: Peasants, the Trujillo Regime, and Modernity in Dominican History*. Stanford, CA: Stanford University Press, 2003.

Vermeulen, Heather V. "Thomas Thistlewood's Libidinal Linnaean Project: Slavery, Ecology, and Knowledge Production." *Small Axe: A Caribbean Journal of Criticism* 22, no. 1 (55) (2018): 18–38.

Vicioso, Sherezada. *Un extraño ulular traía el viento*. Santo Domingo, DR: Alfa y Omega, 1985.

Vimalassery, Manu, Juliana Hu Pegues, and Alyosha Goldstein. "Introduction: On Colonial Unknowing." *Theory & Event* 19, no. 4 (2016). https://muse.jhu.edu/article/633283.

Vitoria, Francisco de. *Relecciones sobre los indios y el derecho de guerra*. Madrid: Espasa-Calpe, 1975.

Wade, Peter. *Gente negra, nación mestiza*. Bogotá, Colombia: Siglo del Hombre Editores, 1997.

————. *Race and Ethnicity in Latin America*. Vol. 3. New York: Pluto Press, 1997.

Walcott, Rinaldo. "Outside in Black Studies: Reading from a Queer Place in the Diaspora." In *Queerly Canadian: An Introductory Reader in Sexuality Studies*, edited by Maureen Fitzgerald and Scott Rayter, 23–34. Toronto: Canadian Scholars' Press, 2012.

Waldby, Catherine. *AIDS and the Body Politic: Biomedicine and Sexual Difference*. London: Routledge, 2003.

Wallerstein, Immanuel. *The Modern World-System: Capitalist Agriculture and the Origins of the European World-Economy in the Sixteenth Century*. New York: Academic Press, 1976.

Warren, Calvin. *Ontological Terror: Blackness, Nihilism, and Emancipation*. Durham, NC: Duke University Press, 2018.

———. "Onticide: Afro-pessimism, ~~Gay~~ Nigger #1, and Surplus Violence." *GLQ* 23, no. 3 (2017): 391–418.

Weeks, Jeffrey. "The Sexual Citizen." *Theory, Culture & Society* 15, nos. 3–4 (1998): 35–52.

Weheliye, Alexander G. *Habeas Viscus: Racializing Assemblages, Biopolitics, and Black Feminist Theories of the Human*. Durham, NC: Duke University Press, 2014.

Whyte, Kyle Powys. "The Dakota Access Pipeline, Environmental Injustice, and US Colonialism." *Red Ink: An International Journal of Indigenous Literature, Arts, & Humanities* 19, no. 1 (2017): 154–69.

Wiarda, Howard J. *Dictatorship and Development: The Methods of Control in Trujillo's Dominican Republic*. Gainesville: University of Florida Press, 1968.

Wilderson, Frank B. III. "Grammar & Ghosts: The Performative Limits of African Freedom." *Theatre Survey* 50, no. 1 (2009): 119–25.

———. "The Vengeance of Vertigo: Aphasia and Abjection in the Political Trials of Black Insurgents." *InTensions* 5 (2011): 1–41.

Wolfe, Patrick. "Settler Colonialism and the Elimination of the Native." *Journal of Genocide Research* 8, no. 4 (2006): 387–409.

Womack, Craig, Daniel Health Justice, and Christopher B. Teuton. *Reasoning Together: The Native Critics Collective*. Norman: University of Oklahoma Press, 2008.

Working Group on Mining and Human Rights in Latin America. "The Impact of Canadian Mining in Latin America and Canada's Responsibility: Executive Summary of the Report Submitted to the Inter-American Commission on Human Rights." April 3, 2014. http://www.dplf.org/sites/default/files/report_canadian_mining_executive_summary.pdf.

Wynter, Sylvia. "Unsettling the Coloniality of Being/Power/Truth/Freedom: Towards the Human, After Man, Its Overrepresentation—An Argument." *CR: The New Centennial Review* 3, no. 3 (2003): 257–337.

———. "The Ceremony Must Be Found: After Humanism." *Boundary 2* (1984): 19–70.

Yaszek, Lisa. "An Afrofuturist Reading of Ralph Ellison's *Invisible Man*." *Rethinking History* 9, nos. 2–3 (2005): 297–313.

Ybarra, Megan. *Green Wars: Conservation and Decolonization in the Maya Forest*. Oakland: University of California Press, 2018.

112–13. *See also* Christian coloniality; colonialism; decolonization

comadronas, 138–39

compartir, 14, 26; defined, 104

congos, 105

Congos of Villa Mella, 134–35

consultas, 30–31, 70, 144

creolization: temporal, 106; of zambo consciousness, 21

criminalization: of queer people, 9n39, 66, 112

criollo resistance, 67, 93, 135

criollo traditions: in the arts, 134; Black sovereignty and, 125; Christian coloniality, rupturing of, 32, 41, 50, 57–58, 125; diminishing of, 127; entities of, 30, 62; erasure of, 102; as folkloric performance, 133–35; nature in, 62; queer freedom and, 125; reading in, 34–35, 37, 50–51; reciprocity in, 137–38; repression of, 63–64, 127, 131; as resistance, 135; as "satanic," 135–36; secrecy of, 132–33, 145; tourism and, 133; visibility of, 144–45; war on, 127. *See also* ceremony

Dakota Access Pipeline, 91

Davis, Martha Ellen, 98

decolonization, 2, 115; Christian theo-philosophical conflicts of, 13; gagá and, 129; queer black, 4–5; the state and, 7; zambo consciousness and, 56

Deren, Maya, 33n8

Desir, Dowoti, 99, 100–101, 149

deterritorialization, 88, 136; of campesinos, 71, 73, 77–79

Díaz, Luis "Terror", 134

differential consciousness, 6n19

displacement: of campesinos, 73, 80, 144; Christian coloniality and, 143

dispossession, 10, 18; of altars-puntos, 135; of body-lands, 135; Christian coloniality and, 6; of queer Black bodies, 61n1; of queer Indigenous beings, 65; war and, 137; of water-memories, 135

Dominican Republic: as arrivant state, 11n44, 13–14, 32, 66, 126; blackness in,

15; campesino movement in, 78–80; citizenship in, 96, 128–29; ecological activism in, 70–71, 88–93; gold mining in, 88–90, 104–5, 142; homophobia in, 119–20; independence of, 119; liberation theology in, 75, 78–79; nationalism in, 72–73, 93, 102, 120, 126; neoliberalism in, 126–27, 148–49; as nepantla, 13–14; queerness in, 15; sugar cane industry in, 127–28; as territory of war, 127; tourism in, 126–27, 135, 141; US occupation of, 74, 75n40, 98, 103

Driskill, Qwo-Li, 4, 5

emancipation, 16

embodiment, 37, 49; of blackness, 111; of queerness, 111

erasure: of Afro-descent, 93; of blackness, 93–94; of criollo traditions, 102; of indigenous sovereignty, 66; of queer Black peoples, 93–94, 144

erotic, the, 29; nepantla of, 117; repression of, 135; sovereign, 5, 24

Estevez, Jorge, 122n20

Fanon, Frantz, 2n3, 113n11

Ferbel-Azcarate, Pedro, 122n20

flesh-soil, 61

Fortuna, Xiomara, 134

Franco, Tomás Hernández, 134

fugitivity, 69

gagá, 127–28; decolonization and, 129; Dominican-Haitian solidarity and, 130; Easter 2013 attack on, 127, 129, 130–33, 135, 149; as site of protest, 129–30; as spiritual war, 128, 130–31

García-Peña, Lorgia, 72n31

gender: binary, 68; ceremony and, 39, 49–50; Christian coloniality and, 30, 50, 68, 112; coloniality and, 22; colonization and, 12; instabilities of, 114; labor and, 40–41; misterios and, 47, 50; race and, 20; sexuality and, 20; in stories, 39–42; zambo consciousness and, 58

Ventura, Johnny, 134
vêvê, 1n1, 26–27, 85, 107
Vicioso, Sherezada Chiqui, 134
Vicioso, Tony, 134
violence: of anthropology, 65n13; anti-Black, 6n19, 66; anti-Haitian, 73; of Christian coloniality, 12, 15, 65, 73–74, 103, 112, 132–33, 149; church-sanctioned, 149; colonial, 113–14; of colonization, 112–13; of myth of extinction, 10–11; non-conformity and, 112, 123; against queer Black body-lands, 132; against queer people, 112–13, 123, 132; self-silencing and, 110; state, 149; xenophobic, 66
Vitoria, Francisco de, 116–17

war: Black sovereignty and, 115; body-land and, 116; Christian coloniality and, 115, 124; colonialism and, 115; as discourse of power, 115; dispossession and, 137; gagás and, 128, 130–31; queer freedom and, 115; sovereignty and, 115, 124; spiritual, 130–31
War of Restoration, 98, 99n25
water-memories, 6, 26–27, 80, 87; as alternative to blood logics, 88; blood logics and, 103; dispossession of, 135; healing

and, 30; Liboristas and, 101–2; logics of, 103, 105–6; meaning, production of, 148; survival and, 93
Weems, Carrie Mae, 2n3
woven density, 20–24; of being, 62; of blackness, 33, 106; of consultas, 30–31; embodying of, 49; hypodescent and, 32–33; mestizaje and, 32–33; of queerness, 106; spiritual autonomy and, 146; of spiritual being-ness, 25; of zambo consciousness, 68

xenophobia, 105; anti-Haitian, 63–64; violence of, 66

zambo consciousness, 21; blackness and, 94; Black sovereignty and, 56–57, 101; blood logics and, 84; ceremony and, 147; Christian colonial logics, inversion of, 147; creolization and, 21; decolonization and, 56; gender, race, and sexuality and, 58; manielismo and, 114; queer blackness and, 94; queer freedom and, 56–57, 101; queer indigeneity and, 94; recognition and, 92; solidarity and, 33, 49, 92, 117; spiritual autonomy and, 146; woven density of, 68